The Way Of The Mystic-Wizard

A GUIDEBOOK FOR CREATING
A NONDUAL SHAMANIC SPIRITUAL PRACTICE

MATTHEW THOMAS BAKER

The Way Of The Mystic-Wizard

A GUIDEBOOK FOR CREATING
A NONDUAL SHAMANIC SPIRITUAL PRACTICE

Matthew Thomas Baker

CLEARSIGHT
BOOKS

Raleigh, North Carolina

ISBN hardback: 978-1-945209-27-7
ISBN paperback: 978-1-945209-28-4
ISBN ebook: 978-1-945209-29-1
Library of Congress Control Number: 2022908639
Published by Clear Sight Books, Raleigh, North Carolina
Illustrations by Matthew Spencer
Book and Cover Design by Patricia Saxton

Dedication

This work is dedicated to the inner world and all those who seek it.

May you find the hidden treasure of your soul.

TABLE OF CONTENTS

FOREWORD

What a beautifully written book, a textbook of a mystery tradition!

For the one who sets foot on it, the path Matthew lays out acts as an archetypal container. I wish I had had this book earlier in my journey. If you have ever felt a longing to have true communication with your Soul (in Jungian language, the Self), this path offers you the chance to go beyond your thinking mind, to find and relax into your inner world as a refuge. Within you there is another realm—a vivid and alive place that informs your outer world and your creative process. Your imagination is the magical vehicle you ride into this archetypal shamanic and mystical realm.

Matthew and I met through a class with nondual teacher Peter Fenner, PhD. We discovered we had a shared excitement and experience with all the principles that compose the foundation of this path. Matthew read my book, and then asked me to join his nondual shamanism group, and I have been part of it ever since. I'm excited to see him combining the nondual tradition with the practices of shamanism, constructing a living link between self, soul, and spirit, a portal to your inner source of inspiration and your own journey of awakening.

With the winds of change currently blowing at hurricane speed, surrendering into that which is deep within you—the place in each of us that is beyond the material world—you will find your own refuge: your soul realm, where guidance, inspiration, help, support, and soothing are constantly available, day and night. From there, you will find perspectives and insights beyond your outer-world senses and create a direct link to the heart source of your knowing.

There is clarity in Matthew's writing and instruction that can only come from diligent study, lived experience, and years of providing instruction. Matthew developed a unique class called Poetry, Myth, Magic, and the Art of Transformation, and for over twenty years has been mentoring and guiding artists, writers, and performers by helping them create an integral daily practice that gives them the foundation for thriving in life. As an example, Matthew shares his own journey to connecting with this path. All of that is in this book—a summary of a yearlong course that acts as an opening to a magical and spiritual creative path!

The mystical is an invitation, a beckoning, pointing to that which is beyond linearity. With this path of the Mystic-Wizard, you have the chance to go beyond your thinking mind, to embody a living creative journey that is Self-revealing. For most today, the path of shamanism represents a spiritual technology of a bygone age, yet you will find that your shamanic consciousness is alive and well within you and that shamanism is on the rise today. The shamanic perspective within all of us is ready to be woven with both our modern perspective and the mystical perspective to form a more integral and informed view of reality and the world.

Our society today is based on the rational stage of mental development, where science and logic act as though the shamanic and mystical are inferior, but these aspects of your being are your human heritage, waiting to be reclaimed. The rational mind does not seem to be finding the way through our current unprecedented predicaments; perhaps our future is better served by integrating our shamanic and mystical selves with the rational, and recognizing the vast archetypal realm within, so that our inner life is as full as our outer life and so the inner world can help us heal the outer world.

Shannon Pernetti
Archetypal Pattern Analyst
Portland, Oregon, 2021

INTRODUCTION

Spiritual awakening can happen suddenly or slowly, but however the process unfolds, it ultimately allows us to move beyond the alienation that the modern egoic self feels. Seeing through to the presence of spirit—what is sometimes called pure or unconditioned Awareness in the nondual awakening traditions—can and does radically transform one's personality and sense of identity. The old self falls apart and a new self is born, like the classic image of the caterpillar transforming into a butterfly.

Before the butterfly can appear, the caterpillar must build itself a cocoon, a container for the process of transformation, in which the creature is slowly dismantled into what looks like amorphous goo. In the goo lies hidden an extraordinary design process that is beyond the caterpillar's capacity to understand. A new form is built, one that no longer must crawl slowly across the world and view it from the limited perspective of one leaf, but rather can fly, travel thousands of miles, and see the vast world more clearly.

This image of the butterfly is a beautiful metaphor for the awakening process. The transformation is managed by our soul, and our daily spiritual practice is our cocoon. Together, self and soul work to dissolve the rigid structures of the egoic self to create a more flexible, open, joyful, and authentic sense of self that can work with the soul to manifest the life potential that has been waiting to be born.

THE AIM OF THIS BOOK

This book is an introduction to the Way of the Mystic-Wizard. Its purpose is to help you build "cocoon" in the form of a mystical (nondual) and magical (shamanic) daily spiritual practice that will help you develop your inner life and become more authentic and empowered. If you engage with the concepts and methods introduced herein, by the end of the book you will have a daily practice that can support your life. In addition, you will have called out to your soul and will have begun the process of creating a direct link to the true source of your own inspiration.

(NOTE: This book is not a basic introduction to nondual mysticism or contemporary shamanism. There are many good books on these topics. If you don't have a background in these traditions, I would suggest at minimum a quick search online to read about the nondual and shamanistic traditions. You may also want to look at depth psychology and archetypal psychology, and their history and main concerns. Once you have a conceptual framework, come back, and you will get the most out of this book and the path.)

WHERE THIS PATH AND THE BOOK COME FROM

My own awakening was both sudden and planned for. Before it, I had spent twenty years on a quest to prepare for and cultivate awakening, beginning with reading Hermann Hesse's *Siddhartha* in high school. By my thirtieth year, I knew precisely what I was looking to accomplish and had built a spiritual container to hold it. Even though I knew what was happening, the awakening itself still radically altered my perspective, and I wished I'd had an instruction manual on how to build the container and how to sustain and manage the process of transformation. This is in fact what I have been developing over the past twenty-plus years and how this path came about.

The Way of the Mystic-Wizard stems from my own spiritual explorations and practice as they have developed. That is to say, this is not a theoretical path; rather, it is based on my experience as a practitioner and teacher. The origin of the book comes from both an instinct and a request from the inner and outer world to share what I have discovered on my journey and through study, practice, and teaching.

The book is the product of years of mentoring and guiding artists through the process of developing a daily creative practice, whether it be in poetry, meditation, pathworking, painting, or dance. In particular, it is derived from a course I developed and taught called Poetry, Myth, Magic, and the Art of Transformation. No matter the creative practice, it is the practice that matters.

This text is also a result of the work I have done since 2018 at the Institute for Nondual Shamanism (NDS) and that of the practitioners who have been meeting with me to deepen this path through regular group practice. I want to thank all who have participated in my classes and at NDS for the contributions they have made to the development of *The Way of the Mystic-Wizard*. I hope this book can be for you the guide that I lacked.

WHY THIS PATH NOW

Thinking is a powerful mode of cognition. However, it is only one mode, and can become as dangerous as a sharp blade when it becomes unbalanced with the other essential ways of knowing. Thinking tends to prioritize its own ideas over other perspectives and ways of perceiving reality and creating meaning. This can easily lead to mental obsession and subsequent suffering. Analytical thinking can reinforce the modern sense of the isolated and alienated self, thus cutting a person off from the other modes of being and knowing. When thinking is overly dominant in human personality, it creates a particular worldview; individualistic thinking is currently the dominant mode in Western culture.

The different parts of consciousness that thinking can block are often the doorway to the inspiration and perspective needed to develop an authentic life. By engaging in spiritual practices such as those provided in *The Way of the Mystic-Wizard*, we can overcome this imbalance and reconnect with the soul, the spirit, and the symbolic world within and natural world without. In essence, the path of the Mystic-Wizard initiates the reader into another way of being. Its ultimate goal is both an awakening to the nondual presence of pure

Awareness and a life guided by your soul that will lead to meaning, purpose, and spiritual empowerment.

By working together on this process, soul and self can avoid the near total collapse of the egoic self that many of the most significant spiritual teachers of our time have had to undergo in order to awaken. As Steve Taylor points out in his excellent book, *The Leap: The Psychology of Spiritual Awakening*, more and more people are going through an awakening process. Humanity is evolving, but we are as of yet ill-prepared to handle masses of people moving through this transformative process. Clearly, it is not helpful for our civilization to have millions of people go through a traumatic egoic destruction in order to awaken to a deeper perspective of reality if they are then unable to function in life.

What we need are containers that hold the process. We need to build our cocoons and allow the transformative work to unfold while we also manage our lives, jobs, and families. And this is what the Way of the Mystic-Wizard does.

WHO THIS PATH IS FOR

The simplest answer to the question "Who is this path for?" is that it is for those called to it. The Way of the Mystic-Wizard, as I am presenting it, is not for everyone. In addition, the book is not the path. Much of the path is determined by your own soul and by the process of development and awakening as it unfolds.

Inherent in this path is a requirement for spiritual independence and endurance. You must be able to endure the rigors of practice, self-education, and transformation, but I doubt this path is any more or any less rigorous than any other serious spiritual path. To make the most of the Way of the Mystic-Wizard, you ought to be open to teachings from all over, as the path draws from many traditions. We are all in some basic sense spiritual seekers, and the soul will call you to the traditions, books, and people you need to find in order to grow. If an intuitive process like this fits well with you, then this path and book may be what you have been seeking. Much that is in this book and this path would be considered part of the esoteric traditions of various religions, and the knowledge being passed on is done with the greatest respect for the ancestors who developed those paths, connected to the inner world, and brought forth the wisdom that we now have access to.

This brings me to my next point. This is also a path and book for people who are comfortable with the idea that the spiritual inner world and the outer world are equally important to our existence and journey. In the ancient world, this view was the prevailing perspective. Today it is rare. The ancient philosophers upon which Western society is based, including Aristotle, Socrates, and Plato, were well aware of the reality of the spiritual world, the efficacy of sacred magic, the nature of our shared Awareness, and the soul. We have not simply grown out of these ideas; due to our outer, thinking focus, we have grown *away* from them. If you are drawn to becoming a person who heals the split between the outer and inner realms, then perhaps this path is for you.

HOW TO READ THIS BOOK

This book is a living object, which means there is an ensouled quality to it. As you read the book, you will slowly come in contact with the wisdom and compassion of the soul behind it. It is also a magic book, a living document that connects to the inner world and transmits wisdom. Many subjects, and even phrases, will come up more than once. That is on purpose, as intermittent repetition is a powerful means of learning and initiation. It is how we learn a language, which is essentially what I am teaching: a language for living a more ensouled and awakened life.

This text contains instructions and a multitude of ideas, so it may occasionally sound like an academic work. It is not. It is actually designed as a mythical journey with a teacher who is having a conversation with you. It may feel disconcerting at times, or as though it is moving in circles. This is on purpose; recall the book is alive, and it moves. Do not be surprised if at some point you put the book down and go out in the world and forget about it, only to come back and realize you just lived through something you'd read. Rather than thinking of this book as something you merely buy, consume, and are then done with, think of it as a portal leading into a way of being in the world. If you truly connect to the stream of wisdom behind the book, it will guide you.

Practically, *The Way of the Mystic-Wizard* is broken into eleven major parts, each with multiple chapters, like a series of short conversations or lectures. They are placed in an intuitive order, and they build on each other. Later chapters make more sense once you have digested the first chapters. However, a later chapter may call to you, so listen for what your soul says. Given that the book is a living conversation between you, me, and the wisdom stream of this lineage, when it is best for you to have a particular conversation is entirely up to you and your soul as well as the conditions of your life. Often a part of the text will have no relevance to you and will then arise later when your conditions are ripe for that section, and you will be led to it.

The book is a summary of a yearlong course and an introduction to an entire spiritual and magical path, so feel free to read it straight through to get an overview and then go back and truly begin the course. There are a variety of exercises and numerous recommendations for texts to read and integrate as you develop a daily practice; the actual inner work outlined here will likely take anywhere from a solid year to three years to complete. Of course, you can also just dip in and get a few nuggets of gold before moving on. Either approach works, or even both at separate times, because for those called to this path, there will be little that can stop you if your soul has signed you up for it.

Any way you find yourself working with the material herein is fine. The real measure of this book's value is only what it does for your particular life and path, and it has been written with that intention in mind.

If you indeed feel called to this path, may it carry you on your own sacred quest toward ever-greater authenticity, excellence, and embodiment of the awakened state. May the journey serve to bring you joy and assist you in contributing something meaningful to the world that only you can offer. May the suffering and challenges that the path inevitably will force you to confront be the seeds that bring forth the power, beauty, and wisdom of your unique expression.

Part One

UNDERSTANDING THE PATH AHEAD

The long path alone
delivers you here
to this.

In Part One, I will outline and establish the essential conceptual frameworks for the entire Way of the Mystic-Wizard. If you would like to get an overview of the journey you are about to take, this is the best place to begin, for the conceptual shifts required to make the most of the path are considerable and affect your worldview from the start.

THE ARCHETYPE OF THE MYSTIC-WIZARD

An *archetype* is the life pattern, or container, that forms your intentions on a path. Just as the archetype of a monk would form your daily life if you joined a monastery, so too the pattern of the Mystic-Wizard helps form the lives of those called to this path. This book's techniques are drawn from the nondual and shamanic traditions, but the Mystic-Wizard archetype is more specific than those wider fields of inquiry and activity. It took years of searching, refining, and trying various other terms and containers before "Mystic" and "Wizard" arose as the core archetypes, and the term "Mystic-Wizard" contains subtle patterns of creative, spiritual, and magical intention and identity.

The first archetype of this path, the Mystic, holds the idea of one who seeks out the mysteries of consciousness and the process of awakening. To be a mystic is to be curious, and a mystic feels compelled to seek out our true nature. The Mystic embodies the intention to generate mystical experiences that alter consciousness and allow for the integration of more expansive perspectives. As one explores various new states of consciousness, one's sense of self is expanded and empowered, and the awakening process unfolds. The goals of the Mystic are greater freedom from avoidable suffering, greater wisdom about how to live, and compassion for oneself and others. The most famous Mystic of our planet is likely the Buddha, as his journey focused on awakening to the truth of our shared Awareness and then teaching others how to achieve this singular goal. His teachings embody the path of the Mystic as both a seeker and teacher.

The second archetype of this path, the Wizard, uses magic in a particular way. There are shamans of many types with many purposes, but the Wizard that has been portrayed by Merlin, Gandalf, Yoda, and Dumbledore is a particular archetypal path with a special purpose. These wizard characters embody sacred magical power, and practical and spiritual wisdom as well as compassion. They use the sacred power mediated from the inner world to help others (and themselves) to grow. They are not primarily shamanic healers, or great leaders; rather they all share the specific calling to mentor others in their own development and life path. For Merlin, it is the young Arthur; for Gandalf, it is Bilbo (and Frodo); for Yoda, it is Luke Skywalker; and for Dumbledore, it is Harry Potter. Wizards in this lineage are mentors who initiate students into their own connection to their soul and, with that, connection to genuine creative, sacred magical power and the responsibilities that power entails. In doing so, they help others seek out and fulfill their destiny. This has been my own primary vocation in life, largely in my role as a professional arts educator for thirty years, but in other ways as well.

The path of the Mystic-Wizard embodies the intention to develop wisdom, compassion, and sacred magical power to help oneself and others to live a more authentic, creative, and fulfilling life that has a positive impact on the world and that cultivates the awakening process. These outcomes are the true purpose of this path and all the practices and perspectives the path engages with.

THE MYSTIC-WIZARD'S INTENTION IS WISDOM, COMPASSION, AND SACRED MAGICAL POWER.

MYSTIC-WIZARD PRACTITIONERS IN THE MODERN WORLD

Throughout most of human history, if you were serious about spiritual practice, you either joined a monastery or you headed to the hills, the desert, or the forest and renounced the world. Why did you leave? The answer is pretty simple: because the rest of life distracts you from your intention to make your life about spiritual practice. It can also be easier to practice in a community that supports that practice. What is much rarer throughout history, yet very much a substream of the pathways of spiritual development, is the *householder*, the serious practitioner who lives in the world rather than retreating from it.

Despite the fact that most of the significant traditions have at times seen the householder as a lesser position than the monk or the nun, we now live in a time in which taking on spiritual practice inside the householder setting seems more appropriate for most people. In fact, I suggest that we have arrived at a time when the householder path may ascend to become the dominant form of the serious practitioner. The householder path holds the key to a transformation of our institutions and the larger culture. The Mystic-Wizard path helps generate individuals working to transform the world from inside it rather than monastics secluded from its demands and deep needs.[1]

---

[1] In many ways, the confrontations that arise from worldly demands actually become catalysts for spiritual transformation, because they facilitate making contact with our deepest wounds and initiate a process of questioning, healing, and changing that propels our practices forward. Much like the ideology of Tantric yoga, there is a leaning into the chaos of human form in order to move through it and become more liberated and whole.

To follow the householder path today is to engage as fully as you are called to in work, community, family, marriage, and the raising of children, all while deepening your mystical and magical practices.

If you take up the Way of the Mystic-Wizard as a householder practice, your relationship with the transformative power of your soul's wisdom will come first in your life and will inform and infuse your entire life with spiritual purpose and power. Just because it takes place in the world and is not hidden in a cave or monastery does not make it any less powerful, challenging, or authentic. What matters is the path and walking it as you come to it.

WHY DEVELOP A DAILY SACRED-MAGICAL SPIRITUAL PRACTICE?

The first reason to develop a sacred-magical spiritual practice is for yourself. You do it to improve your life, to develop your inner-world connection to soul, and ultimately to attempt to become a more wise, compassionate, awakened, and capable being. The second reason to develop this inner and outer practice is to help the world in whatever way your gifts can best be manifested. Thus, our motivation is both for the self and for the other, for these are the two main categories in life—you and everything else.

We embrace both these motivations in the Way of the Mystic-Wizard even though the path we are going to walk leads to our discerning that ultimately there is no difference between the self and the other on the level of Awareness (there is, however, on the level of materiality). We embrace both because to do otherwise is to deny an aspect of creation—either the truth of our unity, or the uniqueness of our individuality. Denying either of these is like rowing a boat with one oar: we row in circles and end up in a whirlpool of delusion of failed or fanatical motivation, neither of which serves us long term.

THE INNER REASON
FOR A DAILY PRACTICE

The inner reason for developing a sacred-magical spiritual practice is to create a deep sense of purpose and direction in your life. All of us want and need to have a purpose, a noble reason for being alive that makes a difference in the world. Creating a Mystic-Wizard practice for the betterment of the self and world is just such a purpose. It is akin to deciding to help solve a significant social problem to better the community you live in. A good purpose gives your life direction and allows you to measure the competing elements of your life against it.

Deciding to develop a spiritual practice is much like deciding to learn an instrument. It will require that you practice every day so you can create beautiful music. In this case, the difference is that your body, mind, soul, and spirit are all part of the instrument you are endeavoring to master. The beautiful music you eventually create will be how you behave, create, and engage with others in the inner and outer worlds.

In spiritual and magical practice, we attempt to become loving, wise, and powerful beings who affect the world for the better. Remember to be clear from the outset that this path, like anything worth mastering, takes a deep commitment that ends up shaping and directing your life. This depth takes time to develop, but once it gets ahold of you, it is hard to abandon.

A GOOD PURPOSE GIVES YOUR LIFE DIRECTION AND ALLOWS YOU TO ASSESS COMPETING ELEMENTS.

Even when your enthusiasm flags and your practice falters, you may discover later that you were still on the path—you were simply led off the trail you thought you needed to follow so that you could see a new one you needed to find.

Such is the way.

Note that you can have more than one practice in life; you can have several that dovetail. Many artists, musicians, actors, scientists, inventors, entrepreneurs, academics, and athletes also have a serious daily spiritual practice that is the foundation of their success and fulfillment. No one made them create these practices; they were instead drawn to them in order to overcome obstacles, generate less self-inflicted suffering in their lives, and ultimately develop a higher degree of mastery in life. Practice is a calling, and often the call is heard only as a result of suffering combined with a deep curiosity and desire for freedom and agency.

THE OUTER REASONS
FOR A DAILY PRACTICE

What good is a daily mystical and magical practice to you in the outer world? The outer world is the place where the rubber meets the road: our relationships, our work, our health, our finances, and finally our happiness. As modern people, we have a practical and utilitarian view of most things, which will serve us quite well in our practice. We do not have a lot of time to spend on activities that do not generate change, so a realistic view of practice helps us embrace those pursuits that garner results and promote our growth and mastery of the instrument that is us.

Practice helps us wake up, not only for a greater purpose, but also to our much deeper identity as a soul and then as spirit or pure Awareness itself. Being aware of our true self is fulfilling and satisfying in a way that cannot compare to anything else we do. As we are almost constantly "asleep" in spiritual terms, we often misidentify with various mental and emotional patterns that continually bring us varying degrees of success and suffering. In this asleep state, human beings are conditioned to look only outside themselves for their happiness and continually seek distractions and surrogates to avoid the anxiety and unfulfilled feelings inside. Simply realizing this process is going on provides a massive awakening; learning that it is not likely to ever end is another awakening. It is then that we can begin to work to transform the process into something more healthy and complete.

This leads us to the outer reason for the inner work and for taking up a daily spiritual practice. Waking up—becoming aware of the soul, of the inner world, and of Awareness itself—leads to a more authentic and powerful embodiment of spirit in the world. You might say that our outer world is a divine art project and that engaging in practice and the path of awakening is about bringing the potential of our earthly lives to fruition.

THE HALLOWQUEST

Central to the Way of the Mystic-Wizard is an annual quest for the sacred hallows. The development of this path began in earnest when I started teaching a course called Poetry, Myth, Magic, and the Art of Transformation. In the class, I used as a template a book by Arthurian scholar-shamans Caitlín and John Matthews titled *Hallowquest: The Arthurian Tarot Course: A Tarot Journey through the Arthurian World.* The Hallowquest focuses on a seasonal process in which sacred self-knowledge is sought after. The book draws on Celtic, Anglo-Saxon, and Arthurian myth and lore, and the Tarot to guide the annual journey. The quest allows you to encounter and develop experiential knowledge of the sacred hallows: the spear, the cup, the stone, and the sword. These objects represent the four Jungian active powers of our consciousness: intuition (the spear), feeling (the cup), sensing (the stone), and thinking (the sword). These modes of interacting with the world are valuable, and yet each by itself is incomplete without the others.

The quest is about creating balance in the self and developing a mastery of the hallows, thereby creating a more stable and capable container to hold the awakening process, which in and of itself releases enormous energy that must be managed and integrated into the newly awakened self. The Art of Transformation course was an experiential quest for the four hallows that used poetry, psychology, and inner-world exploration as avenues for self-discovery, and the Hallowquest concept helped students develop a container for their sacred creative practice.

Part of my contribution to the Hallowquest is the addition of the fifth hallow. The fifth hallow is the nondual aspect of consciousness, alternately called in the nondual spiritual traditions unconditioned Awareness, pure Awareness, empty Awareness, and formless Awareness. In the Western traditions it is called the spirit, an all-encompassing presence of the divine that permeates reality, is ever present, and is, in essence, who we are.

Pure spirit, or unconditioned Awareness, is empty of any form and is often symbolized by a diamond and the clear light it reflects. The quest for this fifth hallow is an exploration of the unconditioned natural state of Awareness, a state in which everything is already always complete. Pure unconditioned Awareness is the invisible, formless, elusive goal of the mystical quest. In Arthurian myth, the fifth hallow is a supernatural presence represented by the white stag that vanishes in the forest after being spotted by the seeker. The stag is impossible to catch because it represents the ever-present quality of pure Awareness. It cannot be captured because the seeker already has it—this is the essence of nondual teaching and truth.[2] It is akin to seeking your reading glasses and then realizing that you are already wearing them. The fifth hallow, spirit itself, weaves in and out of all the quests for the other four sacred hallows. Pure Awareness is where we both begin and end the quest. It is the treasure at the end of the rainbow and the entire journey all at once.

BUILDING THE PYRAMID OF YOUR PRIORITIES

What does it take to enter the Mystic-Wizard path? The answer is somewhat intimidating and counterintuitive, but true nonetheless: the route requires a major shift in priorities. When asked what is most important in their lives, most householders will rightly say "my family and friends." This is all well and good, and even as it should be. But with those things

---

[2]   As we evolve, we begin to develop protective mental, emotional, and physical patterns to help navigate and endure life. These patterns are the conditioning of the egoic self and are useful tools of survival that aid in the construct of separate reality, or dualism, needed to develop and function. When we welcome pure Awareness, the grip of conditioned constructs is loosened and the constructs can be seen as objects arising in Awareness rather than as a single limited reality.

as top priorities, you will have a challenging time developing a sustained practice of any kind or making significant progress. It is an issue of life orientation.

Imagine a pyramid that is missing its middle section. On the bottom is a mesa cut off from the top of the pyramid floating in the sky above it. Imagine that the things sustaining your life—priorities based on earthly relationships—are at the bottom of the pyramid in the mesa. These are the things you love about life and the things you are trying to build your life with and for. They include people and places and finances and opportunities. All this is good; it is the stuff of life. However, as you can see in the image at right, the base is cut off from the top of the pyramid.

The top of the pyramid is where the spiritual energy and guidance for your life and practice is stored. It is waiting to descend so as to guide and empower your life. To link up the power and wisdom that comes down from the top of the pyramid with the life that is trying to flower at the bottom of the pyramid, you need to build the blocks that connect the two. Building those blocks is your daily practice.

The blocks that build the bridge between the inner world and the outer world are made from the time and energy you spend building your practice. To construct this practice, you must make it the first priority in your life. If you do not, then the inherent demands at the bottom of the pyramid will pull you away from your purpose. Simply put, the connection will not increase unless you make it your top priority to increase it. In this way, the connection is like any other relationship, which is also no different from any creative endeavor in life. If you want to be a concert pianist, an Olympic swimmer, or a top student, you must develop the appropriate daily practice before you can place yourself where those opportunities lie.

However, you must also have an equally solid and integrated outer life; otherwise, you risk the possibility of rising up to live

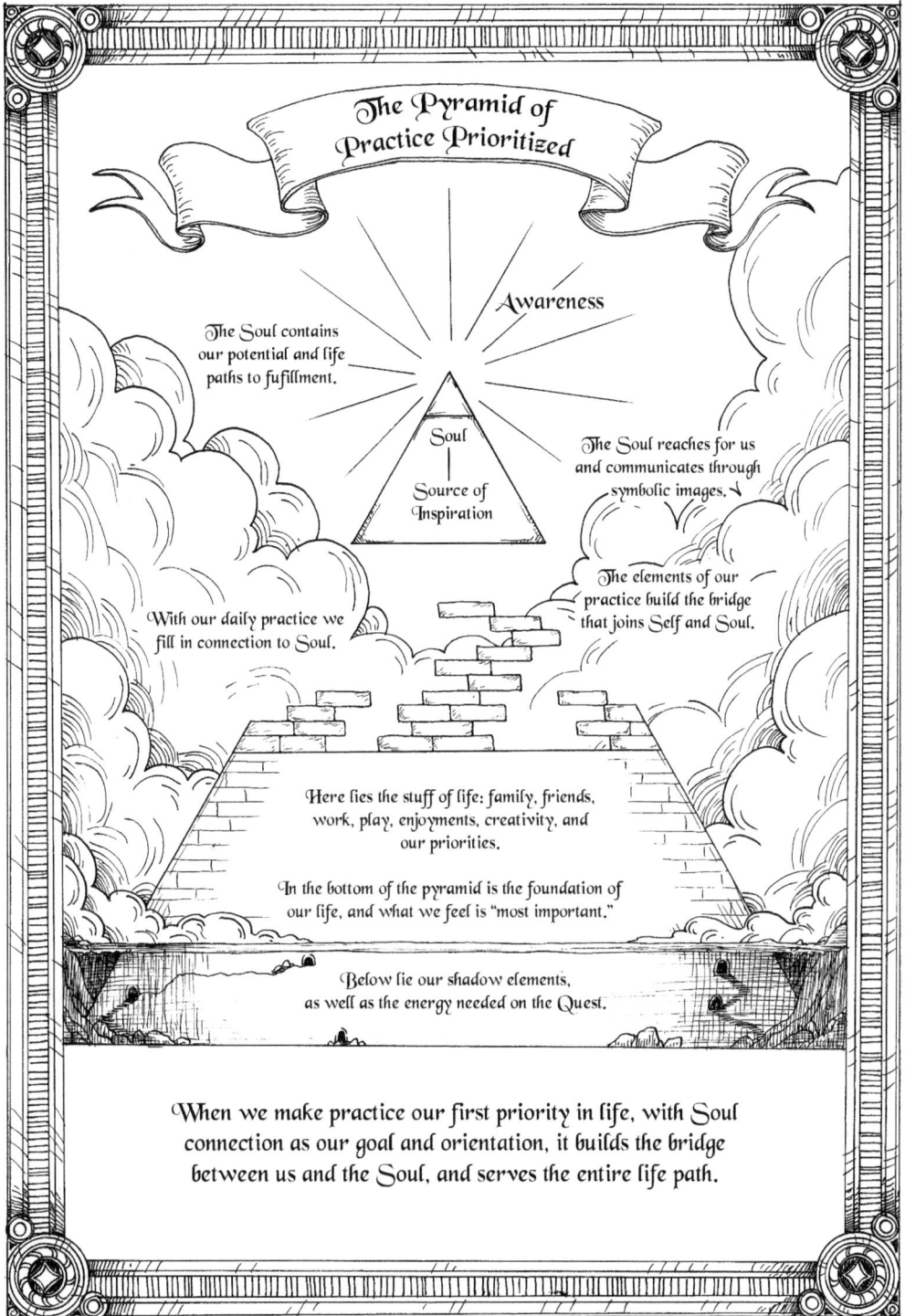

The Pyramid of Practice Prioritized

Awareness

The Soul contains our potential and life paths to fulfillment.

Soul
Source of Inspiration

The Soul reaches for us and communicates through symbolic images.

The elements of our practice build the bridge that joins Self and Soul.

With our daily practice we fill in connection to Soul.

Here lies the stuff of life: family, friends, work, play, enjoyments, creativity, and our priorities.

In the bottom of the pyramid is the foundation of our life, and what we feel is "most important."

Below lie our shadow elements, as well as the energy needed on the Quest.

When we make practice our first priority in life, with Soul connection as our goal and orientation, it builds the bridge between us and the Soul, and serves the entire life path.

at the top of the pyramid, which is an escape fantasy called *spiritual bypassing.*[3]

Making your practice the top priority in your life may seem like you are making the rest of your life a distant second. In reality you are committing to these earthly elements in a more profound fashion. These other elements, be they family or friends, are a very close second. By putting your practice first and your own development and awakening first, you are, in fact, dedicating that process and training to the betterment of everything that exists at the bottom of the pyramid.

Connecting the bottom and top makes you a servant of the entire pyramid, a servant of the soul. With success in this process, you discover that the actions of an awakened and connected you are more compassionate and in alignment with soul and spirit than those of the unawakened, unconnected you.

This shift of priorities is an obvious one if you join a monastery, nunnery, or other spiritual order. It is not so clear for those of us engaged in solo work in the household. However, what is required to complete your pyramid does not change simply because the living conditions have changed from cloister to home. Unfortunately, this reorientation has a number of unintended consequences, which we will look at shortly. But first, to clarify, the change in your general orientation is in no way an excuse to avoid life or your responsibilities in the outer world. In fact, the success of this change in priorities will make the rest of your life that much more relevant and important, since that portion is the source material for the inner work that will take place on the path. Everything in your life becomes fair game for the soul to use to transform you; nothing is exempt.

EVERYTHING IS FAIR GAME FOR THE SOUL TO USE TO TRANSFORM YOU.

---

[3]   *Spiritual bypassing* is the result of becoming too detached from the earthly bounds of our human nature, which then become suppressed deeper into the shadow self as neglected wounds. Putting your practice first means to strive toward the embodiment of your already-awakened self and also continue to see and honor the shadow self, which is made up of past and present wounds.

CHALLENGES BROUGHT ABOUT BY CHANGES IN YOUR ARCHETYPAL STRUCTURE

We are all living out an unconscious mythic story about who we are, where we come from, where we are going, and who is coming with us. All of this will get called into question as you endeavor to make a change in the way you have organized your life. The old myth has a staying power and a deep desire to continue on in the way it always has. The people around you are also invested in the myth of your life and the intentions that the myth holds as well as the behaviors that follow.

When you take on a new archetype, such as the Mystic-Wizard, and commit to the path, a new creation myth for your identity is being generated. It will take about two years for the old myth and the new myth to integrate into a third myth that reconciles the two in any meaningful way. This is normal and natural. However, it will be emotionally challenging for you since your sense of self (identity) is shifting; it can feel like you have two dragons fighting inside you. As you craft the new myth, the practices that support it, and the worldview that goes with it, there will be a honeymoon period, as there is in any new relationship. Then at some point the old myth will realize that you are not kidding about the new path and the new you. The old myth will see that some of the old story of you is going to have to be released. Aspects of you and aspects of your life will fight that change.

So how to manage this tension?

The first way to manage it is to realize it is going on. Then, start tracking the process in a journal where you record and process your transformations. In the journal, ask what the central elements of your old myth are. Who are you? How do you see yourself? How do others (family, friends, coworkers) see you? What is the creation myth of you?

Once you get a sense of the old myth of your life, then begin to imagine the new one into existence and visualize the changes it will create in your life. You will immediately see how this newly imagined life may make you uncomfortable in some fashion. For the first few years of my mystical-magical practice, I hid the depth of my practice and only shared it with those I knew would be supportive. Then, in the middle part of this change, I shared it with a lot more people. By the end of the process, the old myth and the new had synthesized into a new merged myth that I had not fully expected or planned. It was then that I stopped sharing the new myth with others and allowed myself to just live out the new merged myth and let it take its natural course. It became who I was and what I did. Only then did I begin to feel like this new self was authentic and not something I was simultaneously overly proud of and embarrassed by.

It takes time, patience, self-compassion, and wisdom to navigate the transformation. The entire process is the same one you go through when initiated into any new vocation or profession, whether medicine, law, religion, or teaching. It takes about three years of being an apprentice to get some stability with your new identity and develop your skills, and another three to feel like you are actually the being you say you are and act as every day ("doctor," "lawyer," "minister," "teacher"). Be patient, track the process, and have compassion with your own insecurity around the process. Looking back, you may be embarrassed by your early attempts to overembody the archetype; later still, you will forgive yourself for that and be at peace with the process and your journey of initiation. Embarrassing first attempts at embodiment of a new archetypal path are part of the process and later generate some well-earned humility and tolerance for our shared humanity.

THE NATURE OF THE COMMITMENT TO THE PATH

It is common to hear that people cannot find the time to meditate every day, or to do their yoga, or to perform whatever it is they consider their practice. It is so common as to be a stereotype of the modern spiritual seeker. The truth is that we all have, on average, the same amount of willpower, and we burn it up quickly every day by going to work and dealing with life. Thus, it is not that we are not committed or are weak willed; it is a matter of what we are committed *to*. We don't need to gain more discipline; we need to arrange our priorities. We all have about three hours of good concentration in a day. We must use some of it in our spiritual practice.

Habit and structure can carry us a long way once we get a practice going, but it will not go at all if we do not make it our top priority. And later, once you have made your practice a habit and the going gets easier, be prepared to subconsciously let it slip and to notice the immediate consequences in your life. Keep in mind that most professionals in practice-oriented fields, such as athletes, musicians, and so on, all have coaches or teams that keep them going. We Mystic-Wizards have no such luxury. You must be your own coach and make your own decision to take on the practice. Once you've accomplished that, you can eventually manifest some practice companions who will walk alongside you and lend you support when you need it (and you will need it). However, first you must set out on your own. If you are willing to go the path solo, it is a sign of your readiness. If not, you are not ready. You approach the path into the forest alone, just as in the past one approached the door to the monastery alone.

BE PATIENT, TRACK THE PROCESS, AND HAVE COMPASSION FOR YOURSELF.

A pyramid is built upward, one brick at a time, and so is a spiritual practice. It will take at least two years of serious commitment to get the scaffolding up, and for a solid first layer of bricks to be put into place. In those two years, things will begin to change in your life. It is through this process that you begin to discover who you are on several levels of being. You will discover that your soul is your source and that spirit is your being, and that they are more aware of you than you are of yourself, just as when watching a television program you are more aware of the character than the character is. How many times have you said out loud, "No, don't do that," and the character does it anyway? Lessons must be learned the hard way, or they are not earned. It is both humbling and reassuring that your soul has been there all this time, and that it is there to guide you on your way henceforth. Wisdom has a voice and she speaks.

Daily then, the most important thing you will do is your practice. This commitment will serve the rest of your life in ways you cannot yet even imagine. It is the change in priorities that orients your life toward building the bridge between self and soul. From that point forward, the marriage of self and soul is the primary bond in your life. It is the secret marriage, the inner marriage that all romance actually and originally pointed to—the ideal "other" has always been the soul. The troubadours who invented romance knew this, and they buried this secret in their stories so that the path would be revealed to those ready to see it. The great Arthurian romances are in part stories about the relationship between self and soul, and the ways the self loses the soul, sacrifices it, or misunderstands the relationship.

Perhaps the strongest book I have ever encountered about awakening to soul and spirit through an Arthurian romantic tale was *The Speech of the Grail* by Linda Sussman. In it, she writes with analytical, archetypal, mythical, and poetic elements woven together, and deliberately takes readers through a retelling of Wolfram von Eschenbach's epic initiation story[4] of Percival. In von Eschenbach's telling of the grail myth, the grail is not a cup but rather a radiant, celestial stone fallen from the heavens. Sussman recounts the twelve chapters of von Eschenbach's story, and after a summary of each section's action, she follows with an archetypal analysis of the story. In so doing, she reinvigorates the poem's mythic power while also engaging the reader's analytic capacity. She then presents suggestions for a means of engagement with the initiatory themes in practices that will lead to the development of the speech of the grail, which transforms our speaking into something that is inspired directly by the soul. We all know when this happens: words penetrate when the soul is behind them; they transform the listener and the speaker at once. Such is the magic of the soul when it is merged with the self and then speaks or acts in an inspired manner. Our greatest actors, poets, and orators have all drawn upon this merging ability, and so too, our greatest athletes and artists.

The Speech of the Grail is a magical initiatory book like the one you are reading, and I recommend reading it once you have been engaged in practice for several years. It outlines the deep, mysterious process through which our wounds—the ones we receive and the ones we inflict—become the pathways to our healing and empowerment. This is part of the great archetypal mystery of the spear, the grail, and life and human development itself. It is the path of the wounded healer, which is a common initiatory theme in shamanism all around the world, and is an essential part of the Way of the Mystic-Wizard. The outcome of working through the process of healing is a shift to a much deeper and more active connection between self and soul.

---

[4]   An initiation story is one whose plot puts the protagonist through an experience that prepares them for something new. This type of novel is often known as a *bildungsroman* (German), a novel of education or formation.

In return for this profound shift, the soul itself moves to assist you in ways not yet imaginable. It will test your resolve as well. But like all vowed intentions, when you make them, the divine responds in kind; it starts helping you by showing you how to build the living temple that will house the spirit and the soul on Earth. That temple is you.

In the Arthurian myths, these "temples" were the wise old hermits who lived in the forest and that the knights happened upon. Imagine Luke Skywalker showing up at ancient Yoda's little hut on the planet of Dagobah and you will get the idea. That is the archetype of the Hermit. You too will build your own hut, and in that place you will meet the shadow and the light within you, and they will learn to dance together and integrate you into a whole and complete being. The well-known animated show *Avatar: The Last Airbender* is another story that does an excellent job of tracing the path I am talking about. It takes viewers all the way from preadolescence, through the issues of how the egoic self relates to the soul and to spirit, to the importance of practice and seeking balance in the elements of consciousness.

TRADITION AND TRANSFORMATION

There is a natural tension between tradition and transformation. Some readers will have come from and been formed by a specific religious tradition. Some of you will have left a tradition behind, and some will have left and returned after having been away. Some of you will also be like me, having come from not much at all. In each of these cases, you must deal with the inner tension between tradition and transformation.

The instinct to grow and transform is part of our biological and psychological structure; the year itself transforms through the rising and falling of the four seasons. Our own lives as human beings are structured to carry us through major transformational stages—the obvious ones being birth, childhood, adulthood, old age, and death. But many other aspects of life often force transformation on us, such as illness, accident, loss, education, work, dreams, and conflict. All of these forces are at work in our lives at all times. The choice is simple: are we going to embrace this aspect of life, or resist it? The part of us that wants to grow can embrace it, but the part that rightly wants safety, security, and belonging is not too keen on it. Thus we find ourselves inherently involved in a lifelong inner conflict between these two legitimate aspects of ourselves: stability and change. You might say that life itself is a constant dialogue between them in its various dimensions—from relationships to work, to travel and religion, and sometimes even food and clothing.

THE CHOICE IS SIMPLE: DO WE EMBRACE TRANSFORMATION, OR RESIST IT?

So what does it mean to choose to engage in transformation? The essential point is to decide that you are willing to do the work your spiritual practice places upon you. To be open to growth and change, loss and sickness, birth and death means to live willingly in the creative tension of the stream of life. With this attitude in place, you can make a commitment to the art of evolving through the process of living.

This basic stance changes virtually everything you do, from the conversations you have and the vacations you take, to the friends you keep and the plans you make. It becomes a subtle yet powerful intention in your life. We will always have the inspiration to change and also the instinct to stay the same, but we will no longer question why we do, and we can learn to

hold both desires at the same time.[5] That is why you build a daily practice: holding any polarity takes practice to master, and there must be a court in which the two aspects of the self can wrestle. Wrestling and getting angry is a power source to break the stalemate inside you. You will in time become very familiar with your rage at the divine machine that so perfectly runs this show. And after all the stomping and yelling, you will come to a moment of acceptance and letting go of your resistance. It is in that moment that the beauty and perfection of Awareness becomes visible. For that is often when the deepest, most subtle shifts take place and true transfiguration comes about.

Traditions are the bedrock from which we grow and whence we often receive information that forms our essential values. Religions are steeped in tradition and myths that help orient our lives. The need for tradition is strong in us, and driving our attachment to tradition is the profound need to belong and feel safe and secure in a tribe. The tradition and the family or tribe that helped us grow up—if we had one—answered some fundamental questions, such as Where do I come from? Where am I going? and Who is coming with me? These are the essential three questions that every mythological tradition answers. They are the basic questions we are all trying to answer. Thus, once you have a stable answer, it can be hard to let go of any part of that answer and evolve beyond it.

If you feel comfortable in a tradition, there can be a tendency to avoid exploring outside that tradition, even if you are getting clear signals to do so. If you come from no tradition and are desperately seeking a place to land, the tendency can be to dive in headfirst. This can lead to overcommitting and perhaps losing sight of the more significant journey that is reaching for you.

---

[5] Holding the polarity between transformation and tradition can become its own practice of listening to the personal truth in each. Listen for what is right in each moment so that your path evolves into what best suits you.

The deep need to have a stable place where our key life questions are answered can lead to later disillusionment with our tradition. Due to our need, we might not be willing to look at the negative, shadow aspects of the tradition. The idea of looking outside a tradition we were raised in can feel deeply threatening. The feelings it evokes can be much deeper and more instinctual even than the idea that we are betraying our tradition. In fact, it can feel like we are undermining our fundamental stability and identity in life. In either case—overcommitting or long-term attachment—the deeper issue at work here is the need for spiritual independence. A look at all the great mystics, shamans, and wizards throughout our world will quickly reveal that many, if not all, forged vital new ground. That is our calling in the Way of the Mystic-Wizard, and this book is a result of that call.

It is also the call of the creative self and the archetype of the Creator. You are being asked to emulate the creative instinct of the universe itself. There is no older, more legitimate tradition in our universe than to create. Creation is the fundamental and first act of our universe. As far as traditions go, you are in good company if you are creating. And if you have not read many creation myths, take a peek at them. They all involve the creative instinct and a polarity that leads to conflict, which then drives the engine of evolution itself. In a particularly famous mythos, after the divine created its first round of reality, the divine reflected on its own creation and said it was good. What *kind* of good is part of what we are working out in this path. What is good is creativity and conflict and resolution. How can that tension be good? You must believe in the outcome and the creative process. You must choose to believe in the power of creation and its ultimate potential for uncovering truth and for creating beauty, meaning, love, and joy. Even when life falls into dysfunction, which it inevitably does, you must choose to believe in the creative process unfolding and in the fact that you are an active participant in it.

Spiritual transformation requires us to come to a new set of answers for those three fundamental questions: Where do I come from? Where am I going? Who is going with me? It also requires the ability to find a tradition that sustains us while still putting the inner direction we get from spirit first, regardless of whether it forces us to cross into unknown territory or abandon aspects of our tradition or parts of our community that we cherish.

As you engage in the journey, you will face over and over the inclination to turn away from something new from outside the path you thought you were on. It is necessary that you resist the temptation to avoid an opportunity for moving beyond your spiritual comfort zone. Exploring does not mean losing a tradition. It is instead a process of seeing that tradition from another perspective and adding that new viewpoint to your own.

As seekers on the path of the Mystic-Wizard, we stay alert for teachings all around us; when and if we find something that is valuable, we work with it. This is part of the vital work that deeply committed spiritual seekers of all traditions are doing in our world today. We are building a more integral understanding of our own humanity and of the great art of evolving ourselves into compassionate, powerful, and wise beings.

THERE IS NO OLDER, MORE LEGITIMATE TRADITION IN OUR UNIVERSE THAN TO CREATE.

To help in this process, consider that from the perspective of the soul, all the books ever written were simply chapters in one massive human narrative. At any given time, you may need to access one small part of that enormous volume. In such a vision, all traditions are the tradition of humanity, of which we all occupy a part. Today, you have the responsibility to engage from this world-centric perspective and thus utilize all the teachings that will move you forward exactly when you need them. So, give yourself permission to be comfortable with the discomfort that sometimes comes with not knowing how something fits into your path. It is from those moments of discomfort that spirit often delivers the richest new insights about your spiritual life and journey.

ON NEGATIVE CAPABILITY
AND THE MANIFEST WALL

The Way of the Mystic-Wizard has a high demand for several capacities, including endurance, initiative, creativity, autonomy, and *negative capability,* a term coined by the nineteenth-century English Romantic poet John Keats. When a person has negative capability, they are "capable of being in uncertainties, mysteries, doubts, without any irritable reaching after fact and reason."

In our context, negative capability means the ability to sit in the fires of intuition and transformation and not know where exactly you are going or who you will be on the other side. Negative capability requires all the other traits I listed, and you might say it is the natural result of those traits. You must be able to endure for the long haul, to resist having an outer authority tell you the correct answer of how to live, and to engage in the creative process that drives the momentum of personal evolution. In the midst of that, you get a chance to develop your capacity for negative capability.

In my Art of Transformation course, I had an image that captured the process. I used to say that taking the course was like "riding a horse backward while blindfolded"—the idea being that the horse knows where it is going, and all you need to do is learn to listen and keep your balance.

It sounds easy to walk the path of transformation. Sometimes it is, and sometimes it is not. The challenges will vary in difficulty, and the amount of negative capability you have at any given moment will vary. One day I am completely fine with the unknown and the next I am afraid of my future and stuck in a mental trap about it. It is the practice of recognizing the trap, forgiving yourself, and returning to Awareness that shows you the doorway out of suffering. It takes time and practice to develop faith in the process, in the soul, and in Awareness. Trust is an orientation and an ability. The image of the horse gives you a fair assessment of our real existential condition and the surrendering that is required.

As a poet and fiction writer, I can tell you that my poems and stories come alive and have a life of their own. Like the horse, they know where they want to go. And so does your soul. This is the wonder of the soul as the source of your inspiration—it is the true magic of existence. Every moment of life, Awareness is pulling a rabbit out of the hat of formlessness, and the rabbit is reality itself, moment after moment appearing, right now. Somehow it does that without falling off the horse. We, too, can learn to trust and stand right on the "manifest wall," as I call it, the line where potential is made into reality. In the end, wizards, poets, artists, and entrepreneurs of all kinds are all standing on the manifest wall, bringing forth the energies of the hallows and expressing them in our world.

KEEPING A SPIRITUAL JOURNAL

To process your spiritual journey and to capture the insights you receive, find a journal—one you are not afraid to write in to express your thoughts as you go through this course and as you build your practice. The journal is not meant to be a record of the past, but rather a means to express and clarify your questions and answers. I've written thousands of pages, and I seldom look back at them unless I am deliberately tracking something over time. They are simply a place to make sense of my journey. I have hundreds of poems in my journal as well, and letters I've pasted in. All these communication modes are ways to make sense of what you are doing and why. This is important: if you cannot stay clear on *why* you do your practice, you will stop doing it.

· ·

EXERCISE
Reflection Questions

Spend some time journaling about the following:
1. Why do you want to start a spiritual practice?
2. What issues would you like to heal in your life?
3. What would you like to have happen in your life?
4. If you cannot get some of these things, do you want to be free from wanting them?
5. If so, what is the thing you would most like to have or be free from wanting to have?

· ·

PATHWORKING: THE ESSENTIAL PRACTICE
OF THE MYSTIC-WIZARD

Pathworking is an inner-world shamanic journey, in which the energies and beings encountered are clothed by the journeyer's imagination in symbolic forms that make sense to them. This psychological technique—also called *active imagination*—allows a dreamlike state to arise in which the individual is still in control. It is almost like daydreaming, except the eyes are closed, and it is more profound than typical daydreaming—like Alice falling into the rabbit hole. For some people, pathworking is a continuous movie, just like being in the outer world; for others, it is a series of snapshots that contain a lot of information on a feeling level or intuitive level. Shamans and magical and spiritual practitioners the world over use the inner journey to travel to inner worlds. In this inner visionary state, they gather information that they bring back to help those in the outer world. They also gather allies to help them manifest things in the outer world, and amass spiritual power that they channel back into the outer world for various purposes.

Throughout this book, I invite you to use active imagination to travel on guided inner-world journeys. Through the use of the technique, in time you will be able to reach deep into the inner world and contact genuine spiritual streams of wisdom, power, and love, and the beings that embody and transmit these streams. The inner world I am going to introduce you to is a collective landscape co-discovered and co-created through the help of people who have made journeys with me at the Institute for Nondual Shamanism (NDS) and the spiritual beings that guide the process. The NDS inner world is a well-established place; it is a vast realm with mountains to the north, a sea to the far west, plains and a lonely volcanic mountain to the south, and a hill and castle to the east; in the center is a forest with a grove in the middle of it. There are many small sites of empowerment, healing, and wisdom throughout the forest.

This inner spiritual world and the journeys in it were discovered over many years. Since shamanism is a self-revelatory tradition, the journeys needed to be created live in order to be revealed by the inner world. This task was done, in part, by the first working group of NDS that went on a yearlong quest for the five hallows; the journeys and images and inner landscapes were revealed directly to me while I was leading the group into the inner world, and they were recorded as we traveled. Some of the locations are even older, stemming back to the first locations I was shown many years ago as I began leading students into the inner realms.

When working in a journey group, one way you know that everything is being revealed by the spiritual realms is through the check-in process after the journeys. In almost every instance, after our journey one of the six members in the NDS travel group would indicate that they had seen various aspects of the trip before I even spoke. As that type of confirmation process continues over time, you can confirm that you have contacted real spiritual places, beings, and guides. The journeys then reveal a living, active inner world you can contact and commune with.

The keys to following these journeys are to set your intention to learn what you most need to at any given time, to trust your inner guides,[6] and to be open to how the imaginal journey

BE OPEN TO HOW THE IMAGINAL JOURNEY UNFOLDS.

---

[6] Your inner guides are already working with you regardless of your awareness of them, and they can take a wide variety of forms. You may be introduced to inner guides through the journeys in this book, through learning about deities or mythological characters who resonate with you, or through other beings that reveal themselves to you in the inner world.

unfolds. The journeys that I guide you on can be taken multiple times if necessary, until you are comfortable and capable in the inner world, and once you have gone on a journey a few times, you will be able to return to its destination. Once you have established a connection to your own inner animal guide and inner teachers, then despite what journey I begin to take you on, your own guides may take you somewhere else. However, as a shamanic practitioner and teacher, I highly suggest you stay on the paths provided until you are very comfortable with journeying and have strong inner allies.

Some people have an innate visioning ability to experience the inner world like a waking lucid dream. Although this may sound like a great gift at first, it can also be overwhelming, so take your explorations of the inner world slowly and carefully, as you would with any new planet you landed on. And I recommend you find a support person to help you. There are many good shamanic teachers in private practice you can find through the Foundation for Shamanic Studies.

If you are interested in more extensive training, then take a course in shamanic journeying from a live teacher or through a prerecorded course. There are many kinds of inner-world journeys you might encounter today, and each offering has its own orientation, purpose, and process. For instance, in the courses taught by the Foundation for Shamanic Studies, the journeys have a goal or intention but do not have set paths. Those courses are designed from the start to help you connect with your compassionate inner-world spirits and find your own routes to them. Other offerings include *The Tower of Alchemy: An Advanced Guide to the Great Work* by David Goddard and *The Magic of Pathworking: A Meditation Guide for Your Inner Vision* by Simon Court. These are both excellent resources that stem from the authors' extensive work in the Western magical tradition. Sandra Ingerman, a noted teacher and figure in the revival of Shamanism in the twentieth and twenty-first centuries, has an excellent introductory course on journeying, Shamanic Meditations: Guided Journeys for Insight, Vision, and Healing, available at soundstrue.com.

May your journeys be fruitful, and if this path is indeed the way you are called to follow, the inner-world allies encountered in these journeys will make that clear. If not, no worries; seek answers and paths to follow from your own guides. Or perhaps some of these journeys will be of value, and then you will be led elsewhere. Always, always, always, you and your soul and inner compassionate allies are the authorities on what is suitable for you. This is the Way of the Mystic-Wizard and the method of shamans and mystics for millennia before us.

INNER-JOURNEY INSTRUCTIONS

You can read each journey in this book and imagine it as you go, or you can seek out the NDS section on my website[7] to listen to recordings narrated by me. As an alternative, you can record the journeys yourself. You can also listen to the journeys with the recorded sound of a shamanic drum or, if you like, you could play a drum or rattle. The journeys are most effective when you are not interrupted and, ideally, when your room is dark or you are blindfolded. Experiment to find the best set of circumstances for you to enter an altered state of mind but not one so deep that you fall asleep or lose control in the journey.

---

[7] matthewthomasbaker.com

Everyone experiences the inner world differently; some folks are highly visual, some not at all. Some people get impressions and feelings; others hear words. It is all okay. Trust that the inner world is guiding the journey, and if the inner world takes you off the recorded path, that is fine.

When you come back, make notes in your journey journal about what stood out to you. The next day go back and read your notes, contemplate, and write about what the notes may mean, without trying to get a fixed or final answer. Listen for meaning, and let any images work on you the way a poem might. Often the power of the journey will continue for some time, and meanings may unfold in the outer world via signs, synchronicities, and sudden insights. The soul level of reality communicates through symbols, which always have many meanings, and the act of interpretation is actually the art of opening yourself to being moved by the images rather than wrestling the images into some pre-existing conceptual framework.

And now it's time for the first journey.

Journey One
TO THE FOREST EDGE

Set your intention to enter the inner world and discover the next step in your spiritual journey.

Take a deep breath, relax, close your eyes. You find yourself floating down through a mist. *Five, four, three,* deeper, *two,* deeper, *one.*

You appear in front of a beautiful, large oak door. There is a symbol on the door. Notice the symbol, and then place your hands on the door on either side of the symbol and feel the door. You hear the lock in the handle of the door click, and the door opens. Take a step through.

You find yourself in a long corridor made of stone. It is your inner castle. At the far end of that long corridor you see light. Start walking down the corridor and reach out with your right hand, dragging your fingers along the cool stone. You see your fingers are leaving behind trails of light on the stone. Walk forward about five paces until you come to an arched opening on the right side of the stone passage; it leads to a stone staircase that goes down.

Walk down the staircase. It spirals down one full rotation, taking you down one level. When you exit the stone staircase, you find yourself in a large, comfortable living space lit by sunlight streaming through the tall windows set high in the walls. The room is called the common room. There is a medieval-looking fireplace with a large chair and a couch in front of it and a rug on the floor.

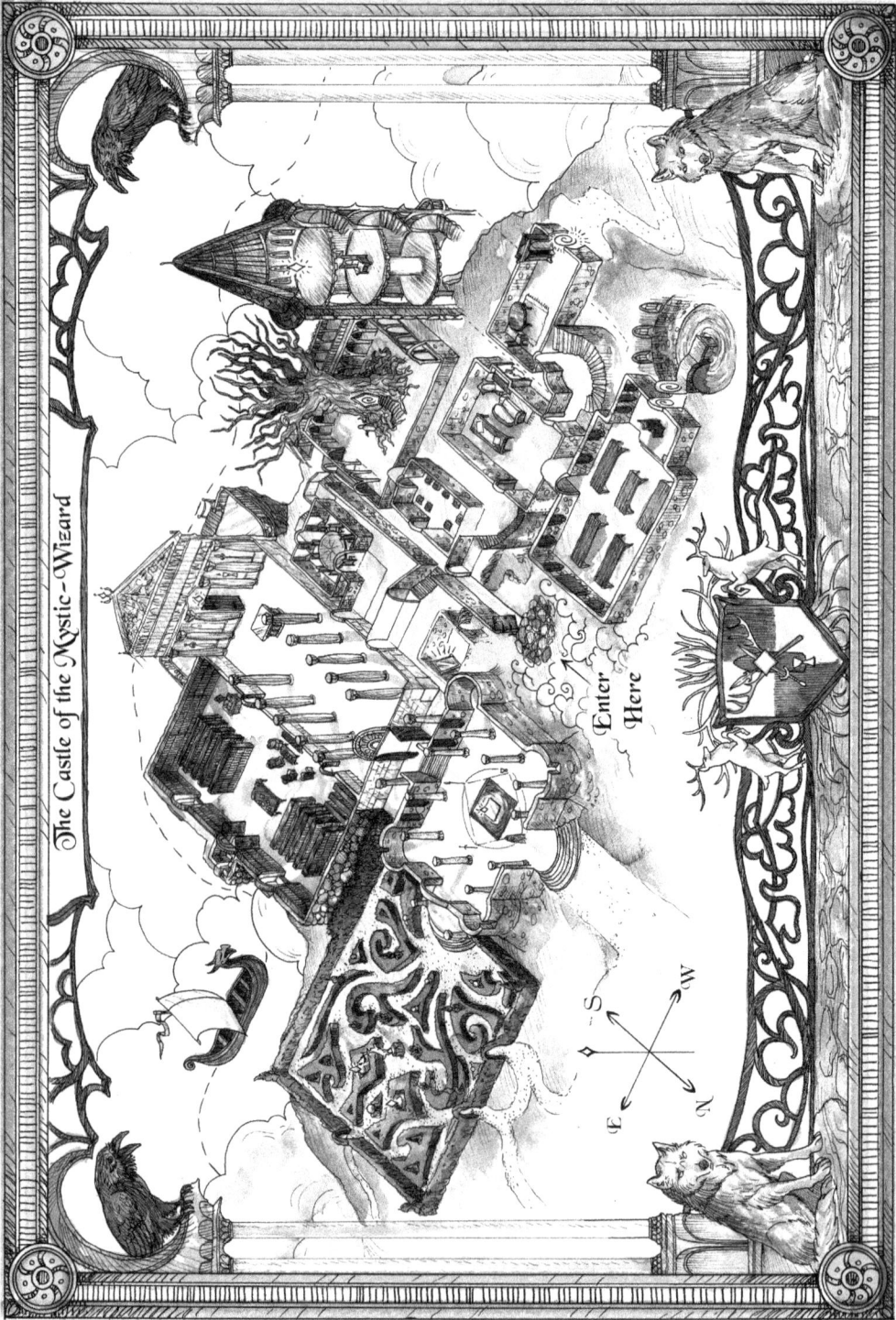

The Castle of the Mystic-Wizard

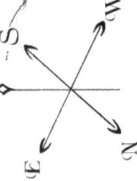

Enter Here

About five paces behind this setup is a large table with an ancient map laid out. You can see only that the map seems to detail a vast forest landscape. Before you can look too closely at the map, you notice movement, and you see a cat sitting on the chair by the fireplace. The cat notices you and seems interested that you have arrived. Take a moment to interact with the cat.

At this point you see there is an exit from the common room directly across from the point you entered. It is a doorless archway with a stone staircase that spirals up. Go ahead and leave the common room and step up the staircase, spiraling around once until you come to a landing with yet another open archway. Step through the archway and turn to your right.

You are in a long, narrow room that has a shimmering portal at the far end. To the left of the portal is a standing closet. Go ahead and approach the portal. Put your hands up and feel the energy of the portal. This is the portal to the inner landscape. Before you step through the portal, turn to the closet and open it. Inside hangs a set of traveling robes. Put them on, and observe that they fit you perfectly. Now step in front of the shimmering portal and gently push your hands into the energy of the portal. Allow the energy to fill your inner-world body. Once you are attuned to the energy, step through the portal.

You are standing on a hill, looking over a vast forest—a beautiful scene— and below, at the base of the hill, is a field. There is a pathway that leads from where you are down the hill and across the field. Start following it, winding your way down, until finally you come to the bottom and start walking across the field. You are drawn closer and closer to the towering trees at the edge of the forest. As you approach the forest, you see there is a wide, mist-filled path that leads into the forest. Two birch trees stand at the edge, arching to create a gate into the forest. In the distance, along the misty path in the forest, you see a white stag with enormous antlers. He looks at you and then turns and vanishes into the mist.

And then you notice that next to the path entrance is a large standing stone with an intricate ribbon of interlaced carvings going from the base up to the crown of the stone. Walk up to the large stone; there, as you get closer, you see inscribed in the stone the same image that was on the front door to your inner world. Place your hand on it and sense how the two are connected.

Suddenly, to the left you see something step out of the forest, an animal of some kind. Notice what kind of animal it is. Then take a moment to connect with this animal who, for now, is your animal guide in the forest. Go and sit and be with this animal; see what message it has for you.

Then you take note of a spot in the ground before you. You and the animal become aware of it together. Reach down to the earth and scrape off some of the dirt; there is a little hole with an object of some kind inside. Pull that object out. Here is the answer to what is next in your spiritual journey.

Now, it is time to return. Bring the sacred buried object with you. You find you can simply absorb it into your hand, where it makes a tiny golden tattoo of the image of the object. You and the animal walk across the field together and back up the hill. You come to the top of the hill, and there is the shimmering portal. Turn around and look out over the forest and the enormous landscape with the animal by your side. To the right, far to the north, are snowcapped mountains. Halfway up one great mountain you see a glimmering blue light and what appears to be some kind of cave.

Now, thank the animal for your connection with it, and promise that you will return. Look out over the forest one more time. Sense that this place is familiar, that it calls to you, that you have some part you are meant to play in this inner world, even though you are unaware what it is yet. Turn and step through the shimmering portal.

You find yourself back in the long, narrow portal room. Turn to the freestanding closet, take off your traveling robes, hang them up, and then walk back out of the portal room and down the stairs into the common room. There is your cat again, on the chair watching you. And there is also the large table with the map on it. Go over to the table, and on the map, you see that by the edge of the forest the standing stone has been marked, along with the path that mysteriously leads deeper into the unknown. There is much to discover here, but that will wait for another time.

It is time to return. Leave behind the map and the common room and go up the stairs into the hallway. Turn left, and walk to the back of the door; it magically opens on its own. Step through, and the door shuts behind you. Turn and place your left hand on the symbol on the doorway to your inner world and say, in your own mind, *It is done.*

Now you are rising up through the mist. *One, two,* higher, *three,* returning to this world, *four*. You are integrating all that you've seen and learned. Stretch and wiggle your fingers and your toes until finally, *five*, you open your eyes, and you are fully returned to the outer world.

Finally, take out your journey journal and before the central images fade, write down what stands out as most important about the journey. If you like, you can draw key objects or moments, or write a poem that captures the essence of your experience. The key is to get the meaningful symbolic images down. You don't need to know what they mean, and likely cannot know right now. Also record how you felt. What did it feel like to be in relationship to the cat, the animal guide, and the stag? Lastly, what object did you dig up from the earth and what tattoo do you now wear on your hand?

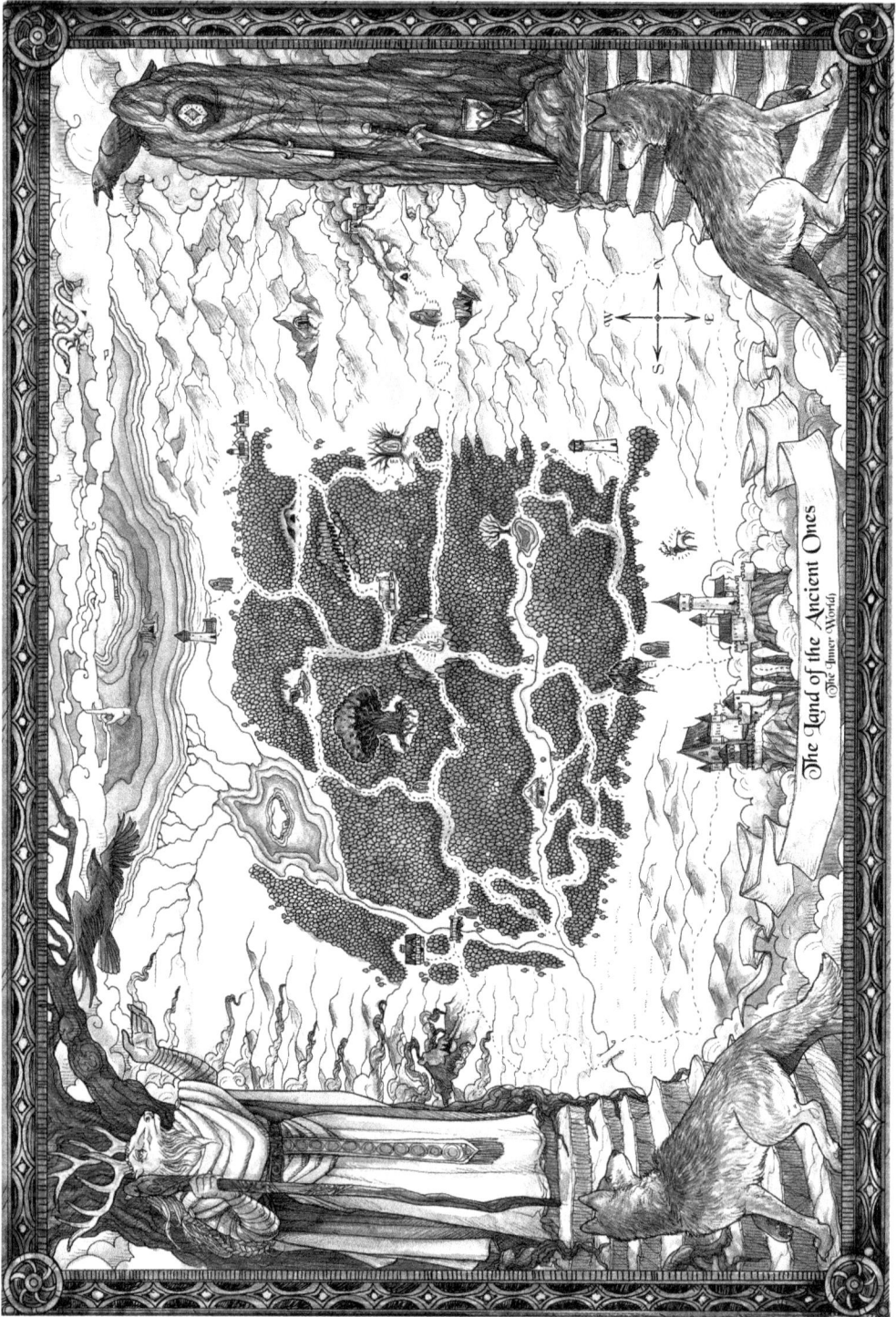

The Land of the Ancient Ones
(The Inner World)

Part Two

A WORKING PERSONAL COSMOLOGY

In the evening's cool breeze
we have become our own opposite—
utterly complete.

In Part Two, we will explore how we conceive of the universe and of ourselves. The concepts in this section expand our sense of self and our perspective considerably, so please take them in slowly. As you become aware of aspects of yourself you have not hitherto known, it can be disconcerting. Be respectful of your own resistance and doubt—they are normal and serve a purpose.

WHAT IS A PERSONAL COSMOLOGY?

We all have a way we believe the universe works. Most of our beliefs were formed through experience in the outer world as well as from how we were shown and taught to experience the outer world. Therefore, we all have a personal Way, a personal cosmology, that deals with reality. It stands to reason that our Way is not complete or entirely accurate, but rather a working version of a Way that we are using to manage our journey through life. Since it is a working version and not a final version, it can be updated, transformed, and made more accurate and efficient in ways that could help us succeed, suffer less, and become more prosperous and joyful. The process of updating our Way is the process of acquiring wisdom.

I will also posit that there is, in fact, a way the universe *actually* works, and that the closer our personal cosmology is to how things actually are, the more empowered we are likely to become. This is the premise in science, mysticism, magic, and shamanism. We can certainly see how this idea of reliable knowledge plays out in our tremendous scientific and technological capacity today. We are superbly successful in that dimension right now, but we are far less developed in the spiritual dimensions of reality and in seeing how things connect and influence each other.

So the universe is chugging along exactly as it is, following its own rules. These rules include the manifestation of beings such as ourselves. Amazingly, we, as self-conscious, thinking beings, are allowed in this universe to create our own rules—even when they are utterly contrary to how things work. We are also allowed to discover the *actual* rules through trial and error, inspiration, and luck.

This claim I am making also means that, since we are inside a system of actual rules about how things genuinely work, we can never really get a complete view of the system from the outside. In fact, nothing in the universe can see everything in the way we can see something held in our hand. And even when we hold an object in our hand, we are looking at it from one perspective and cannot see the other side of the object.

HOW WE THINK
THE UNIVERSE IS,
IS, IN PART, HOW
THE UNIVERSE
APPEARS TO US.

Your personal cosmology is a rule structure and a way of managing your journey. The question is, is yours working well for you? It is highly probable that, as with most people, some of your belief patterns are successful for you and some are not as successful. Then there are those beliefs that are a complete and epic failure. And, ideas that were successful in the past might not be so useful now.

Our goal as we move forward in this section is to attempt to understand the working model of your personal cosmology and to make it more open, flexible, guided, and empowered.

Our cosmology guides our actions and helps define what we pay attention to and what we believe. So our personal construction of how we think the universe is, is, in part, how the universe will appear to us. This idea is at least a little bit true for all of us. To a certain degree, what we believe is what we see—or in this case, what we pay attention to. However, this statement fails to encompass entirely the concept I'm getting at. If you do not see a bus and you step off the curb, the bus will still run you over. The bus still exists despite your oversight. If you deny a feeling you have, suppress it, and then believe it does not exist, it may appear to go away, but it is instead relegated to the subconscious, and eventually it will emerge and be expressed somehow in the body, mind, or emotions. So, clearly, "out of

sight, out of mind" is something we can do, a useful magic trick, but it is not a great long-term solution to problems, just as never leaving your house is not a great long-term solution to avoiding being hit by a bus.

Our personal cosmology, as well as what we sense is possible on any given day, determines our beliefs and guides our actions. It therefore makes sense to identify what your cosmology is and how it affects you. One way to do that is to compare your own beliefs to the ones that will follow in this section. The personal cosmology that I will lay out is based on my own experience with a working cosmology that is able to manifest excellent results for those on the path of the Mystic-Wizard. It is not a standard modern cosmology. It draws from the wisdom of ancient shamans, philosophers, and the inner world, as well as the insights of many modern mystics, psychologists, and scientists.

A couple of core cosmological and mythological questions to think about before we jump in . . .

THE FIRST QUESTION:
WHERE DO YOU COME FROM?

First, where do you believe you come from? That is, what is your source?

Many modern people, despite what they may say, operate under the unconscious belief that their source is their parents, that is, their family. That is the operational reality programmed into most modern people. The majority of people do not, for instance, operate as if they are the direct manifestation and incarnation of a deity or an immortal being made of light. Most do not say and think this because most folks do not experience this. But what if you did? What if you felt that, knew that, and therefore could see yourself that way? What if you had been taught and shown the presence of your own soul from day one, as well as the presence of the divine, that is, pure Awareness? Some people have had this training all their lives.

Many Tibetan monks are brought up with exactly this kind of central mythological and cosmological foundation. In fact, the entire Tibetan culture is based on it. You can imagine that this belief system would have an effect on your vision of yourself, your identity, and your sense of what is possible and important in the world and in your life. It is a fairly empowering, stable, and uplifting foundational myth and cosmological outlook, but it is no more complete than the standard Western view. Though it has many valuable insights, it, too, is the product of a specific time and place.

If, for instance, your parents are your origin, and they damaged your psyche somehow, you could then spend your entire life being angry about that fact, or motivated by it. If, however, you are the creation of an immortal soul that chose your parents and life conditions, you could see the same difficult situation as part of the challenge that your soul decided to engage in during this life. Your soul, not your ego-personality, chose to engage with these life conditions.

Let us be clear here: in this cosmology, the human personality is a construct of the mind, the soul, and the body, and it is not responsible for the conditions it finds itself created in. It is, however, occasionally able to take responsibility for attempting to deal with those conditions and become empowered through that process. I call that viewpoint the foundation stone of the Way of the Mystic-Wizard. *Your life is an act of incarnation of the soul, not an accident of birth.* I choose not to have a myth that the universe is an accident, or that I am an accident, because that is not an empowering belief. I choose to take on the myth that I am the incarnation of a powerful immortal being that is living out an incarnation with me as the front man on the tour. It is not I who possesses a humble, mute soul, but rather the noble soul who possesses a humble human vehicle for its exploration of this reality.

Which would you rather have as a part of your cosmological perspective? Are you a creation of an immortal being? Or are you a blank slate that your parents and culture wrote on? Why not take the one that empowers you rather than the one that keeps you in the narrow confines of your biological and social sources? A good myth is one that emboldens and empowers the human personality to engage with life and to not blame others or fall into a narcissistic or nihilistic loop of despair. The myth we choose matters. It determines what we will pay attention to as we go. You cannot be a Mystic-Wizard if your birth is not seen as a fundamentally important, magical act of creation by a celestial being that had both purpose and power in its choice. So, I ask again: Where did you come from?

Here is a note on the birth of heroic mythic characters: There is a reason that in mythology, heroic characters—King Arthur, Leia and Luke Skywalker, Harry Potter—always discover that they are the children of nobility or powerful beings. In the stories this is a symbolic way of expressing our own noble origins as a soul. The soul is our true parent, true divine nobility. *It is not literal nobility on the earth that matters; it is our spiritual nobility, lineage, and inherent divinity that is being pointed to in those stories.* The symbolic mind and heart know this instinctively, which is why we relate to those characters.

The logical mind struggles to understand how everyone can be a noble, heroic character, but if you could look at the universe from the soul level outward and see all the brilliant immortal souls of our world manifesting and incarnating personalities, you could bear witness to the extraordinary nobility of the entire human species. Now *that* is a cosmology to live with and by, is it not? In fact, you could say that the entire movement and expansion of individual rights as citizens is an intuitive reflection of this great truth of our internal nobility.

YOUR LIFE IS AN ACT OF INCARNATION OF THE SOUL, NOT AN ACCIDENT OF BIRTH.

Thus, it is enshrined in many constitutions the world over that we all have the right to life, liberty, and justice. Before these ideas were developed by modern self-citizens, these were not rights, not shared ideas; only the blood-nobles in the leading family hierarchies had those rights. In some basic sense, our political structures have been trying to catch up with a more accurate myth of the spiritual realities of our existence since society began. It has been a long road, and the process is still unfolding all around us.

THE SECOND QUESTION: IS THE UNIVERSE ON YOUR SIDE?

The second question to ask yourself is about the entire universe: Is the universe ultimately friendly, or not? Is it ultimately on your side, or not? Despite all the terror and madness and setbacks and pain, is the universe—spirit and soul—at some basic level on your side, or not? Einstein said this was the most important question a human being needs to answer. Why would he say that? Because he was speaking about the importance of your cosmological outlook in determining what is possible for you to see in your life. Will you decide that the universe is working with you, or not? Answer quickly, from your heart or gut, not by thinking about it.

Okay, now you know where you stand today. The answer to where you stand at any given moment can come easily or not, depending on the situation, and this is a very human phenomenon. But really, the key point is not what your answer is today, but rather what could unfold if you answered consistently with "Yes, the universe and vast spiritual forces are always watching over me, working with me, even when I am clueless and have no idea they are there."

What are the implications of that cosmology?

The first consequence is that you are not alone in this life. When human beings are alone or abandoned, it can generate serious existential anxiety. Given that life will deliver up times when you really *are* alone (in the sense that other humans are not around), then the shamanic-wizardly view that you have a noble soul and many inner-world allies and spiritual buddies is quite empowering. Why not choose that idea instead of the one where we are living in an empty void of space and there is nothing and no one there for us? The latter is not an empowering myth and in fact is a relatively recent one invented during the Enlightenment; anyone living before about 1850 would have thought it a completely outlandish concept. Yet today it is a common cosmological stance. Even people who are religious, who say they believe in God or angels, often hold an unconscious stance that none of that ideology is "real."

What would happen if you could live in a multifaceted universe populated with innumerable beings to support and help you? That idea would dovetail with the answer to the first question—the idea of your being the direct manifestation of a celestial being.

On a final note, it is easy to decide to agree with this worldview and cosmological foundation, to say, "Yep, I got that. In fact, I have thought that way for many years." However, that does not mean you are programmed that way or that you actually live that way. The only way to change your programming is to rewrite the code. Rewriting code is a lot of work, and you have to go line by line. The way you do that is by building a daily practice that redefines your cosmological stance, and in time your view and experience of the world is changed. When I say "in time," I mean about a decade, unless you are one of the populace who has had a near-death experience and remembers it, and as a result was utterly changed in an instant. If you choose to read the literature on the near-death process, you will understand what it takes to do a redesign of one's cosmology in an instant. However, since most of us are not interested in falling off a horse and hitting our head in order to see the entire celestial world and hear a divine voice, we must take the path we have in front of us. We must practice the new view, and *act* as if we have fallen off a horse and seen the celestial universe so that we can slowly begin to genuinely sense it. The Way of the Mystic-Wizard relies on the ability to embrace this process of transformation. In the end, it is a path of genuine transfiguration of your actual perceptions and therefore of life itself. It is a path on which we are no longer the being we once were, and the world is no longer the place it once was.

Let us now dive into the potential implications of these two ideas—our source and the friendliness of the universe—and the construction of the personal cosmology of a Mystic-Wizard, without apology or embarrassment. We are, after all, following in the footsteps of the greatest scientists, writers, and philosophers in history, from Newton and Einstein to Shakespeare and Plato.

FROM SPIRIT TO SOUL TO SELF TO SHADOW

The next cosmological subject we need to address is the nature of our various selves. In the modern secular world, it is common to believe that we exist on only one level of being, and that there really is only one legitimate level of being. As I mentioned before, even in religious environments in which the spiritual realms are theoretically embraced, there is little understanding or exploration of, or even a conceptual framework for investigating and understanding, our various levels of being. Therefore, there is little knowledge about how those levels of being can help us live our lives. So we find that in our modern technological world, many materially successful people rarely feel joy, never feel bliss, and have no idea that love is actually divine compassion and not attachment. Of course, how would they know? They have not delved into their own being and discovered the higher perspective beyond the ego-self.

In the West we have just begun to explore meditation, just begun to investigate our being. Other cultures have been aware of multiple levels of being for several thousands of years and have developed techniques for accessing these levels. Fortunately for all of us, we have access to that inner technology now, just as we have access to our outer technology. That is a nice combination for developing a genuine mastery of the actual rules of both the outer world and the inner world.

The cosmology of the self I lay out below will help give you a conceptual structure for these levels. It is a ladder or framework in which you develop an understanding of who you are. This framework becomes extremely important as your practice develops, for the relationship between the self and the soul is as important in spiritual growth as a parent is to a child's development. Without the help of the soul, the path of awakening can get derailed over and over again, circling many conceptual cul-de-sacs. These dead ends amount to forms of spiritual bypassing or despair. *Spiritual bypassing* is a term that describes ways in which we (our ego-self) can subconsciously use our spiritual path to avoid engaging with the parts of ourselves and of life that we would like to avoid. The point is to understand that without a spiritual guidance system and outer spiritual companions on the path to verify and reflect back to us our true situation, we are more likely to remain stuck in conceptual circles of denial and avoidance. Thus we need to connect to the source of our true inspiration, the soul, so as to keep evolving and transforming.

Let us then investigate this conceptual framework of being and how it helps to support our practice, our growth, and our eventual awakening and empowerment. We will start with the self, then examine the soul, the spirit, and finally the shadow. We will look at how each aspect works and relates to the others.

THE SELF

The *self* is what we consider to be "us." It is what many often call the ego, but because that term has multiple meanings and often has a negative connotation, I prefer to simply use the term *self* and define it myself in order to create conceptual clarity.

In my definition, the self is both your sense of identity and your sense of being present and awake. In other words, the self is your pure awakened Awareness looking out through the rich and highly individualized matrix of memories, concepts, desires, dreams, fears, and potentials that you think of and feel as being *you*. In this view, the self is, in fact, an extraordinary art project that moves, thinks, expresses, and creates.

We all, then, are human selves evolving and moving toward fruition as best we can inside a set of often necessarily contradictory and challenging conditions. All of the tough aspects of the human condition are built into the project. Biological, mental, environmental, and social limits are all challenges the self faces. However, it is, in part, these challenges that provide the grist for the mill and help us grow psychologically and socially. Challenges can develop grit in the personality and, therefore, the possibility of developing the willpower to embrace personal spiritual evolution when the time is right. Overcoming challenges helps the self develop endurance, which is the most important trait for the Way of the Mystic-Wizard. When your faith in yourself and your soul fails you, your simple endurance can help you finish a race.

It is important to say at the outset that there is nothing wrong with being a self. Yes, we are limited, but that is our design, and spiritually our project is to "upgrade" ourselves so that we can become more compassionate, wise, powerful, and, ultimately, more happy and fulfilled. These goals are in service to the self, the soul, and the world. The end goal is a merging with the celestial self or soul potentials in all of us so that we might arise in a more refined and powerful manner. This is traditionally what has been called becoming a saint.

THERE IS NOTHING WRONG WITH BEING A SELF, BUT WE CAN CHOOSE TO UPGRADE.

The Way of the Mystic-Wizard is in some basic sense an attempt to democratize the path to this outcome and no longer reserve it for the spiritual elite who live in caves and monasteries and have access to esoteric ideas, practices, and spiritual teachers. Historically it was quite common among such circles to believe that the only thing the average person was really good for was to financially support the endeavors of the spiritual elite. At one time, people even felt that way about artists and craftspeople as well.

As a longtime arts educator, I feel that we are living in a time when not only does everyone have the right to life, liberty, and the pursuit of happiness, but also the right to pursue genuine awakening, wisdom, mastery, and spiritual and creative accomplishment. I believe that this second pursuit is the best chance we have to address the larger problems we have as a species on Earth right now. This is my deepest motivation for writing this book and sharing the Way of the Mystic-Wizard. I want more Mystic-Wizards in the world! And I firmly believe that you, if you have come this far, have the right and the ability to be one.

Finally, the self is the main character in the story of our life. This may seem obvious, but some folks try to rid themselves of the self because they see it as flawed. It is *not* flawed. It is rather

an evolving entity with many contradictory elements that can become integrated and refined into more beautiful and elegant forms. It is a work of art. And in the primary metaphor of the old alchemists, the journey and process here is to turn ourselves from lead into gold. Refusal to embrace this unfolding process of the self is a refusal to enter into the transformative evolutionary process that is taking place in humanity; it is a denial of the primary impulse of creation. To reject transformation is to reject life, and although this rejection is allowed in the rules of our universe, it rarely creates happiness or the evolution of the self or the world. In fact, it usually generates pain, often in the name of ideology.

Throughout life's journey the self is transformed. In that process it goes through many forms of "death" and "rebirth," and a developmental stage that leads to greater integration as well as an expanded view of what the self is. In this process, one expands and then includes and integrates the previous view, holding that earlier view with compassion.

Philosopher and writer Ken Wilber described the nature of this self-transformational process as one that transcends the old view and yet includes it as a subset of the new view, rather than being one that transcends the old and then kills it. When we don't include the old, what was left behind tends to come back, and when it does, it is usually pissed off that it was left out of the process and sacrificed on the altar of the new you. Remember, the old myth and the new myth must wrestle like two dragons inside you, or like two kittens if you prefer, but the idea is not for the bigger kitten to win; it is for them to play, fight, wrestle, and flex their uniqueness before, in the end, they lie down together in peace beneath the tower of the self. Therefore, in reconciliation they become a new foundation for the tower. But that foundation takes time to solidify, and while the fight is going on, the tower shakes, the windows crack, and the villagers run screaming in fear that the tower is coming down.

In practice, some degree of sacrifice of the old self to the new self always takes place. Yet I have found, as with most processes, if you can identify it, name it, and thus distinguish it, then the negative results are far less damaging to us and to others. A more compassionate process is to allow the neglected parts of the self back to their seat at the table, to be included when you are better able to give them the attention they need. This leads us to the next step in our discussion of our multidimensionality—the nature, role, and reality of the soul.

FROM SELF TO SOUL: THE FIRST STEP IN AWAKENING

The soul is you at another level of being. This may at first seem odd, since you are more familiar with "you" as the self we just discussed. Yet once you look inside a bit, you will be surprised to see that you have always known that this other you was there and has always been present.

The easiest metaphor for understanding the nature of the relationship between soul and self is that of an author to their character in a novel or a movie. The essential perspective is that the soul generates the energy and direction of the self inside the level of reality that is our earthly life. Typically people say that they have a soul. But to be more blunt and honest, if we are going to express the idea of ownership at all, then it would be more accurate to say that your soul has a self, a you. For your life and your purpose, your powers and challenges, the very value of your life depends on the soul's intention to incarnate at all, as well as on its immortal existence. The soul is the author; the self is the character.

THE SOUL IS THE AUTHOR; THE SELF IS THE CHARACTER.

At first this may seem weird, because as modern people we have been developing a powerful sense of an independent self-identity for the last four hundred years or so. This modern sense

of self has been slowly evolving and creating a concept of its own inherent value as separate from the larger social-class system since the Renaissance and, later, the Industrial Revolution. We have gone through a powerful and important development in the growth of the idea that the self has rights that are imbued by divine design. We have now developed to such an extent that we can begin to turn back around and reengage with our own celestial origins without fear of being totally reabsorbed and losing a sense of our importance and potential destiny. It is much like a child learns in the middle school years to distance themselves from their parents and then in their mid-twenties, after the identity project of adolescence has been solidified, they can return to having a new but different relationship with their parents. So, too, the modern empowered citizen-self has evolved over hundreds of years, and we now take our modern sense of identity for granted. Most of us, once adult, can now reach into the deep well of our inner being and rediscover the soul without losing our own hard-earned sense of identity. With direction, we can instead discern a deeper, more authentic purpose for our lives beyond fulfilling our social responsibility to family and tribe.

The soul is a powerful force in our existence, just as an author is the powerful creative force in a character's existence. Thus the marriage of self and soul is the most important awakening process that a human being can have right now. Its practical value outshines even an enlightenment experience.

Awakening to the spirit and the unity of pure Awareness is so radical that without the guidance of the soul, that awakening can be catastrophic for the self. What is seen and realized about the nondual nature of the self (and all of reality) can be co-opted by your own shadow[8] and undermine your development or even shatter your self outright. Waking up to pure spirit or Awareness is such a radical identity shift that most

---

8   Parts of yourself you are afraid to face, including trauma, guilt, and loss.

people need to talk about the truth (sometimes leaving the rest of humanity thinking they are delusional). It can also lead to inflation of the self, and the personality thinking that it, the self, is actually God. This happens because such a person does not have the words to express the truth they saw, so they misunderstand it and co-opt it, turning it into a spiritual weapon. Development of self and connection to soul become essential to creating a container that can hold the process of awakening to pure Awareness.

The soul can lead you to an awakening of the spirit's presence when you are ready and deeply aligned with the soul. This happens, in the best case, after much inner work has already been done to integrate your shadow. You become much less likely to suffer an existential spiritual crisis when you powerfully sense spirit for the first time if your self and soul are integrated and more whole. In other words, the soul helps prepare the vessel of the self to hold the realization of its own divine foundation. The soul is the parent of the self, as well as the beloved, sister and brother, best friend, and spiritual spouse of the self. The soul is the individualized immortal source of all your inspiration.

My own introduction to the soul came when I took my first creative writing class in my sophomore year of college. Two important things happened in that class, and they were keystones to the conceptual framework that I would later build to hold the creative process and the start of the marriage of self and soul.

The first event was when my creative writing teacher told me to always treat my characters like they were real people. It was his only overarching comment about my story, which we had all read for class that Thursday. He said nothing of the theme or what my story meant, which I found insulting because I was trying to say something deep and important through the story. But I had made the serious blunder of sacrificing my characters to that end, a classic creative error. What I meant the story to be about did not resonate with my teacher because he could sense that none of it was real. He could feel my hands on the handlebars of the story trying to steer it the way I wanted it to go, so the story felt manipulated. Not because there weren't some well-rounded characters or nice sentences. It felt wrong because I had those things and yet I had jerked those characters around without respect for their autonomy. I made them say things they would not, things I myself was saying to impress my teacher with how clever I was. I was not clever; I was instead revealing my insecurity and lack of wisdom about the sacred nature of the writing process and the creation of a legitimate reality.

My story was a thing that did not lift off the page with life energy, which is the hallmark of true art. It was a humbling moment. My teacher went on to look at the first sentence, and we spent the rest of the class in a myopic and infuriating marathon investigation of the crafting of the first eight sentences in the first paragraph of a fifteen-page story. It was a lesson shown to me that was never explained and never spoken of again. It was not one I understood well at the time. In fact, I would not understand much of it for another decade.

Later that fall came the second event. It was midnight, and my second story was due the next day at 10:30 a.m. I had nothing. With an air of subtle despair, I went into the computer lab. Nearly ready to give up, I wondered if I would fail this class. I was exhausted and shut my eyes. Out of nowhere, I saw a man driving down a snowy, winding road. He was in an old, brown Jeep Wagoneer. Somehow I knew he was in New Hampshire, headed toward a hotel. It turned out it was Christmas Eve, which I did not know when I began writing. Every time I shut my eyes the story unfolded, a new scene opening in my mind from the mysterious source of all things. I was somehow *connected*. There turned out to be all these odd folks at the hotel who were hiding out away from everyone else. Some had no-where else to be, and some had places they should be but didn't want to be.

I stayed in that writing lab all night and all morning writing a twenty-four-page story that unfolded and refolded and folded over itself with grace. It was written, then shaped, then rewrit-ten, and then edited all in one sitting. It flowed from a place I couldn't identify, but I can tell you I was alive in a way I had never been before while writing. I knew this story was better than anything else I had ever written.

I left the lab at 10:00 a.m., made my ten copies to hand out, and even got to class on time. It would be another week before I got the results of my classmates' reading.

Seven days later, we began with a long silence at the start of class, and then I got the highest compliment I would ever re-ceive from my teacher: "Now *this* is a *story*..." I don't remember the rest of what he said, only that he made it clear in his tone that the story was something real, something that lifted off the page like magic, something worth working with.

Later, at his office desk, he would teach me how to work on the story line by line, how each line was a living brick in the cathedral of a story. Little did I know that he was initiating me into a writing practice handed down to him from writers such as Tobias Wolff and Raymond Carver, and to them from John Gardner, one of the great creative writing teachers of the second half of the twentieth century. Gardner was a man with a deeply religious instinct to his soul and his craft, as evidenced in his short but brilliant book *On Becoming a Novelist*. I later decided to dedicate my life to becoming a novelist based solely on Gardner's book and the experience of the story I had written that night.

Today, as I am writing this book, it is thirty years later—thirty years after that critical creative breakthrough to the source of my inspiration. I still remember the circumstances under which the soul came to visit and the portal opened between her and me. I had no real way of understanding what had happened, just the realization that of all the work I had ever done in my schooling, writing that story all night was the most important thing I had ever done. I would follow that golden thread for a decade and go on to get an MFA in creative writing. I wrote a novel, many stories, and hundreds of poems. I still write to this day—poems, journals, and, in this case, books on magic and spirituality. All of it was practice, a practice that built the bridge between self and soul.

In the end, the connection to soul and the creative process became a living link through which other areas of my life could be transformed. Ultimately, I turned this creative character-invention and story-writing process inward toward the self and thus began the spiritual journey that resulted in the book you are reading now. In some sense, Gardner's promise of what becoming a novelist could deliver to a person has come to fruition.

At the end of *On Becoming a Novelist*, Gardner writes,

> Novel-writing is not so much a profession as a yoga, or "way," an alternative to ordinary life-in-the-world. Its benefits are quasi-religious—a changed quality of mind and heart, satisfactions no non-novelist can understand—and its rigors generally bring no profit except to the spirit. For those who are authentically called to the profession, spiritual profits are enough.

Little did I know at the time that what he was pointing to was a kind of inner union of self, soul, and spirit, but this single paragraph dramatically affected the course of my life and eventually this text. All of my path—from novelist to poet, to educational leader and teacher, to finally Mystic-Wizard— can be traced from this one paragraph, which spoke to the fundamental capacity for the arts and a creative practice to deliver up something other than simple material rewards. It spoke to my desire to connect with my soul and to spirit and so awaken my true self.

Any creation, even a minor character in a novel you may be writing, is, if it is inspired by the vision of the soul, a legitimate and authentic creation of source. It deserves the respect that such a being deserves, as does every personality and being. Creativity and its many children are essentially a reenactment of the continual outflow of spirit-force that issues forth from the formless source of all that is. The soul is the source of you, and of your creative power and energy. It is your home and origin.

Yet most people do not think of the soul as being real, or as real as we are, and so, as with anything we do not think of as real, we spend much less of our attention on it, even allowing it to fester. The relationship with the soul rarely develops to real depth. The soul sits and watches, and whispers and guides, and sometimes creates a major course correction. Meanwhile, the self barrels forward into life, clueless of its origin, power, or sacred creative potential. This state of affairs tells us much about the conditions of our universe and the rules of engagement (so to speak). We will expound more on that later. Suffice it to say that much depends on our willingness to engage and ask for help so that help can find us.

As you awaken to the presence of your soul, you are, in essence, a character-person awakening to the presence of your author. And just as when writing a story, when you treat your characters like they are real, they start to tell you what they want to do and show you where they want to go. So, too, when you begin to turn toward your soul, you are awakening to the story of your life and you begin to sense the realness of your soul, finally allowing it to have a "real" effect in your actual outer world, your "real" life. You can then start to tell your author what you want. You can learn to get what you really want, or get past the wanting of it. Either way, the result is the same;

your desire is complete and you can move on. And after many, many false desires are burned away, the real things you want will emerge from the soul, and they will manifest, just as in a great novel, with a kind of inevitability. You will even become thankful (eventually) that you did not obtain your false desires, for they would have been diversions and distractions taking you off the path your soul has for you.

Your soul gains traction in the story of your life once you begin to work with it to manifest what it desires and, as such, what you *truly* need or desire. For what the soul desires, which rests in your heart, is what will unfold in your life—if you can manage to get to the real true desire hidden there. For all of us, many of the true desires of the soul are hidden under a variety of false images and attachments, but they are still there, existing, waiting to be uncovered. In fact, the journey of uncovering the authentic *expression* of the soul is an important part of the process of becoming *integrated* with your soul.

A pearl begins in an oyster with a grain of sand that irritates and spurs the growth of the pearl; so, too, with awakening to the soul and the evolution of the self. The false aspects of the self are the grains of sand, which represent the hurdles to becoming authentic. The process of overcoming the false, conditioned layers of the self is the process that makes us authentic. So, in some interesting story-making sense, the false layers are not actually false—they are, in fact, the plot drivers of the story. The imbalances and falseness still reside there, and this fact creates much suffering in our and other people's lives. And yet we all have these imbalances, so we are all driving each other to become more awake, integrated, and capable.

We are the art project of the soul.

WE ARE THE

ART PROJECT

OF THE SOUL.

THE SOUL

Naturally, the self wonders what the *soul* really is. The easiest explanation, perhaps, is that it is an awake and aware matrix of conscious and unconscious energies manifesting in a body. This could be a fairly good definition of what our own self and body are as well. The real difference is the level of frequency at which the two different aspects exist. Imagine the difference between self and soul as similar to the difference between a dolphin and an eagle. Both creatures are able to touch the element that the other lives in, air and water, but they are each designed to exist in their own element.

The soul is created to exist outside the human domain of experience. In mythology this other realm and aspect of us is often represented by birds and the sky they fly in, so it was intuited that the soul exists at a more refined, or less dense, frequency than we do. Our issue then is being able to communicate across that "wall," or frequency change. Luckily, we have our imagination, the all-important faculty that helps us have real communication with the soul. Without imagination, or symbolic consciousness, we could not access our inspiration or get a single new idea.

The challenge most people face as they begin the marriage of self and soul is that they do not feel that the soul is as real as they (the self) are. One idea that helps to adjust this natural and normal perspective is the idea that the soul is, in fact, *more* real than you are. In an ultimate sense, this is false, for all of us are made of spirit, but in another, more essential sense, it is true, since the soul gives birth to your existence. In addition, there is ample modern and historical evidence from those who have had near-death experiences that the realms we enter after we leave our physical manifestation are in fact more luminous and vibrant, more real-seeming, to us than our own world and experience. Of course, "luminous," "numinous," "awake," "filled with light," and "immortal" are only a few ways to describe something as being more real. However, these are the ways humans have tended to describe what is most real and essential and imbued with life. For beings with a limited life span, it is natural to think of immortality as falling into the "more than" category. But in truth, it's just different.

The point here is to see that the soul and the soul realm have as much ontological reality as our own world. In fact, they may have *more*, for if the way something is constructed is outside the decay of time, then it is eternal. On that basis alone we could say that the soul realm has a lot more staying power than our own world, which always falls apart and will end in fire in a few billion years.

The *nature* of the soul, then, is of course something of a mystery, and always will be for us, yet much can be sensed and lived into. Let us just call it "our immortal aspect that manifests us," and acknowledge that it lives and speaks to us through our heart, mind, and imagination.

The *role* of the soul, we will posit, is to guide and co-create our life with us. The soul is the author and we are the character, and we will work together to transform the self and the world around us. We work to embody as much of the divine capacities of the soul as we can while we are here on Earth. There is no rush to do this, but each human life has a precious quality to it because it happens exactly this way only once.

The *reality* of the soul is more essential than we are, being immortal and our source, so we have the opportunity to focus a lot more attention on it than we have up to this point. How we do so will be a major aspect of our practice and the reorientation of our waking life once our spiritual practice is up and running. The practice will be one in which the innate miracle power of the soul to manifest practical and transformative results seemingly out of nothing does in fact manifest in our lives. This is what we humans call "magic"; hence, the path of the Mystic-Wizard.

From the soul's perspective, magic is simply how to get things done for the self-character it has created.

The operating system of the soul and self married together can perhaps most easily be described as divine magic. This system connects us back up to the fundamentally mysterious and magical capacity of the spirit to bring forth objects and ideas from formlessness. Just as a magician pulls a rabbit out of a hat, so too does pure unconditioned Awareness give birth to things from the mysterious nothing of itself. It is this power of creation to which the soul has direct access, and through the soul, so do you. The soul is the genie in Aladdin's lamp that has been trapped for a thousand years (or a hundred incarnations) before the young aspirant finally discovers and rubs the lamp. Spirit is the lamp itself, the space inside and outside the lamp, and the innate ability of the lamp to create a genie, you, and everything else.

By connecting to the soul, we awaken the genie and the relationship begins, leading to the question, of course, of what to wish for. For me, the lamp I rubbed was writing fiction, and so the genie arrived and gave me a Christmas present. What I asked for that night was a story to tell that was worth telling. You are reading it now and will be your own judge of whether the genie's gift was worthwhile.

Fortunately for us, the soul, our own personal, immortal genie, is on our side and does everything it can to lead us to our true wishes (which the soul gave us) by slowly and sometimes painfully detaching us from the delusions we have about what we think we want, what we think we need, and what we think will make us happy. It is a good thing the soul knows what it is doing and what we really want, because most of us do not. However, do not feel bad about that lack of knowledge; we were built from ignorance so that we could go on the journey to discover these personal truths. The beautiful irony is that what shapes us is not the accomplishment but the journey. In other words, the journey is a process that unfolds and always starts with classic misdirection, like a good mystery novel. You are at A, and then you set out to get to B, only to find that once you arrive at B you can now see C. So off you go after C, knowing that it is a more genuine destination that, ironically, you would never have seen unless you had first quested for B. In fact, by traveling from A to B you become a different person, and only that new person can see the new objective at C. This is usually because B fails or disappoints you in some irrevocable fashion.

The path to authenticity is an ironic one, and it must be, for if you knew where you were going, you would likely balk and refuse to go.

THE SPIRIT

The last aspect of our multidimensional being we will discuss is *spirit*, or pure Awareness. It is perhaps the simplest aspect of all. It is also the most essential and the most powerful, yet of the entire plethora of beings that we are, it is the least directive or insistent.

The spirit-self can best be described as that part of you that rests in a state of peacefully witnessing your life and the life of your soul. It is not involved in what is taking place, but rather holds the space for it to unfold. In meditation it is possible to be aware of the self, the soul, and the spirit simultaneously. You can climb the ladder of being until you sit on the high throne of the spirit-self and see the other aspects below or within it. From that place, a deep peace can arise, along with a subtle bliss in the heart, followed by a magnificent joy in the throat. In this state you can imagine simply sitting in meditation forever, with no reason or desire to leave.

This is a powerful and important state of self to uncover, for it is deeply regenerative and allows the self and the soul to be

SOMETIMES YOU CAN ONLY GET FROM A TO C BY GOING THROUGH B.

at rest. It helps solidify the realization that everything is utterly fine as is and was already always complete. At the same time, once you descend from the throne, the self is ready to go again, because at the self level there are responsibilities to take care of and a life to be lived. One of the great mistakes you can make as a mystic, and it has been made countless times, is to reach the high seat and see all as pure spirit. Then the self decides that the "answer" to life is this and so attempts to destroy the self and the soul. The self sees this as an escape from pain and suffering and believes that life is not needed. It is like a fish realizing it is in the ocean, deciding it will dissolve itself into water, and telling every other fish that it should dissolve as well. This is a false narrative. Why would the ocean need to dissolve its own fish?

Thirty years ago, while I was wrestling with this very mystical conundrum, one of my mystical druidic teachers, Philip Carr-Gomm, asked me a key nondual question. We were on a druidic retreat on Iona, an island with a long mystical druidic history. The spiritual power of Iona naturally increases the tension you feel between the opposites you are holding inside you. This results in a rich, if challenging, atmosphere for transformation. Philip, an author, spiritual teacher, and the chosen chief of the international Order of Bards, Ovates and Druids (a position he held for thirty-two years before he handed it on), was patiently listening to me trying to resolve the conundrum between doing and being, the soul's deep impulse to incarnate, and spirit, which has no need to at all. I was trying to drive myself toward some kind of ultimate freedom in order to resolve this tension and was going a bit mad in the process because of Iona's intense field of influence and my own desperation. As we sat at a table by the window having tea, the speech of the grail suddenly issued forth from this wise mystic teacher. "What is the rush?" he asked.

And with that simple question, he oriented me toward facing life on its own terms and engaging with it despite the pain.

What is the rush, when you are already fully here? is, of course, a mystical question. My own awakening was some months away, but that question started me down the road that led to it.

The mystical instinct tends to push toward an ascension out of life and pain; it thinks something is wrong or broken here that needs to be transcended. But there is nothing wrong or broken. It all just *is*. Druidry and other shamanic paths descend into life and see nature and us humans in it as sacred expressions of the formless mystical source.

In the Way of the Mystic-Wizard, we hold both instincts in the palms of our hands as we live and meditate and practice. We recognize the desire to escape and seek the formless realm of spirit, as well as the deep desire of the soul to delve into existence and manifestation. This tension of ascending and descending impulses is the primary driver of incarnated, self-aware existence, and it is the reconciliation of these two deep desires that is the fruition of this path. For when you do manage it, you live in the world of the nondual while simultaneously embracing all life and all its suffering, joy, and beauty. What then arises is profound gratitude that anything exists at all. *Because nothing has to be*. Spirit is, was, and always will be already complete without the manifest world, which is why life, in the spiritual traditions, is considered a gift of the divine, because the divine doesn't need it and never will. However, the divine performs the action anyway; you could say the divine is making cake for no reason at all. The cake of reality is simply good. It is no better or worse than formlessness. It is simply good to have cake and human beings, despite all the pain and suffering that might go with them. Long ago, Ralph Waldo Emerson wrote that we suffer and toil so that formlessness can become vocal with speech. I believe he was correct, and I would add that this is not because formlessness *needs* to become vocal with speech, but rather it is happening only because it *can* happen.

The power and peace of the spiritual self are an important

backdrop for the journey that is the marriage of self and soul and the manifestation of the soul's life plan for you. It is from this deep place of your multidimensional being that you can begin to discern the true desires of the soul. Developing a meditation practice that allows you to access this state of being eventually becomes essential to the unfolding of your life as well as to the ability to manifest actual change in the world of the self. Once you can rest in this place of the spirit-self during meditation, then you can integrate the soul and the self and stay aware of all their aspects as they merge into one being. From that place the creative miracle power that your various selves are designed to be able to implement can come forth. That power will emerge in the way that *you* are designed to express power. We are as unique in our expression of spiritual power as we are in our spiritual paths.

How you will ultimately mediate power from the inner world into the outer world is the great mystery of your innate uniqueness. The way you take inspiration and turn it into manifestation is the really interesting aspect of being a human being.

WHAT IS THE RUSH, WHEN YOU ARE ALREADY FULLY HERE?

THE SHADOW

We are all aware, thanks to Freud, that we have unconscious desires and motivations. What most people are not aware of is that we also have a veritable theater full of unconscious characters or suppressed self-parts in us that would like to run the show of our life. Collectively they make up the aspects of our *shadow*. In keeping with our theme of respecting aspects of our being, it is best to assume your shadow is as real as you. When it is in control of you, you think and feel like it is you. Only later, after you stop being possessed by your own shadow, do you sense that something inside you hijacked your Awareness and acted out its own regressive agenda.

In essence, the shadow is the you that is repressed and kept down by the many faces of your socialized self, who tries to orient and control what you do in life. All of this effort at control is so that you survive socially, belong in your family, and can master whatever "success" means in your culture. The trouble is that the shadow also contains enormous repressed energies that want to run things as well. These energies are essential for making the journey of awakening and completing the marriage of self and soul.

Common energies that are held by the shadow are all the aspects of our wounded self that we would rather not look at— our angry self, lustful self, greedy self, fearful self, jealous self, and many, many more. These aspects are like little goblins living in the basement of our house. Each one wants up and out into the light to express itself, but we have blocked and locked them away. As our self grew up and was socialized, these aspects were repressed and put in their place down in the basement of our being. This is a normal and natural process, but so, too, is the process of becoming intimate with these goblins and recovering the energy used to fully repress them. There is also hidden wisdom that emerges in these awakened aspects that can teach us about the nature of our journey and about energy, power, desire, growth, and integration.

HIDDEN WISDOM EMERGES FROM OUR SHADOW ASPECTS.

For example, the angry self, when integrated, becomes the empowered self that defends boundaries and calls out injustice. The self-loathing or shameful self, when integrated and brought into consciousness, can evolve into the compassionate self. The anxious self that worries about everything, when integrated, can arise as alertness and insight into the patterns of reality that are used to chart safe passage. And our embarrassing lust, in its awakened nature, becomes the engine and source of all our power. It has the power to purify each body center it manifests through and to open a new power and perspective. Each center then becomes a sacred expression of spirit and soul.

The internal mastery of the primal energy of biological life, when blended with the energy in the top of the pyramid, becomes the building blocks for an entirely new self, an immortal self of energy and light. When we begin the journey, the energies are all over the place and are being run by confused, automated, conditioned patterns. At the end of the journey, we have become a well-tuned instrument through which the energy of life joyously cascades and plays. The energy itself is experienced as an awakened expression of wisdom.

Each one of the repressed aspects of our emotional life can be reintegrated and expressed by a soul-guided personality. In doing so, the aspect expresses itself with wisdom and compassion. Mastery of this process of integration and enlightened expression is the inner work of the Way of the Mystic-Wizard. Working to accomplish anything less is an avoidance of our responsibility as aware beings. Not everyone has the capacity for this level of awareness or mastery, which makes the art of inner work even more essential for those who can accomplish it. Life continually challenges us to engage with new situations that trigger more unconscious material to surface. So there is no final destination, just the continual process of development, much like any other artist seeking mastery over their specialty.

The work, then, of the marriage of the self and soul is about integrating our celestial aspects. The work is also very much about integrating our shadow aspects. It is important to know that you cannot walk this path to awakening and integration without facing the disowned parts of yourself. However, we have a great ally in this process: the teacher, guide, and healer that is the soul. Thus, the shadow and the self can learn to dance with the music that soul sets for them. It is still not easy, but it is much easier than trying to do it on our own.

Over and over in my own life, my soul has brought me to deeper levels of healing by revealing the parts of me that have been left behind. The beauty of the soul is that it can see when the exact right time is. The beauty of the soul is that it can see the exact right time and circumstances for drawing up another layer of the shadow to be processed, named, and known intimately. It is a remarkable and challenging process.

Self, soul, spirit, and shadow—these are simply one way to look at the aspects of our being, one set of words to describe them. They are terms I have found helpful to describe actual realities that I have discovered on my path. How exactly any of this is truly structured is, of course, a mystery, but one thing is clear: we and the cosmos are constructed in a particular way, and this way can be uncovered and (to a certain extent) made sense of.

The essential rule of thumb I have used for my cosmology of the self is this: Does the system provide results? Does it *work* as a way to do the work of transformation and manifestation of my life path and self? I am not interested in whether it is perfectly accurate in every sense. No matter what we do, we are always looking through a clouded lens at states of being and realms of being that are dimly lit for us at best. We are fish speaking about the sky. But I do not choose to make this a big issue. As a Mystic-Wizard on the path of awakening, I am more interested in gaining traction in the process of transfiguration than in anything else. The structure as laid out above is always being tweaked and updated as I deepen my own experience and gain new insight from doing the actual work and reading about the work others are doing.

Journey Two

THE GROVE OF THE WISE

Set your intention to go to the Grove of the Wise and ask what you need to know now. Close your eyes, relax, take a deep breath, and find yourself floating in the mist. You are floating down deeper, *five, four, three,* deeper into the mist, *two,* deeper, *one,* until finally you find yourself in front of your inner-world door. Land on the platform there, and go up to the door. Place both hands on the door; feel the entrance to the inner world and sense the world that is beyond the door.

You hear the door click, and it opens into the corridor of the castle within. Step through the archway and into the corridor, and start walking along the stone floor, reaching out with your right hand and dragging your fingers along the stone wall. Notice your fingers leave traces of light behind as you go.

You come to a stairway to the right; it spirals down. Go down the spiral stairway until you come out of it into the common room. This is a beautiful room, where there is a fireplace, a couch, a chair, a table, and graceful windows letting in light.

There is a cat sitting somewhere; go say hello to the cat. Then look around the room a little bit and notice that the quality of the light has changed slightly, something about the shift in the seasons.

Now go across the room. You find another staircase made of stone that spirals up. Go up that stone staircase until you come to another platform; then go through the archway and turn to the right. Now you're in the portal room, and you're staring at the shimmering portal on the other side of the room. To the left of the portal, against the wall, is a standing closet. Go over to the standing closet and open it. Find in there your traveling robes. Put them on. As you do, feel a sense of empowerment from the robes.

Then go and stand before the shimmering portal. Reach out your hands and put them into the energy and light of the portal; feel that light and energy move through your own inner light body. Attune yourself to the energy of the portal and the world that is beyond the portal. Then step through the shimmering portal.

You are standing on the hillside, looking out over the vast forest. Below you, at the bottom of the hill, is a beautiful field. There is a breeze that brushes your hair, and you can feel a coolness in the air, a shift toward autumn. Off to the right you see the great mountain range; the tips of the mountains are already covered in snow. Start walking down the hill; follow the path till you get to the bottom of the hill. And then start walking across the field till you get closer to the edge of the forest.

As you get closer to the edge of the forest, you see the pathway into the forest, and there is the standing stone. On the standing stone is a symbol, the same symbol that is on the door into the inner world. Go up and touch the standing stone with one hand; just feel the stone.

Out of the forest to the left steps your animal guide from your first journey. Go over and say hello to your animal. Stand at the gateway of the birch trees next to the standing stone.

Set your intention to go to the central grove, the center of the forest, the center of all things. Then start walking into the forest along the forest path. It is a beautiful day, cool underneath the trees as you walk along and go deeper into the forest. In the distance up ahead, you hear the sound of a stream. Eventually you come to the stream; it is not wide, and there is a stone in the middle that you can step on to cross. But before you do, lean down and wash your hands in the stream; drink from the stream, and wash your face. Feel what it is like to be present at the stream and cleansed by the sacred waters. The water is cold and pure, clean. Then stand, step across onto the stone, then jump across to the other side of the stream and keep walking deeper into the forest.

The farther you go, the more the forest changes. It appears to get older, and the trees even larger. Then you see out in front of you what seems like a pool of light. It is pouring into one area of the forest, and you come at last to the edge of what looks like a clearing. It is a wide clearing surrounded by a circle of enormous old trees. You look out to the center, and there you see an old woman sitting by a fire over which she has placed a small cauldron.

Here at the center of the grove, she sits. Approach her and sit in front of the fire. She reaches into a pouch at the side of her waist, and she drops some herbs into the fire; they spark up, wafting incense through the air. You become aware that the old woman is aware of you and your life circumstances right now in the outer world, and so she offers to answer any question you might have or help you with anything you need to process. Anything you let go of can be put into the cauldron to be bubbled away. Go ahead and communicate with her now as long as you need . . .

And now it is time to take your leave. The old woman reaches into a pocket in her robes; she pulls out a gift for you, and opens her hand and gives it to you. Give thanks to her.

Get up from the fire and move to the edge of the clearing and back into the forest. Start walking along; before you know it, you have come to the stream. There by the stream you find a little vial with a cork stopper. Go ahead and open the vial and fill it with water from the stream so you can bring some of it with you; put the vial in the pocket of your robes. Then start walking away from the stream toward the edge of the forest.

Quickly you come to the edge of the forest, and there is the standing stone.

It is time to say goodbye to your animal guide. Give thanks to your animal, and tell your animal you will return many times. Then turn and walk across the field and go up the hill, until you reach the shimmering portal. Before you step through, look out again over the forest and realize that you now know how to get to the center of the forest, out of which all four sacred paths and directions flow. You sense that there is some way in which the four directions come together, which someday you will discover.

Now turn and step through the shimmering portal. You find yourself in the portal room. Take off your robes and put them in the closet, then retrieve the vial of water and bring it with you. Leave the portal room and go down the stairs into the common room and walk over to the table. On the table is a large map of the inner world. There you can see the castle that you are in and the hill and the forest, and now the trail that leads to the central grove. There is much yet to discover.

To the left of the map is a small glass vase. In it is a flower that looks like it is thirsty. Open up the glass vial you brought from the stream, and pour the water in. You watch as the flower is quickly rejuvenated. It has been brought back to life. Finally, put the vial next to the vase.

Now it is time to leave. Leave the common room, go up the stairs into the hallway until you come to the back of the door. As it opens on its own, step through and turn; the door shuts on its own. And there is the symbol, once again, of your entry into the inner world. Place your left hand on the symbol on the door and say in your mind, *It is done*.

Now you are drifting up away from the door, through the mist. *One, two*, coming back, *three*, reintegrating into the outer world. *Four*, wiggle your toes and fingers. You are coming completely back to the outer world, completely present with all the memories you need. *Five*, open your eyes, and you are fully returned and back to the outer world.

Record what stands out to you in your journey journal.

PART THREE

THE NATURE OF REALITY

The impossible creatures gather,
for the uncanniness of their own existence
unsettles them.

In Part Three, I will introduce you to the nondual element and provide some exercises and instructions for how to explore the nature of Awareness. There are specific moments in this chapter intended to begin opening your perspective beyond the egoic structures that we all are built with. Awakening is a process. There are many steps as it unfolds in your life, and they are unique to you.

UNDERSTANDING THE NONDUAL PERSPECTIVE
AND THE PROCESS OF AWAKENING

A critical element of understanding and integrating self, soul, spirit, and shadow is the concept of nondualism. The nondual perspective says that everything is one. On some level, many of us already suspect, or even know, that everything is somehow connected to everything else. But on a day-to-day basis, this understanding means nothing unless you can actually sense this reality and live from this view—and only then can it help you.

What follows are "pointing-out instructions" about nondualism. Please note that the way this next section is written is constructed in a specific fashion and includes long, redundant sentences. This is on purpose. Just keep reading, even when the language seems to be repeating itself. The structure of the writing is intended to induce a shift in view. It is designed to help you see that what is reading this book is what wrote it.

The genius of the nondual perspective is quite simple.

You know you are awake because you are reading this. You also understand that you are you and not someone else across the room. This is self-evident in your experience. This is not an argument; it is merely the fact of your experience. There is a distinct sense of *you* being here reading this right now. And right now, as I am writing this, I also have a unique understanding of *me* being here writing this, as does everyone else who will ever read this. We refer to this, as we often do, as your awareness.

But what if your awareness didn't belong to you alone?

You are aware and awake. If you were not, you would be asleep or unconscious.

Here is the nondual insight:

The awareness that you are using right now to read this sentence is exactly the same as the awareness I am using to write it. We are all expressions of the same awake, aware, ever-present, unending, spacious Awareness. I do not mean our thoughts and personalities are identical; only our awareness is identical, and there is a big difference between your pure, empty, open awareness and your thoughts, feelings, and personality. It is so simple and obvious an observation that, after a moment's reflection, the mind typically rejects it outright. Ask yourself: If we did not share the same basic awareness, how would we even be able to communicate?

Another way of saying this is that you already contain and have 100 percent of spirit, and 100 percent of the radical awakened, enlightened mind is already you, here, right now. It is not hiding; it is *this*, the this that you are using right now to read this sentence. No upgrade is needed. No breakthrough, no purification is needed for this to be itself, and for you to be this. It, our Awareness, is reading this and aware of this thought here right now that is flowing through your mind.

I know—it seems too simple. The awakened state is supposed to be far away, hard to achieve, and so on. However, it is not. It is right here, right now, witnessing your mind reading this. It is only a thought that spirit is far away, and that thought is moving through Awareness like all the other thoughts you have ever had or ever will have, leaving no mark whatsoever on pure, untarnished, open, immortal Awareness—your own natural state. It is this, utterly present, right here, right now. If you seek it, you might miss it, because the treasure is already here. You are it. We are it. Nowhere to go. We never left. This is it, right here, right now. How can that be? Sense it around you, or sense it in yourself—either way is fine.

When you were very young, maybe one year old, you knew this. Then, as your personality grew and your ability to think and name things developed, you, the thinking mind, in a sense, took possession of your Awareness and claimed it as your own—sort of like a land grab, or going for the ultimate cookie. You created a belief that stated that this, Awareness, is mine. I am me. I am (*insert name*). That conceptual grab is all right and suitable for a toddler, for it appears to help us develop into an adult personality.

The premise here is that an idea that you made up when you were one or two years old is beneficial for forming an identity and a sense of self, but can become a pretty cumbersome idea much later in life, especially if it is fundamentally not true. Your thinking that you possess Awareness provides the necessary training wheels for forming a personality, but once you are grown and can ride along with balance, then you no longer need the extra side wheels. "This Awareness is mine, and only mine" is a useful developmental view, so to speak, from ages two through eighteen. However, Awareness belongs to us all equally and is all of us equally. Your sense of being awake and aware is identical to everyone else's.

If you look carefully inside right now, you will sense that "your" Awareness is the part of you that makes you feel like you are you. In other words, the thing you treasure most, your Awareness, is the same Awareness as that in your friend and your enemy, your dog, and, in fact, even in the sky.

Awareness is like the Force as it is described in *Star Wars*. It permeates all things. When that spacious, open wakefulness is infused in the body, mind, and soul of a human being, it also develops a personality with desires and dreams and all the myriad and wonderful uniqueness of every single human being.

WE ARE ALL EXPRESSIONS OF THE SAME UNENDING AWARENESS.

There is near infinite variety in human beings and in beings in general, all founded on a uniform and utterly identical pure, open Awareness that permeates all things. How do I know this? Because I can sense it and see it. This is not just a theory; it is an actual view or perspective that can be developed slowly over time or can be suddenly seen in an instant—or both.

The first time I saw this perspective I was under a lot of stress, and I read some traditional pointing-out instructions in a book by Ken Wilber called *The Eye of Spirit*. By reading the chapter in the way that Wilber instructed (just as I instructed you), I became aware of the ever-present. Something in me let go, and Awareness was simply there—everywhere—awake and present in everything. I knew instantly that this was what and who I really was, and so, too, was everyone else.

My reaction was to laugh, because it seemed so absurd that this had not been utterly clear all along. I realized that we human beings, due to the nature of our development, had become really good actors. We had invested deeply in our personality and merged our mental self-form with Awareness but had subsequently forgotten that we had done so. At some point early on, we stopped seeing our personality as something inside us, and instead merged with it and became it. It is fine we did so, since it seems a natural human developmental stage. However, the value of seeing through this early merge is profound if the time is right for it.

THE TREASURE IS
ALREADY HERE.
YOU ARE IT.

The Wilber chapter on pointing-out instructions is now available free online, and I quote the opening section to give you a taste of the writing and of his instructions. If you want to stop and go read this chapter online now, please do; or simply save it for some other time. From *The Eye of Spirit*, the chapter "Always Already: The Brilliant Clarity of Ever-Present Awareness":

What follows are various 'pointing out' instructions, direct pointers to mind's essential nature or intrinsic

Spirit. Traditionally this involves a great deal of intentional repetition. If you read this material in the normal manner, you might find the repetitions tedious and perhaps irritating. If you would like the rest of this particular section to work for you, please read it in a slow and leisurely manner, letting the words and the repetitions sink in. You can also use these sections as material for meditation, using no more than one or two paragraphs—or even one or two sentences—for each session.

Where are we to locate Spirit? What are we actually allowed to acknowledge as Sacred? Where exactly is the Ground of Being? Where is this ultimate Divine?

The Great Search: The Realization of the Nondual traditions is uncompromising: there is only Spirit, there is only God, there is only Emptiness in all its radiant wonder. All the good and all the evil, the very best and the very worst, the upright and the degenerate—each and all are radically perfect manifestations of Spirit precisely as they are. There is nothing but God, nothing but the Goddess, nothing but Spirit in all directions, and not a grain of sand, not a speck of dust, is more or less Spirit than any other.

The Oneness referred to here is actually your most essential, awake Awareness. It is the you that is reading this book currently, not some hidden or distant Awareness that must be found or recovered or was lost. All those times you have spaced out and had no thoughts but were still there, that is it—just that. Utterly and ridiculously common, like the air we breathe (or if we were fish, it would be the water we swim in) and finally are made of. Who notices the water if you are a fish? Or the air if you are human? It is there, but we do not see it because we delude ourselves into the mistaken notion that Awareness and thought are the same thing. But they are not. If you look right now, even if you think about it logically, you will notice that you are still here when you are not thinking about anything, so you must be more than your thoughts. You are that. You are this, silent stillness, right now. That which is aware as you are reading this right now is Awareness. You already have 100 percent of it. Just this.

As mentioned, these are called pointing-out instructions, and they mean just what they say. They point out the nature of ever-present Awareness. This entire section was a simple way to explain and point out to you what is already here. What do you do with this insight? You gently cultivate your awareness of Awareness. To help that process, look at the sky. See the vastness of it; just explore and open up to the sky's spaciousness while sensing the awake Awareness. As we move through this journey, we will return to becoming more aware of Awareness.

. . . .

EXERCISE
Exploratory Nondual Exercises

To help you understand the idea of nonduality, here are two exercises. If you don't like the first, try the second. Finding the right nondual exercise for you can take some time, and using one that triggers you is counterproductive. The idea is not to blast through your denial with dynamite but rather to see through it from a new perspective, like looking at a Magic Eye picture that from one angle shows one image and from another angle shows a different image. We want to see, without damaging the mind.

Exercise 1: One-to-One, Person-to-Person

Use this exercise if you like intimacy and can partner with someone who also likes intimacy. Do not try to force this exercise on someone who is not intimacy-oriented.

With a willing partner you trust, do some nondual sharing. Look into your partner's eyes and start by seeing them as a person, as you know them. Just look and see what is there while they do the same back to you. At first, looking at each other can be uncomfortable, but if you stay with it, you may discover a kind of simple, childlike innocence and connection. Awareness in you is looking at Awareness in them. You may also feel awkward because you are suddenly very close, very intimate; that is because you are occupying the same Awareness.

The truth is, everyone has already practiced nondual sharing many times before. It happened often when you were a baby, so you have already seen through this Awareness thousands of times as a child; you may not remember it right away, but the patterns are there in your brain, already laid down.

Take some time and rest in that space together.

Then, after that, talk about what it is like. What is it like to have this essential self that you share with another? How does it feel? What part of you can relax or be at peace in the natural state? What part of you is terrified you will be overwhelmed or die? Just observe. You are like a fish sensing the existence of water for the first time.

Exercise 2: Ocean or Sky

Use this exercise if you would like to explore nonduality without another human being or cannot find a partner. This option is also a good one for nature lovers, since nature mystics already sense the presence of Awareness as it manifests in the natural world. The idea is to go one step beyond nature mysticism and into formless mysticism.

Go to the beach—physically or in your imagination.

Notice the waves. Pay attention to the sound, the sight, and the feel of the rolling waves as they come in. Connect with the rhythm and flow.

Then look farther out for the waves; slowly move your gaze farther and farther out in the ocean until finally you see the horizon where the water meets the sky. There, at that point, rest your sight and Awareness. In the background will be the sounds of the waves and in the foreground of your consciousness will be the vastness of the sky, and the ocean, and the line where they meet. It will be just there, where the sky and the ocean meet on the horizon and there is a stillness where nothing moves—no waves, nothing—that the two things are one, both two things and one thing. And you are that. You are the silence and stillness of the horizon. You are the vastness of the ocean below, and the vastness of the sky above; you are form and formlessness meeting on the line of the horizon, the line where creation is and is not at the same time.

Rest in that, and be complete. There is nothing beyond the horizon, nowhere else to go, nothing left to do or accomplish. At the end of the world, you find your true home.

. . . .

THE BENEFIT OF CULTIVATING AWARENESS

What does cultivating an awareness of spacious, open Awareness do for us? For some people, it might do nothing at first. For others, Awareness may be obvious, and they have always known it. Whatever the case, the point of culti-vating the natural state is that you are totally complete in that state. There is nothing to do, nowhere to go, nothing else that needs to be known or done. It is, in a fundamental sense, a subtle, healthy bliss of completion and coming home.

This resting in the natural state, with others or the self and nature, can be profoundly rejuvenating. It does not solve your existential problems any more than a warm bath solves your ac-tual problems, but it does clean off the endless agendas, plans, and intentions. You are simply complete. In that state it is re-markable how inspired you can become; for instance, problems may suddenly have solutions you would never find in a state of dualistic separation.

Cultivating the natural state is also called "developing the view." It is the view from the end of the quest. It is the view you already had before you set out on the search. In Tibetan Buddhism, it is the idea that you begin at the end and get the highest, most advanced, and most refined spiritual teachings (read "most simple") at the start. Just start at the end. Then you can see it and cultivate it. And if you are ripe and ready for that view, you will value it at least a little bit. But if you don't, no worries, there is no rush; just keep on living your life until you do value it and then you will come back to it.

The results of practicing the natural state are that you be-come more and more aware of Awareness over time.

And how does this help?

Have you ever felt alone, abandoned, insecure, overwhelmed, desperate, betrayed, or confused?

Yes. And no doubt you will feel all those things again some-day, as they are prevalent occurrences in life. The natural non-dual state will not make them go away or stop coming, but you will have an ally when they do come at you. You will have this Awareness that permeates the field of your universe. You cultivate Awareness because the natural state is the profound ground upon which all reality exists. In fact, reality as we know it is a manifestation of Awareness, an ornament of beauty and terror that has arisen right out of this ordinary ground of being.

This book is not just about your natural state and cultivating awareness of Awareness. That is only part of the story, but it is the foundation on which the rest of the story rests. In Tibetan Buddhism, the realization of the view is called "the ultimate medicine." This is because the ultimate medicine corrects the fundamental misperception of our mind. It is this misperception that often drives us to seek an endless assortment of things to satisfy our deep hunger for feeling complete. The view satisfies that hunger.

You will still need to go to the doctor to get medicine for your body and a counselor for your mind and heart. But the ground-level misperception of Awareness can be corrected when it is engaged with and cultivated. And guess what? Awareness begins to support its own cultivation of the view. Awareness wants to be found out, wants to be recognized. It wants to return to the home of its own ground, which it never truly left.

Why? Because all distortions of view are a kind of energetic contraction that takes energy to sustain. They are like a clenched fist. The fist wants to relax and move to a state of least tension, to the zero point. This is part of the way our universe is constructed; all things move toward entropy. As they do, tension is released, and so are we released from the mental suffering that our ideas and beliefs about our life create. As you cultivate Awareness, even the tension that is the self-sense begins to loosen and can finally vanish for brief moments. A release of tension energy occurs when you notice the presence of Awareness before it settles into peace. It is a gift to be released from mental contractions, even for only a moment. Over time, the moments will stretch out and become longer.

The Mirror

After having done some nondual sharing with your friend or nature, try it in the mirror.

Look in the mirror past or through yourself to Awareness. Notice that Awareness is seeing you through you, and you are seeing it back. That is how close you are. So close that it is, in fact, you. It is the you that is reading this right now, and it is the same you that wrote this very sentence.

UNDERSTANDING THE WORLDVIEW OF A MYSTIC-WIZARD

The perspective of the wizard is derived from the nondual. Many shamans and wizards of the classical sort have had a significant illness, often intertwined with a near-death experience, that made them into the shamans they are. This ordeal also sometimes allows them to see through blockages to unconditioned Awareness. Amidst their illness, they sometimes see past the conceptual block of separation and sense that reality is infused by one infinite, formless spirit. They also often see the multidimensional nature of the universe. This vision includes many levels of reality; however, we will use a simple system to help clarify these many levels and group them into two basic categories: the inner world and the outer world. You already know about these two worlds and have been working with them all your life, but you likely don't fully appreciate them because of the moment in history in which you were born.

The outer world is the physical dimension of the planets, stars, people, cats, bananas, your body, and so on; it is clearly accessed via your five senses. The inner world is the symbolic world and is accessed via your imagination; it includes all your inner voices, dreams, feelings, and fears, and your entire experience of reality. You never really experience the outer world as it actually is, because you are always only experiencing it inside you as a sensation that you interpret.

We have an outer objective reality that we all can sense even though we can't fully know it objectively. There is, however, much agreement about how things are and work in the outer world. In other words, there are rules for how this outer world works; we call this science and wisdom. There are also rules for how the inner reality interprets it; we call this psychology.

There is a way that things actually are, and we as humans are good at working with that. Everything is not an illusion; everything is an authentic ornament of Awareness, and it all works in a very particular way. The old mystical maxim "everything is an illusion" is a bad advertisement for mystical insight. The idea is not that everything is an illusion and therefore not real, because clearly that is not a tenable explanation for the condition we find ourselves in. What is meant is that how we perceive reality is incomplete. Our perception of reality from our view of separateness could be described more accurately as "delusional." The world is not an illusion, but we are partially deluded about how things are, who we are, and the nature of reality itself. This is hardly a big surprise, as we are inside the thing we call reality. If a fish could talk, it would not be a big surprise if the fish had no idea what water was. How would it know after all? Water has always been right there, closer than its own fins.

What does the wizard perspective add to our nondual view? The first essential idea is that the inner world is not just in your head. Your mind and imagination are needed to perceive the inner world and outer world. Still, just as the external world does not require your mind to exist, there is an internal objective and collective universe. It is as natural as the outer world and exists before you and after you. That is what the shaman-wizard perspective adds back to our worldview. The symbolic realm is not only in your head; it is everywhere, and your imagination is simply the tool you use to access it. This is not a belief from the shamanic perspective; it is a factual reality based on experience. This is because shamanism itself is practical and reality-tested in its approach. If the shamanic worldview were a fantasy and didn't create concrete results in the outer world, it would have been abandoned long ago. Like science, shamanism is an approach to helping people survive and thrive in the external world. A wizard uses inner-world science and the technology of the spirit world to accomplish outer-world objectives. Those objectives can be tactical, such as finding where the fish are in a lake, to existential, such as discerning the meaning and purpose of a particular person's life path. Answers to both of these types of questions can be discovered by traveling inward and communicating with the beings that we encounter in the inner world.

EVERYTHING IS AN AUTHENTIC ORNAMENT OF AWARENESS.

Having access to the inner world helps you gain information that can be known only from outside time and space as we perceive it. A simple comparison is that we have more information than fish do about how things look from above the water. So, our perspective and the way we exist give us specific capacities that fish do not have. So, too, does existing only in the inner world give particular perspectives and insights that are hard for us to access on our own. When that information is provided to us, it can help us make decisions, solve problems, or guide us to find what we need to thrive. Inner-world beings can even

help us fulfill deep, compelling longings for things that are not realistically achievable in the outer world, simply because the outer world, no matter how good it gets, is not an idealized version of reality.

The outer world is a place of remarkable possibility, yet to try to create things under the outer-world conditions is challenging. These conditions require significant effort, struggle, and often great risk. The results of events in our lives shape us, empower us, and give us an experience that is sometimes equally difficult and profound. The challenges of the outer world can provide us with real depth and can generate both wisdom and compassion in time, if such are cultivated. They give the higher self, the soul, the opportunity to experience something beyond the idealized spiritual worlds. This, it turns out, has value to the soul.

WHAT IS REALNESS?

One of the fundamental questions that comes up when people begin to journey into the inner world and interact with inner-world beings is "Is this real?" Thus, a discussion of what "real" means is helpful to integrate the experiences.

Rather than thinking in an all-or-nothing, real-or-not-real binary, I would like you to imagine that what is "real" falls on a spectrum from 0 to 10.

Human beings are designed to look to the outer world to stay alive, and they acquire food, shelter, and companionship in order to do so. Therefore we see the external physical world as a 10. At 9 or 8 are the word-labels we use for the outer world.

For instance, a rock is not the word "rock." "Rock" is just a word we use to describe something; a stone just is what it is—it is not "a rock." This seems obvious at first, yet see how hard it is to think about a rock without the word-label "rock" popping up? See how hard it is to experience the truth that a rock is not "a rock"? The mind rebels.

The mind does not like to have its categories and names shattered, leaving it with nothing to know. The mind likes to be right. Furthermore, the mind likes to believe its labels are the truth, and only truth, about reality. The mind likes to believe it is accurate with its labels; however, many of these word-names are utterly arbitrary and their origin is lost in the ancient past.

Try to see a rock without the conceptual overlay your mind crafts, and you will understand how powerful that instinct to overlay a label actually is. It is much harder to *not* think of the name than you probably think it will be. Once you have tried a rock, try a cup. Look at a cup without knowing the label or its use. See it the way a master painter sees it, as a shape, a form. Then, once you have practiced, try this exercise with a person your mind thinks you know well. Imagine they have no name, because they don't—at least not really in the ultimate level of real, which is a 10. They are not their name. Pretend you forgot their name and see a human being without an overlay; observe how much more you notice about them.

So the framework we lay over the top of the world—the concepts we have for the world—feels very real to us, but it is only in our minds. It is a lot less solid than matter, but for us these overlays are a 9 on our real scale—meaning still very real to us. Because of this unconscious belief that we know something with our overlay, word-names have a massive effect on our lives. We have other ideas about our word-names that we call "beliefs," and when we think those strong thoughts, it seems to make our thoughts as solid as rocks—enough so that people will die for ideas that have become deeply reified.

Then there are all those feelings we have that come and go. They could be anywhere on the scale from 3 to 9. What is interesting is that when you feel something, it also affects your body chemically. You could have a feeling that might feel like it's a 6, 7, or 8 on the real spectrum and it could have a consequence of a 10 in your body. You feel something that you are nervous and embarrassed about at a 6, and your body has an anxiety reaction with a realness of 10.

THE INNER AND OUTER WORLDS ARE TWO FACES OF THE SAME COIN.

What about the inner world, which is a lot like dreaming? When in a dream, most people believe the dream is real, and so we have physiological responses to that realness. Often, people wake up from dreams or nightmares and think, "Thank goodness that wasn't real." So something in the dream world can start at a 10 and then suddenly drop down to a 2 on the spectrum. There are some people who have lucid dreams, where they wake up in the middle of their dream and realize, "Oh, I'm dreaming." That makes it seem like the dream is less real, in the sense that they know that they are actually in the dream world.

When you interact with a being in the inner world, you are interacting with something that you might experience as between a 3 and a 9, depending on the depth of your immersion. If you put yourself into a "trance" by closing your eyes and focusing on your inner world, changing your brainwaves a little bit as you go further in, you might experience those things in the inner world as 5, 6, 7, or even 8 or 9 on the realness scale. But very few people experience them as a 10, because being in a shamanic trance is like lucid dreaming. You are awake in the dream and have an awareness of what you are doing. Even when you have entirely lost track of the outer world, there is a part of you that still knows that this inner world you are exploring is not the same as walking around in the external world. This knowledge keeps us grounded and embodied.

Eventually, we learn that the inner and outer worlds are two faces of the same coin with slightly different rules. The inner world is much more flexible and symbolic, and the exterior world is much more solid and literal. In other words, one is mind-based and the other is matter-based. They are both made of the same water, just different manifestations of the formlessness that is the source of everything. Therefore the maximum that a person usually can experience in the inner world is a realness of 9. Once a practitioner is well established in the inner world, they typically no longer compare outer and inner, just as you do not need to compare your outer daily life to your dream life—each has its own rules, possibilities, and functions. That does not make the inner less important; it simply means we may perceive it as less solid on our scale of realness because of our embodied nature. And, how we value something is not necessarily correlated with its realness number; for instance, we can value a belief that sits at 9 more than we value our body, which is at 10.

What is important is that anything you experience in the inner world can affect your physiological state, mental state, and emotional state. Your inner experiences can therefore be empowering and full of positive energy. You can be infused with that energy, and you can bring that out into your outer world. This can affect your body, your view of the outer world, and ultimately your entire life.

People use this technique of inner-world imaginal exploration and practice all the time. Athletes use it to train themselves to perform better; speakers use it to prepare themselves to give speeches; other people talk to inner coaches, wise people, and therapists. The question is, when you go into the inner world, are the beings that you interact with *real*? The answer is that it depends on where they fall on your own realness scale. Are they ultimately real in the way we mean it, as a 10 on the scale? Are you?

Nothing is ultimately any more real than anybody else is real, in the sense that we all share the same Awareness. We are all amazing ornaments of unconditioned Awareness, and in the outer world we happen to have bodies of matter. So, are inner beings real in the sense that they have a body of some kind? Sure, they have a body of symbolic energy impressions. Do they have a physical body exactly like ours? No. Can their actions affect our physical bodies? Absolutely. Are they aware that they are also made of pure Awareness? Maybe.

This leads us to the final question: Are inner-world beings autonomous?

Many times, what people mean by "real" is "If they are figments of my imagination, then they are not real."

When you interact with an actual inner-world being that is objectively part of the inner world, in the sense that it exists whether you are there or not, then it is essentially not much different from interacting with someone in the outer world. You want to be aware of that being's autonomy and capacity for working with you, just like anyone in the outer world. The only way to determine the nature of what's real is to do the exploratory work and find out for yourself.

Most modern people come from a place of "the inner world is not real," not meaning they believe it can't have an effect on them but rather believing that those beings do not have an autonomous existence. My only warning would be to be careful with that idea. From the shamanic perspective, inner-world animals and beings are real indeed, and autonomous. If you have doubts about autonomous realness, let that doubt push you to search for an experiential answer rather than taking my word for it. While your jury is still out, *act* like inner-world beings are real, and they will act like you are real. When you experientially have enough data to allow your mind to open to inner-world beings having a higher realness number, you will not be in shock; you will just have moved your worldview into a more expansive version of the universe. As you expand your experiences, you will develop inner-world relationships that guide you and help you, relationships with parts of your own soul as well as with beings that are teachers and allies.

But what if you are only daydreaming?

Most of the time, when you first enter the inner world, you are inside your own autonomous, imaginary egg. That's the simplest way of describing it. So when you are daydreaming, you are working within what is right around you and in you. That egg is almost like an art studio, where you can imagine things into being and create infinite possibilities. I call it "the common room," and I conceive of it as the first room in an inner castle that has various rooms for a variety of purposes, which we will explore later.

Let us say you are in your crafting studio working on a creative problem. You are trying to figure out the solution to it, and then you essentially pray, "Hey, I need help." Awareness, which is aware of everything, can manifest help coming to you through pure inspiration. That can come directly through the top of the egg, right into your own head.

Or, let us say a particular artist inspires you, and that artist passed away at some point, maybe Michelangelo or Leonardo da Vinci, and you have been studying their work. You want to connect with that being's learning and knowledge. There is no reason to believe that anything gets lost. So you are in your egg, and you are sitting there in your studio (which is your imagination), and you start thinking, "I wonder what Leonardo da Vinci would say about this." You decide to connect with Leonardo da Vinci and the essence of what he would bring to the table. There is no reason to believe you could not do that. If you get some great idea and you begin to have a conversation with Leonardo da Vinci, then it is working. And in order to get the best out of that imagined incarnation, you would want to treat Leonardo as though he really *is* Leonardo.

Leonardo is dead, but in the inner world he is accessible, depending on how you approach the inner world. So at some point, once something feels like it is functioning in an authentic way that's supportive of you, you grow out of asking the question "What is real?" because you simply do not care anymore. What you care about is whether or not you can do anything productive with the information or experience.

So let us assume that everything is on the realness scale somewhere, and nothing is not real. In fact, anything that is 0 on the scale would not be perceivable at all. Treat everything on the scale, in the inside world and the outside world, with respect. This is essentially a shamanic perspective. Shamanism is practical in producing results and having respect for what spontaneously appears to us in both worlds.

Of course, you still need to have boundaries and take responsibility for yourself in the inner world, just as you do in the outer world, so call upon powerful, compassionate spirits and ancestors and animal spirits that support you.

Journey Three
THE WHITE STONE BRIDGE

Take a deep breath. Relax. You find yourself in the inner world floating in the mist, and you begin to descend through the mist, *five, four,* deeper, *three,* deeper, *two,* deeper, until, *one,* you appear in front of the doorway to your inner world.

Approach the doorway and gently place both hands on the door. Notice the symbol at the center of the door and attune yourself to the energies of the inner castle. Set your intention to travel to the white stone bridge in the southern part of the forest to meet the Inner Beloved. You hear the door click and it opens; you step through and into the castle corridor. The door shuts behind you. Step forward and reach out your right hand to trace your fingers along the stone wall. Notice that your fingers trail light behind you.

You come to the stairway that leads down to the right into the common room. Walk down the stairs, which curve around once. You come into the common room, and there a dog lies in front of the fireplace. It immediately gets up, wags its tail, and comes over to meet you. You notice that the cat is over on the table, where the map of the inner world is laid out. The cat is walking along the edge of the map of the world. It sits and notices you.

It's time now to travel . . .

Go across the common room through the open archway and up the stairs.

They curve around once until you come to a landing. Step into the portal room, turn right, and there at the far end of the room is a shimmering portal. Walk to the portal and then turn to the closet. Open the closet door, take out your traveling robes, and put them on.

In the corner leans your traveling staff; take it up. As you do, notice that etched up and down the staff are runes, various kinds of symbols. You intuitively understand that they are runes of power that can direct the energies of the inner world that flow through you. They were carved into the staff by the ancient One-Eyed One. In time they will reveal themselves to you, for each rune is alive with sound, power, and form. They cannot be mastered with the mind; rather, they become a part of you in time, and you intuitively come to know them the way you come to know the wind, water, fire, stone, and pure Awareness.

Stand before the shimmering portal and place both hands, including the staff, into the shimmering portal and feel the energy. Feel the energy move into the staff, into your arms, into your body, purifying you and connecting you to the inner world beyond the portal. Let this light infuse your nervous system and the subtle body of energy that you use to travel into the inner world. Then step through the portal.

You find yourself standing on a snowy hill, overlooking a wintry forest and a field at the edge of the woods. Set your intention to travel to the south, to the white stone bridge, and then start walking down the hill; feel your staff in your hand. As you get to the bottom of the hill and step onto the pathway that leads across the field, become aware of the spaciousness around you. You sense that this open spacious field is awake and is aware. It welcomes you.

This sense of awareness is always with you. Even when you are focused on something else, it's always surrounding you and is you. It walks with you across the field. It is present and complete.

You come at last to the edge of the forest, and there is the standing stone. Perched atop it is a raven that looks down with a gleaming eye. You sense something vast watching through that gleam. Notice again the door symbol on the stone, and set your intention to travel to the white stone bridge.

Then you notice movement to your left, and out from the forest steps an animal ready to guide you to the bridge. Go greet the animal, then together step onto the forest path. Start walking deeper into the forest with the animal. On either side in the woods, you sense the presence of the two wolves tracking you and protecting you as you go. And above you, two ravens are flying through the forest treetops, also protecting and guiding you.

You come to the stream and there you meet the Washer, who sits in winter meditation, legs crossed and snow piling up on her shoulders. She is aware of you. She opens her eyes and gently indicates that you should follow the frozen stream southward; there is a path along the stream edge. It will lead you to the boar paths. And so you set out along the path through the woods, following the frozen stream. It is an extraordinarily beautiful pathway through the woods, calm and peaceful, and the forest is mostly asleep.

You come to a place where you can jump across the stream to reach the other side; you do that and then follow the path again, farther south, until you come at last to a small hut. It seems to be the home of a hermit perhaps, a forest wizard, a druid. You recognize this place somehow, but you do not yet belong here. So pass across the open space in front of the hut. The trail goes deeper and narrows as it turns into the woods away from the stream, and you realize you're following the ancient boar paths, the hidden ways through the forest that lead to the deep places that touch other worlds.

The trees grow taller, and you come at last to a curve in the path that joins a much wider path. You walk along for some time until you see yet another standing stone, and you realize you've come very near the southern edge of this forest realm. You look at the standing stone and see again the doorway etched into the stone. Touch the symbol to connect this stone in the south to the stone in the eastern forest edge and to the front door to the inner castle. Now all three are connected.

Then step forward and around one last large tree. You see a beautiful white stone bridge and the river that flows beneath it, unfrozen by some magic despite the cold. The bridge arches, and there's snow along its railings. Stop at the edge of the bridge with staff in hand. The animal that guided you steps back, for it cannot pass. You must go alone to the top of the bridge to meet the Inner Beloved. And then you sense a presence on the other side of the bridge. The beloved has arrived from deep in the forgotten forest beyond the river and is aware of you.

Now start walking up the bridge toward its apex. As you do, you see a shimmering figure coming closer as you rise to the highest part of the bridge, until finally you are right across from each other. The beloved reaches out one hand and gently takes hold of the same staff you are holding, and you feel the connection. Then they reach out with their other hand and take hold of your other hand.

Connect with this part of the soul now, the Inner Beloved. Let this part of you express how much they love you, exactly as you are. Take as long as you need.

And now it is time to return.

Step away and know that the beloved will always be with you, always within you, holding, supporting, guiding. Say your goodbyes and descend back down the bridge to where you find the animal waiting for you. As you walk away from the bridge, you sense the beloved's presence with you at all times.

Start walking the path until you come to the standing stone. Reach out and put your hand on the stone; gently, through this stone, connect to the stone on the far eastern side of the forest. Now, will yourself to transport there to that stone.

And suddenly you find yourself on the eastern edge of the forest with your hand on the original standing stone. There you stand with your animal, and you recognize that you have returned to the eastern side of the forest: there's the field and the hill behind it and the castle on the hill. Now give your thanks to your animal guide. It's time to return.

Walk across the field with your staff and then up the hill until you arrive at the shimmering portal. Step through the shimmering portal, and you find yourself in the portal room. Return your staff to the corner and your traveling robes to the closet. Walk out of the portal room and down the spiral staircase and into the common room. There again, the dog waits, then stands up and comes to greet you. The cat watches from the table. Walk over to the table with the dog, and look down at the large map spread out on the table. There you see the forest and to the left at the southern edge of the map, the white stone bridge, the bridge of the beloved.

Now it's time to return to the outer world. Leave the common room and go up the spiral staircase into the stone corridor and turn left. As you come to the front door, it opens. Step through, and there you see the mist. Turn, and the door closes behind you. Reach out your left hand and put it on the symbol. Say in your mind, *It is done.*

You are rising up through the mist. *One*, *two*, returning, *three*, higher, returning to this world, *four*, wiggle your toes and your fingers, bringing everything you need back into your waking awareness until finally, *five*, you open your eyes and are fully returned to the outer world, aware and awake.

Take out your journal and record what stood out to you about this experience.

Part Four

BUILDING YOUR PRACTICE

They continue down the street,
an imaginary menagerie burrowing into
their attempt to set things right.

In Part Four, we gather the elements of a spiritual practice so you have a method of developing a relationship with your soul and can begin the process of building the sacred container that will hold the deep purpose and direction of your life. This will result in a scaffolding being put up around your egoic self, which then allows the soul to dismantle the self and rebuild it as the awakening process takes hold, without a total breakdown of your life. This does not mean you will not be broken apart—you will, over and over—but the practice container, the cocoon, will hold that process and allow it to unfold with a greater chance of success and with your full awareness that you are in it.

DEVELOPING A RELATIONSHIP WITH YOUR SOUL

There are many elements in a spiritual practice, and many aspects in the conceptual foundation for a practice, mindset, and life. We began in Parts One, Two, and Three to acquire the conceptual and motivational foundation for daily practice and for living a Mystic-Wizard spiritual life. We also need to establish the foundation for you to develop a living relationship with your soul.

It is essential to realize that at this point you could begin to receive inspiration and evidence of the existence of your multidimensional nature. Your soul is listening, watching, and waiting to create your practice with you. You would not likely still be reading at this point if this were not the case. Therefore, do not be surprised if various intuitions, signs, or synchronicities begin to manifest, in the material world or in dreams, that reaffirm your soul's presence and its support and guidance as you take the first steps in creating a new orientation for your life.

Lastly, keep in mind that like a parent waiting for a child to learn to walk, the soul waits patiently for the self to begin to wake up, turn toward it, and make a connection from this dimension to the soul dimension. But the soul has always been there, watching you, loving you, and supporting you. It has been waiting all your life for this time to arise.

FIND A SACRED SPACE

The first step to building a daily spiritual practice is finding a sacred space. This space can be any place in which you can have uninterrupted time and in which you can create a simple, temporary altar and have a place to sit. It can also be a more permanent place in your home if you have the means to find a spot that will not be disturbed—a corner of your room, an entire room, or even a closet you clear out for this use.

The purpose of creating a sacred space is to help us encounter the otherworldly or, in our case, to connect to the mystical realms of the soul and spirit. We go to our sacred space to connect with the divine, and in so doing, we align the different levels of our being and become whole. Anyone who has been to a sacred site and felt the difference has come away changed, understanding what is possible at a holy site. There are places where the inner and outer worlds are more aligned and in which it is easier to communicate with the inner realms and easier to do our practice.

Like any special spot set aside for a particular activity, space becomes an intentional container for working. Teachers set up their classrooms to encourage learning. Doctors and nurses set up surgery rooms to perform operations. We manage space this way in every central activity in life, so the concept of creating sacred space should not seem odd to modern people, but it does, because they have not felt empowered to create their own sacred space. In the ancient and medieval world, it was common to have space for practice and connection with the inner world and the divine. Every household in ancient Rome had a shrine to the local deities and ancestors. As we lost our connection to this kind of veneration of the sacred, we lost a pathway to the soul and to our inner wisdom.

The foundation of our practice is not a new invention but is instead what human beings have been doing since they created sacred altars in caves many thousands of years ago. We are returning to our shamanic roots, the time long before religion turned into vast organizations with rules and regulations and specialized priests. We are reaching deep into our ancestral knowledge for the instinct to create sacred space and to claim our fundamental human right to develop and express ourselves in a way that supports our practice and our connection to the inner world. It is your right to do so, and while on this path it is your responsibility to do so. You cannot connect the top and the bottom of the pyramid without creating a sacred place to practice the art of communing with the inner world and the divine.

Artists of all kinds need their own space where they do their work. Any serious artist has a studio; even if they paint or draw on the road at times, they have a home base where the work gets done. When artists train in graduate schools, they each get their own studio space. The need is so evident that schools devote many resources to creating these spaces.

The need for space for the mystical and magical arts is no different, so it is necessary that you invest in it and insist on it, and do not apologize for creating a sacred space to commune with soul and spirit. It is unfortunate that, as modern people, we are so disconnected from our spiritual instincts that we feel guilty or ashamed about wanting to embody them in a tangible studio for the soul. We were trained to believe that only in a church or temple can significant spiritual intention be engaged, yet all the ancient mystics and wizards went to caves or monastic cells, or built rooms in towers to practice the mystic and magical arts. The tower is a classic archetype of the abode of the Mystic-Wizard because it reaches upward and

DO NOT APOLOGIZE FOR CREATING A SACRED SPACE TO COMMUNE WITH SOUL AND SPIRIT.

emulates a mountain or the top of the pyramid with which we are trying to connect. And a cave represents a turning inward to our source and the inner world. Both are equally important in our work.

Because the world is an ornament of pure Awareness, no one place, person, or thing is ultimately more sacred than another. On the other hand, there are some places, persons, and objects energetically more in alignment with ideal archetypal forms than others. Items and beings in archetypal alignment channel divine energy more smoothly and efficiently, just like a clean engine or a healthy body works better than a dirty engine or diseased body. Spaces also work more smoothly when they are closer to the ideal.

In terms of space, the difference depends on the area's physical attributes but also on people's intentions. The water is the same, but what is floating in the water—the intentions, thoughts, and actions of the people who inhabit the space—can make it cloudy or clear. These two truths—that there is absolute space and relative space, an absolute universe and a relative universe—are not in conflict. They overlap, so there is no need to prioritize one view of the truth over the other. Hold them both. It is all one, all the same water, and it is also infused with varying degrees of energetic expression. You do not need to resolve this puzzle, because it is already always resolved, and only your logical mind wonders why or how it can be so. Your comprehension or lack of understanding of this resolution does not affect reality one bit. Simply rest in the space of nondual presence, and the mind will stop asking how both views can be.

Many questions are irreconcilable at the level at which they arise in consciousness. For instance, our friend the metaphorical fish that wonders what it's like to live above the water will never know the answer from below the surface. Only by flying free, even for a moment, will the fish experience and see the answer. This leaping beyond is what it is like to see beyond the muddy water of a mind. In the Dzogchen tradition of Tibetan Buddhism, seeing beyond the dualistic mind into nondual perception is called seeing the Great Perfection.[9]

Sacred sites embody a person's intention to open deeply to the soul and spirit dimensions and become aware of Awareness. In time, your space will resonate with a perpetual tone of sacred purpose because of the intentional way you enter and perform your practice. The standing wave, or frequency, that embodies your intention is there to help you connect to the divine and become more aligned to soul and spirit and thus become more whole. It is when you least want to practice that this frequency and intention of space become immeasurable help in sticking with your commitment to practice.

If you have a temporary space that you set up every time you do your practice, the very act of setting up your altar creates the space and sets the tone for your practice. A temporary space can be in your home, your office, your yard, or really anywhere you can lay out sacred objects to create the space and intention to practice. You can build a portable altar that you carry with you as well. All you need is a cloth, some sacred objects, and setup and takedown rituals.

Traveling can seem like an impossible time for spiritual practice, but it is vital to develop the ability to practice on the road and practice when you are least capable of doing so. We practice to master ourselves, and mastery counts most when you are under stress.

On the days you are not at home, or you least feel like practicing, simply decide that you will sit and practice for one

---

[9]   This tradition presents a spiritual shortcut, which is a radical and direct approach that cuts through confusion and directly points out unconditioned Awareness.

minute.[10] Unless you are profoundly ill, anyone anywhere can practice for one minute. You can close your eyes in a coffee shop and start your practice. One minute later, you are complete. You will find in time that these mini sessions of training can be utilized throughout your day while washing dishes, folding laundry, cleaning, or even while watching a show. You learn that practice and life can be integrated together seamlessly, and no one but you knows you are doing it. In time, you will be able to practice with your eyes open, and then eventually even while you are speaking to someone. You can develop the ability to be aware of what is in the foreground of your perceptions, such as a person or place, as well as in the background, which is unconditioned Awareness. This double perspective allows the shifts that occur when you are awake to the presence of Awareness. Being awake in your everyday actions affects your heart (feeling), throat (speech), mind (thinking), and body (energy) in a beneficial way. With time, you will realize that *you* have become the moving altar, and in that state you are more capable of hearing the soul's guidance and of spontaneously feeling joy and compassion.

---

[10] It is easy to fall into the same patterns we have built in school or other areas of life that have supported determination and continual output in those areas—doing your homework or producing your work product. While these skills can and will be applied to your practice in the beginning so as to kick-start the process, it is important to note that your practice is not another output. Ironically, it is instead a surrendering to receive that which will actually motivate the many outputs of your life. We need not become emotionally intertwined with our practice in the same way we would with homework assignments or work projects where there is a consequence if they are not done well. It may take time to undo these conditioned patterns, but eventually the feeling of pressure to "do" your practice will shift into a natural allowing of the practice to unfold as it needs to.

ASSEMBLE AN ALTAR

Once you have located a space, the next step is assembling the materials for an altar, which is the focal point of your sacred space. You will place your sacred objects on it, things that connect you to your soul and spirit. Your altar can be a simple cloth you lay on the floor, or a mini table, or a nice piece of wood, or perhaps a larger table if you have a dedicated room.

Once you have the altar, set it up. You will need something to represent your true spiritual self or pure Awareness (perhaps a sphere of stone) and something to represent your soul (perhaps an image). You also might choose to find pictures or statues of various holy beings who inspire you. These can be anything from beings from long ago, people still living today, or any sacred being with which you feel intuitively connected. I believe that being guided by more than one tradition is one of the rich religious opportunities of our time, so connecting with multiple traditions is certainly acceptable, but so is sticking to one tradition if that is what you feel called to do right now.

In my sacred room, I have images and statues of these holy beings from many significant traditions: Avalokiteshvara, Siddhartha the Buddha, the Nazarene, White Tara, Vajrasattva, Vajrayogini, Isis, Osiris, Anubis, Horus, Maat, Ganesha, Odin, Freya, Frigga, Hel, Sif, Bast, the Fates, and Thor. These beings have played a major role in my life over the last thirty years. Each has brought something different to teach me about myself and my path. Every day I spend time with them in my sacred room, and thus, every day, I am in their excellent company from a spiritual standpoint. Over time, I was drawn to spend more and more time in the sacred room I constructed until finally I began sleeping in the room, the way a monk in a monastery might. Eventually, the place sort of woke up around me, and the intuitions and communication with the inner world became a constant connection. There is a reason such a place is called *sanctum sanctorum*.[11]

The room of the Mystic-Wizard is a room that exists in duality—that is, it exists in two worlds that are intertwined, allowing easy access to both worlds. Shamans and mystics from ancient times have both found and created such places where the wall between the worlds is thinner and the work can be done more easily. From those places, the magic and alchemy of the Mystic-Wizard can unfold. From the *sanctum sanctorum*, you will someday craft your life like an artist crafts a painting, and you will do so not only for your benefit and for those you love; you will, as the Tibetans do from their temples, perform powerful rituals for the benefit of the entire world and all sentient beings in all places.

Lastly, the layout of your sacred space requires knowledge of the four directions and the ideas associated with each. What each direction represents can depend on your tradition and on where you live. I place my altar table in the north and my meditation seat in the south; in the west is a window and in the east is a door. I did what felt right, which allowed me to create a pleasing sacred space where I wanted to practice. (Later I will speak more about the four directions and how they can be used to help you manage the energies and commitments of your entire life. The tool for doing so is called the Life Compass, a device that allows you to see what has been in shadow for most of your life and to validate all the critical aspects of your entire life in one glance. The Life Compass has become an invaluable asset in maintaining balance in my life, and we will devote time

IN THE *SANCTUM SANCTORUM*, THE WALL BETWEEN THE WORLDS IS THINNER.

---

[11] *Sanctum sanctorum* means holy place, sanctuary, inner shrine, the most holy place or thing.

to it because of its importance in helping to manage your life and thus sustain your practice.)

SEEK TEACHINGS EVERYWHERE

When I was in college, I was fortunate to have a religion professor who was also an extraordinary mystic. His name was Ralph Slotten, a six-foot-six Nordic giant of a man, in his late sixties when I met him, with a great head of silver-grey hair. He had to lean over a bit to talk with you because his hearing was going. Professor Slotten's existence permitted me to explore all of the "earth's traditions," as he called them. They were all, in his mind, fascinating, and worth studying and experiencing. He had spent considerable time in India with various spiritual teachers, Hindus, Muslims, Jains, and Christians. He also regularly visited all the major denominations of churches and temples in the town of Carlisle, Pennsylvania, where our college was. He suggested that I could respectfully engage with all the traditions that called to my heart.

Professor Slotten told me of a tremendous nondual and soul-awakening experience he'd had that lasted a full five days. He said he had simply walked around in a golden sea of energy he called the bliss-field. It had happened years before I arrived, and his eyes sparkled and his laugh was infectious because he had spent so many years successfully embodying the revelation. The most challenging part, he said, was the month after the bliss faded. He had gone so high that when he came down, he became depressed. But in the end, he rose back up and settled at a more elevated station than before the breakthrough. He was one of the people I was lucky to have contact with who already knew the truth of both the formless presence of Awareness and the existence of the soul. However, he never let on about what he had learned to anyone who was not inclined to know. Instead, you simply felt more at ease and hopeful around him, as if the space near him was itself endlessly full of possibility.

The Druid leader Philip Carr-Gomm writes in his book *Seek Teachings Everywhere* about the fortunate contemporary spiritual impulse to explore multiple traditions. Part of the blessing of our time is that we can seek teachings everywhere without being antagonized or attacked by a religious authority. Seeking teachings everywhere is a significant element of the Way of the Mystic-Wizard and of all spiritual and religious innovators who put inspiration before dogma and transformation before tradition.[12]

Throughout my journey, there were indeed times when I sincerely wanted to limit myself to one tradition. In each instance, the spirit realm revealed that I needed elements from various traditions to synthesize new spiritual insights. This book is, in fact, a reflection of that inner-world teaching. Today we are called to discover new ways to access the inner world. The mixing of people from all over the world in our great cities has brought about a creative fusion of music, food, art, and so on, including wisdom and spiritual practice.

Eventually, at some point I stopped resisting the spiritual direction, and I allowed myself to walk a syncretistic path of integration and discovery. *Syncretic* is an important word for us Mystic-Wizards, for it validates the multitraditional path of the Way of the Mystic-Wizard. Words embody intention, and

---

[12] In fact "seek teachings everywhere" comes from Tibetan Dzogchen and is a line in a poem by Tibetan master Chögyal Namkhai Norbu.

syncretic names the processes involved in this way. Syncretic means something that is influenced by two or more styles or traditions. The word has a noble heritage. It stems from the ancient Greek word *synkrētismos,* which means an alliance or federation of Cretan cities working together. In our modern era, the word syncretic retains this intention of working together. It was not easy for Greek city-states to ally with one another when the competition was fierce between them. It is the same with religious traditions. Some religious traditions fiercely defend dogma as if it is spiritual truth, much like a city-state defends its territory, as if their existence depends on the idea that their tradition is the only truth.

TO SEEK TEACHINGS EVERYWHERE MEANS TO SEEK SPIRIT AND SOUL EVERYWHERE.

Today, the use of the word syncretic applies to societies, music, religion, and even linguistics. Syncretism also reflects the natural process of change that develops through time and through the creative interaction between various earthly actors and the inner spiritual world. The Way of the Mystic-Wizard fully embraces the inherent creativity of the universe, which includes the constant advancement of knowledge, insight, and wisdom through the synthesis of living wisdom streams.

No longer arguing with divine beings about my path turned out to be a good decision. Instead, I spent my time working with them to advance my development and help the world. We can use multiple traditions without appropriating or commercializing; we can approach each path with respect for its sacred nature and origins. Moving with sensitivity and guidance is part of the challenge and responsibility of our time. To seek teachings everywhere also means to seek spirit and soul everywhere. Where you find spirit and soul, respect for the tradition will naturally emerge.

FIND IMAGES FOR YOUR SOUL AND SPIRIT

Once you have created a layout for your space and have a small shelf or table or bookshelf for an altar, you can start seeking images that inspire you. Seeking your soul images and spirit images is a process, and doing so is part of the start of the marriage of self and soul. Some people know right away what those images are, while others take a long time to find them. Still others find images slowly, and the images may even change over time. I have been through all of the above, and offer here some simple ideas that may help you discover the needed images.

The first is to speak or write to your soul, especially if you never have before. The idea is to ask to be led to an image or object that represents your soul. A soul image can and often does appear as a beautiful being. It is not uncommon for it to be a beautiful woman or man who is in many ways the embodiment of what you imagine to be the perfect soul mate. It is also not uncommon for people to have always had the image of their soul mate in their imagination and to have projected it out onto actual people. This projection rarely works out well, as you ultimately end up concluding that the mortal does not embody the ideal—and, frankly, no mortal does. This projection can help you fall in love, but eventually it must be withdrawn and you must learn to love others for who they are, not for who you would like them to be. The soul, however, expresses your idealized vision. Your goal is to uncover that soul mate image and place it on your altar so that you can relate to this idealized divine beloved in a way that reflects the power, beauty, wisdom, and compassion of your divine self.

At times my soul has taken a masculine image, and at other

times feminine, depending on my needs at that moment. No matter what energy the soul image is embodying, the essential compassionate intentions are the same. In my study of Tibetan Buddhism, my teacher, His Eminence Garchen Rinpoche, always clarifies that all the enlightened Buddhas share the same Awareness. Yet, each deity is a unique pathway to awakening, and each one calls out to a different kind of person.

Part of your homework is to begin by looking for a soul image. Perhaps you already have one but never understood it until now. In different traditions, the beings that hold the vision and energy of the soul have various names. In Christianity, it is most often associated with the term guardian angels; in Tibetan Buddhism, they are called yidam deities; in Norse cosmology, they are called *fylgjur* (singular *fylgja*). In the end, what matters is the relationship you build with your soul, however it may appear for you. Ask your soul for help, and then be open to seeing and being led to what needs to come next.

EXERCISE
Outline Your Noble Spiritual Biography

In your journey journal, create an outline of your life that recounts it from the perspective of the soul. See the story as a heroic spiritual pilgrimage that has led you to where you are now—a person building a spiritual practice. This view gives your life a noble cast, as it should. You should be proud, in a healthy way, of getting to where you are now. It is also important to honor those who have helped you get to this point, both the helpers and the troublesome catalysts of change and loss of innocence.

PRACTICE PROSTRATION TO REALIZE YOUR PLACE IN THE BIG PICTURE

Prostration—bowing to the floor—is an act that humbles the self before the soul and the spirit. For a modern Westerner, prostrations can seem awkward, because our political evolution has taught us to bow before no one, especially not a tyrant. That is a good ideology in the relative political world, but in the spiritual world, it is the opposite. I do not know of any profound contemplative religious tradition that does not engage in some form of reverence for our source and true identity. Some forms are much more elaborate, and some are simple, but everyone recognizes the essential need to remind the egoic self of its proper relationship to the divine.

Additionally, our Western egoic self is often uncomfortable with bowing before its own divine self, largely because we do not understand the nature of the divine. This resistance also stems from the modern person's view, which is unaccustomed to the presence of pure Awareness. The modern egoic self may refuse to accept that the universe is more powerful than it is, which is like refusing to admit that the moon is larger than you, despite the implications of that size difference. If you cannot imagine humbling yourself before your own divine aspects, then it is best to turn around and stop moving along this mystical path altogether. It is usually a sign that the self is not yet developed enough to withstand the realization of its relatively small size compared to the soul and pure Awareness. It can be frightening for the self to realize its mortality and actual size.

This is one reason why developing a relationship with the soul and spirit is critical. When you do this, you realize that the soul and the spirit love the self unconditionally—much more than the egoic self loves itself. The self and the shadow are split, fractured, contradictory, and in turmoil. The soul can sit and hold that situation with complete compassion, and the spirit allows it to arise within a vast field of complete peace. The implications of this are pretty remarkable: it means that what we are up to as a self is so important and influential as an act of creation that these different levels of our being will allow the wacky nature of the self to evolve in the messy way it does on Earth. That is a promising notion.

So, learn to prostrate yourself in front of the truth that loves you more than you ever will, and not in front of another human being. At this point in history, avoiding prostrating to another person is sensible on most occasions. (An exception might be a deceased person, perhaps, if you think they embodied the whole truth and were a great soul.) To bow to another person on this path today is to abrogate your responsibility to do the work of developing spiritual authenticity and autonomy. However, if you do find yourself prostrating before a great living teacher, such as HE Garchen Rinpoche, my Tibetan teacher, as I have done many times, please do so in the full acknowledgement that you are bowing to your shared Awareness, not to the human being personally. The Buddha is a term that means "Awakened Oneness"; it is not pointing to the human personality. A person is not an Awakened Oneness, for, by definition, there is only one Awakened Oneness, one Buddha Awareness, one Buddha Mind. In the relative universe, some beings embody an enormous capacity to recognize this fact continually, transmit this recognition, and sometimes act from the Oneness with complete compassion and care. But they are still human, still have a self, still have a shadow, and still get sick and eventually die.

A prostration is simple enough. You start from standing, go to your knees, put your forehead down on the rug or ground (use your hands to brace yourself and lower yourself down carefully), and then return to standing. A variation is to start from your knees. The usual minimum is three prostrations, but doing even one prostration, slowly and with deep intention, can be immensely powerful.

The first time you do a prostration, you may feel silly or awkward, but I assure you that such feelings dissipate quickly. You are, after all, alone in a room, or perhaps a grove, with the soul and pure Awareness. They are just fine with recognizing you as them. You can prostrate to all of nature as well, since the word "nature," in its ultimate nondual context, encompasses all created and uncreated reality, including trees and unconditioned Awareness. There is a reason the Buddha became enlightened under a tree. Trees have an astonishing capacity to embody and hold a sacred space for accessing the natural state of our unconditioned Awareness. So to prostrate to a tree and then meditate under it is an entirely reasonable thing to do—so too an ocean, a mountain, the moon, a pond, a cave, or a cliff. In all cases, be aware of the natural landscape, the soul that animates the landscape, and the spirit out of which it all spontaneously arises in the moment. Just as you become aware of the self, soul, and spirit in yourself, you can sense these three levels in the natural outer world and revere all three as sacred. No level is better than the other, because form and formlessness are mysteriously and ultimately the same. This realization is usually only accessible by direct intuitive transmission from the inner world or a teacher.

To prostrate yourself is to remind yourself of the natural limitation of the self, of being human, which is a healthy thing to do because your sense of self-importance can get inflated with spiritual practice and spiritual power. This is especially true as you begin to be able to manifest spiritual and magical power in various ways. It becomes all too easy to unconsciously begin to assume you are the source of that power rather than a being who channels the power into the world through co-

THE SOUL AND THE SPIRIT LOVE THE SELF UNCONDITIONALLY— MUCH MORE THAN THE EGOIC SELF LOVES ITSELF.

creative alignment with the divine. The unconscious inflation of the self is subtle and easy to miss. Prostrations remind you continually of who is ultimately in charge.

In my case, as my practice matured, and with it the ability to manifest various outer-world changes, I found one day that I had not done a prostration in two weeks. I also found that I did not think it was a big deal. Just a few hours later at work I made some unwise decisions. It is humbling to suddenly see that you have become inflated in your sense of self-importance. Prostration is an essential remedy for self-inflation, which almost always happens in spiritual growth at some point or another, and is always a danger.[13] If I can do nothing else in my daily practice, I do one prostration, and I usually do three to ten a day. They help silence the mind and wake up the body, and are an act of love for the divine. An act of love does not always mean you feel love while you are doing it. An act of service is an act of love, even when you do not feel like doing it—perhaps even more so.

One student of mine says that, given her personality, prostration is one of the most foundational parts of her practice. She must go all the way down to the ground and place her forehead on it or else she is unable to surrender to her own soul and spirit. Keep in mind that it took many years to build up a sense of autonomy, agency, fierceness, and power in the self-structure. So mixing in surrender and letting go can feel instinctually wrong. But developmentally, at a certain point, this act is, in fact, empowerment at another level. When we bow, it is not about destroying what we have built; it is about

---

[13] Self-inflation in spiritual growth can be an essential part of developing the story of our lives. In the same way that King Arthur was boisterous and proud as a child in order to accomplish great tasks, we too have to feel this way on occasion in order to do what needs to be done for growth. However, Arthur would later realize whom he really served and become a genuine symbol of power in the form of care instead of control and inflation. Being grounded on some level in this truth will help us to not get stuck in self-inflation.

adding in the ability to let go, and allowing Awareness and the soul to become active in our lives. Think of prostration as falling in love with your own deeper self. We bow, and we offer the gift of the self to the aspects of our own being that love us.

In my experience, after I overcame my feeling of being an awkward secular person, I eventually felt a great release. I did not realize it, but my cultural and educational training had taught me to hold up my world by myself, with my own ego. However, it doesn't need to be this way; letting go and asking for help is a massive step in the marriage of self and soul. It is also a huge relief to realize you do not need to be totally in charge. Your soul has the map of your destiny. You have to work to accomplish it, but it is just as important, if not more so, to learn to listen. In the end, you must become willing to be directed as well as to lead. Prostrations are a great way to break down the modern Western secular assumptions of radical independence and replace them with a more workable approach that allows for a co-directing relationship between self and soul.

I learned when writing a novel that my characters were not mine; they belonged to themselves and, in time, they showed me where they wanted to go. So, too, will the inspiration that flows from spirit inform the self and soul. Every level of being is involved in the process because no level is unnecessary; if it were, it would not exist. The outer self is the aspect of your complete being that is "on the ground doing the work." The soul is the pilot watching from above, and spirit is the ocean that the ship of you is sailing on. That ocean has deep, hidden currents that it maintains just for you.

Sometimes the nondual insight of your shared Awareness with all life can seem freakish and terrifying, especially at first. But in truth, it is a remarkable cure for the underlying existential illness of your being, which is the belief that something is missing and that it must be your fault. The Tibetans call the awakened view "the ultimate medicine" for a reason, as it reveals that nothing is missing, there never was anything missing, and you are not at fault. You were always, in fact, just this, right here, right now. Just this simple Awareness reading these lines here and now—nothing more and nothing less.

The great quest for unity with existence is destined to fail, all so you can fall over in laughter and tears, recognizing you have been in unity the entire time. Even your belief in your separateness is in accord with all that is. Who, after all, is reading these words, right here, right now? It's you.

. . . .

EXERCISE

Humbling the Self to the Soul and Spirit

Begin with one prostration and feel it. You do not have to use any words; just silently honor the divine within you—the one you placed a symbol of on your altar. Do this and note how it feels, and then record it in your journal.

Then do three prostrations per day for a week, and see if you feel different. See if you sense a subtle bond between you, the soul, and spirit beginning to awaken. Record your experience in your journal.

. . . .

Journey Four
THE LIBRARY AND THE SWORD

Take a deep breath, and close your eyes. You find yourself floating down through the mist. *Five, four*, deeper. *Three*, deeper. *Two*, deeper. *One*.

You appear before the door to your inner world. Place both hands on the door. Become aware of the solidity of the door, its form. And then become aware of Awareness. Notice how Awareness shines right from the form without any need to dissolve it. Awareness's capacity to hold form is effortless, as is yours. You hear the door click, and it slides open. Step through into the inner castle.

Start walking down the corridor. Reach out your right hand and touch the wall. Feel the solidity. See the light behind your fingers as you walk. Keep walking. Toward your right is the stairway to the common room, but keep walking past it. You come to an opening, a passage on the left with stairs that go up. Go up the stairs until you enter a vast temple. Light is pouring into this beautiful space.

Start walking down the main aisle toward the center of the temple. As you get closer, you can see a stone altar in the center with a sword stuck straight into it, shimmering in the light. It seems to be almost alive. It is not yet time to approach, but you sense the presence of this sword throughout the entire great hall.

Now, turn to your left; you see a door that leads out of the central room. Walk toward it; as you do, it opens. Through this doorway you enter into a library. To the right there are several chairs and a small fireplace that keeps the place warm. And there are tables set out, long and wide, with books on them. On the wall at the far side of the stacks of books, there are great windows that let in the light. This is the ancient library. It is the accumulated wisdom of not just your soul, but all of humanity. Anything and everything you would ever need to know can be found here.

As you walk toward the stacks, the librarian steps out on your right and welcomes you. All through this part of the quest, you will work with the librarian to find the wisdom and knowledge you need for your life and your transformation. Go to the librarian now, with your palms up and your heart and mind open, and ask your question. What is it you need to know? What knowledge do you seek? Do this now.

Once you ask your question, the librarian goes into the stacks and finds the book you need. The librarian brings that book to you, gently hands it to you, and tells you to bring it into your heart. You do so. Know that the knowledge you need will unfold perfectly in its own time, that now it is within you. And then the librarian invites you to sit in one of the chairs next to the fire. Here, in this simple place, you can find and discern the answers you need.

Take some time now to be with the librarian in conversation . . .

Now it is time to return. Thank the librarian for the communication and the time spent with you. Know that you can return here to be in dialogue and have wisdom talks as needed. Give the librarian the gift that appears in your hand—some piece of knowledge or wisdom that you transmit to the library of humanity. Take one last look around the library and set your intention to return here soon, whenever you need to know something. Then leave the room.

As you go through the door, you see the sword still in the altar, glowing, full of light. This, the symbol of the divine mind itself, descended into matter, into the earth, to bring about life, humanity, evolution, creation, and the beginning of all things.

Now, walk back out of the great temple hall, and find the exit. Step down the stairs and into the hallway; take a right and head toward the doorway out of the inner world. The door opens, you step through and turn, and the door shuts. You hear it click. Place your left hand on the door and say in your mind, *It is done*. As you do, notice that at the top of the door the symbol of the sword and the stone appears.

And now you are floating up through the mist. *One. Two*, returning to this world. *Three*, bringing all you have learned with you, integrating it into your physical form, bringing with you the higher mind into form. *Four*, becoming aware of your form, your body, aware of Awareness and its awareness of form merging with every cell, never separate, always one. *Five*, open your eyes, and you've fully returned to the outer world.

Take some time now to write in your journal about the inner library.

Part Five

DEEPENING YOUR PRACTICE

What if all this loneliness
was the echo of a love that waits
beyond the bridge?

In Part Five, we begin to look at the complexities of a spiritual practice and ways to deepen it. There are major shifts that take place from an archetypal pattern perspective and also in terms of how your life looks and feels from the inside. It is not unusual for major synchronistic experiences to unfold and for you to begin to live in a world in which such things happen regularly. You might be unable to explain to yourself these magical events or the means by which you are able to accomplish certain things in life. As your perspective widens and deepens, and your capacity to work with your soul deepens, you begin to be able to affect reality in the outer world in undeniable ways. Ethical issues arise, and the core of your daily practice becomes even more important.

ARCHETYPES AND THE TWO MOUNTAINS

The famed Swiss psychologist Carl Jung used the term *archetype* to describe master patterns that human beings interact with throughout life. Examples of archetypes include the Mother, the Father, the Child, the Old Wise One, the Warrior, the Artist, the King, the Creator, the Orphan, the Innocent, the Hero and Heroine, the Scapegoat, the Villain, the Wizard, and the Fool. You can see all of these archetypes as characters in books and played by various actors in innumerable movies. These archetypes also play out in our lives.

I find Carol S. Pearson's *Awakening the Heroes Within* to be an essential book, in part because it includes a survey that allows you to evaluate which archetypes are active in your life. Pearson also breaks the journey of life into three stages. In part one, you're developing and preparing for the journey of life. During part two, as you move into adulthood, you go on the quest to succeed. Finally, in part three, the completion of that quest is to become authentic and connected to the soul. Each part of the journey has some archetypes that unfold in it. In the first part, we have the Innocent Child, and then the Orphan when we inevitably lose our innocence. We have the Warrior as well, because after we lose our innocence, there is a sense of having to activate power and become, if possible, capable in the world and to be able to deal with life's adversity. The other main type in this preparation phase is the Caregiver, which is about learning how to give care and be compassionate. Each of these archetypes has its positive side and its shadow.

As we move through the first set of archetypes, we eventually come to the next set of archetypes; the Seeker, the Destroyer, the Lover, and the Creator. All of these are important for developing and following our path. The Seeker, of course, is the one looking for meaning and purpose. The Destroyer is that portion of ourselves that wants to, and sometimes needs to, break things apart; it is the wounded self. The Lover is the one that allows us to fall in love with a variety of different things, with people, places, and life paths. The Creator is about what we are going to make in the world. It could be children. It could be a business. It could be art or math—it could be anything.

We go through the second set and then have the opportunity to engage with more complex and integrated archetypes, including the Ruler or Leader, the Magician or Wizard, and then the Sage (or the Wise One, Wise Woman, Wise Man), and ultimately the Fool, or what we might think of as the Awakened One. The Fool knows the truth about reality, the world, and Awareness itself. It has attained wisdom, compassion, power, humor, and freedom. Yoda from *Star Wars* is the perfect example. This archetypal path that Pearson lays out is a long journey through life, and her book becomes an excellent guide on how to move through the archetypes.

In the Way of the Mystic-Wizard, the entire journey breaks into two crucial stages, each with its own operating system. The first stage embodies the heroic archetype of climbing mountain number one to success and accomplishment, getting educated, finding work in the world, and building a sense of self. Then, something happens. You come to a moment when career and relationship and success no longer feel so fulfilling, or perhaps when you fail at something significant in life. You realize that things are not going as you planned. This upsetting process is an awakening to the power of the soul through suffering of some kind. In most cases, if we did not suffer, we would keep using the old operating system and keep on succeeding with it.

Therefore, something must go wrong in our life story for us to change and begin to walk up mountain number two.

"Need" is the source of initiative and growth. This is a fundamental part of the human condition and life. Without feeling like we need something that is missing or that must go away, we step away from the creative challenge that change offers. The egoic self is there to protect us, and unnecessary change is a waste of resources. Change for its own sake can cause unnecessary drama and suffering, so most people veer away from it. Need is a sign that something more resounding calls.

If you live long enough, you will get to this moment. It might happen in midlife, but it might happen earlier due to some kind of loss. Suddenly, what you have accomplished or where you have gotten loses its meaning, and you end up on the second mountain of life. So the first mountain is the archetype of success and achievement. The second mountain is the archetypal mountain of authenticity, meaning, and purpose. You are called by the soul to climb it, or else. Fortunately, a calling may well use many of those skills that you developed on mountain one in authentic service to the soul.

The processes required to master mountain one build a strong sense of self-identity. You hear this all the time today as people claim how they self-identify. They are clarifying their right to be identified by themselves and not by society. This is a decisive first step in preparation for the presence of the soul in your life. When you get to mountain two, some of the outward orientation that allowed you to move up mountain one no longer works. A new myth is in order, and a new orientation that points inward at the heart and the soul. The new attitude becomes about being a servant to your own soul, which requires surrender and real courage. Having spent so many years working hard to advance ourselves, we are suddenly being asked to go inward and listen. There can be a deep fear that maybe there is nothing there, that underneath it all you are a fraud.

In a sense, you *are* partially false—or more accurately, you are incomplete in your self-knowledge and in embodying your most profound capacities. The ego-self, devoid of the soul, is missing its divine foundation. If this gap is not addressed, you will continue on and become more and more alienated from your source as time passes. It should not be a surprise that the soul requires continued growth all throughout life.

When you look in one direction long enough, it is easy to forget that there is anything in the other direction. Underneath the self, the soul sits right there and provides that sense of purpose, meaning, and value. All of us are born in the state of our own inherent infinite value. We are Awareness itself, and we are also the extraordinary manifestation of pure Awareness, an expression that will quite literally never be seen on Earth again. Each of us has a unique form and destiny. In the quest to become a self, we lose contact with that innate sense of completeness and profound value that is inherently a part of pure Awareness and our natural state. This is why we work on noticing the fifth hallow and practice becoming aware of Awareness in our body, heart, and mind. In each case, we can eventually return to an awareness of an embodiment of our natural state. When we do, we stop hunting for completeness, and the coping patterns of our hunt begin to unravel and reveal the innate love and joy all around us and within us. This is a significant part of the practice of the Way of the Mystic-Wizard. We use the elements of life to practice, both in our sacred altar space and in the arena of life, to learn to embody the truth of our natural state.

The transition from mountain one to mountain two can be disconcerting. The process you used to get up mountain one, self-starting and initiative-oriented, can fail you on mountain two. The more initiative you take, the less you might accomplish on mountain two, or the more empty any accomplishment might become. What you are learning to do on mountain two is to listen for and decode the symbolic messages of the soul and to integrate your unique soul potential and your already-present completeness, all so you can become a being that mediates the deep and powerful energies of the inner world. You bring that power into the outer world in your own particular way.

That path and process is, in part, a kind of mystery journey. It is not easy, and many fail, because we have no myths that tell us how Yoda became a master, and without a good story to help us along, we can get lost on the way, or just give up. Some fall into despair that there even *is* a way. The point of the Way of the Mystic-Wizard and this book is to build a way to become your own version of Yoda. We are creating a new personal myth to live by. This is what the path is all about. It is about inhabiting a new deep story of your life that outlines and encourages you to climb both mountains at once. The first mountain is pretty straightforward; climb away! On the second mountain, we learn to "fall upward," as Richard Rohr calls it in his excellent book *Falling Upward: A Spirituality for the Two Halves of Life.* The second mountain is not a self-made ego process. Falling upward makes no sense to the operating system of the ego-self that made itself by sheer effort. Mountain two is a soul-directed process in which the self and soul collaborate and generate the means for movement and transformation. On mountain two, we move toward our inner wounds, not away from them—and not toward our surface wounds and frustrations but rather our deep inner fixations and orientations that keep us seeking pure Awareness everywhere but where it is: here.

Of course, the gold of Awareness has always actually been right here, right now. So in this second-mountain process, we slowly unravel the patterns and pains and hurts that drove us to seek it elsewhere, and we learn to inhabit and embody the natural state. Then we begin to arise as a new being, with the powers of our old self in service to the soul. The things we wanted most are then given to us if they are ours to have, while our false images and desires become the fuel to greater liberation. As they arise and we lean into seeing that they cannot ever satisfy us, they become vehicles to practice our awareness of Awareness.

For example, suppose you seek fame, and it is not yours to have. When that nagging desire for fame, power, safety, or love arises, use it as a simple trigger to relax back into your pure Awareness. Then breathe deeper and let the instinct to hunt for your false grail dissolve in the radiant presence of your true nature. And so, in the most seemingly bizarre way, the thorns of your life become the pathway to the bliss of your liberation as they are used to slowly reorient your attention from false outer goals toward the soul and pure Awareness. It is the soul that helps the thorns be pulled, one day at a time, one moment at a time, until at last you hold in your hand the old thorns, and laugh and thank them for their relentless commitment to your freedom—freedom from the illusion that there was something else you needed other than this, right here, right now, freedom from the illusion that you actually *were* your fixations and fears. So much suffering fades. Stranger still, the thorns rejoin your being as flowers so that the actual higher form of your self-soul can begin to emerge. The redeemed thorns themselves become an integral part of your being and of how you will appear in the world. The marks of your painful passage become part of the gift that you embody and the truth that your presence delivers to the world. In this way, the soul and Awareness's brilliance are discovered, and you realize that nothing on the journey was wasted.

THE THORNS OF YOUR LIFE BECOME THE PATHWAY TO THE BLISS OF YOUR LIBERATION.

Mountain number two requires building a daily practice that embodies an awakening process, which breaks some of the tools and attitudes you used to get up mountain number one. The soul does this to the individual ego-self to bring it to a more empowered and authentic place. However, it is discon-

certing; it is challenging. That is why spiritual practice becomes essential. In essence, the Way of the Mystic-Wizard is a path that embodies the myth of the two mountains. We are to build into our lives the processes and attitudes that allow the soul to be our pilot up both mountains from the start. One important skill for that journey is the ability to work with an oracle.

ORACLES

Oracles were revered in the ancient world because they were endowed with prophetic powers, and they were often called upon to intercede with the gods. Theirs was a mystical shamanic capacity and is the essence of what we will try to develop by working with an oracle system.

Many iconic individuals of the ancient world—Greek, Roman, Egyptian—regularly visited oracles to try to get a feel for what the patterns of the universe were around their destinies and to help them make decisions. The Oracle of Amun at the Siwa Oasis, in the Egyptian desert near the Libyan border, was held in such high regard in Greece that an Athenian ship was built to convey envoys to the Oracle in order to ask essential questions. Alexander the Great traveled to the Oracle of Amun to discover if he was indeed the chosen spiritual son of Amun and, therefore, the legitimate ruler of Egypt—and, by extension, the known world. Eventually, the Oracle was absorbed into Greek religion and associated with Zeus, who became associated with the Egyptian Amun. Many other oracles of the ancient world existed outside of Siwa. You've likely heard of the Oracle of Delphi in Greece, probably the most famous oracle in history. There were also oracles in Persia, Libya, Cumae, Samos, Tibur, Cimmeria, Marpessos, and Phrygia.

With the rise of rationalistic thinking and the materialist worldview, oracles dropped out of favor as a way of divining the patterns of fate. However, when such a tool suddenly recedes due to the philosophical development of a culture, it's smart to take a look at the lost practice to see why it once had value. Just because something disappears does not mean it is wrong or is not essential to humanity. And if it is a crucial process, you can be sure it will find its way back, as oracles have in the past thirty years.

In today's world, typically an oracle is not a person but is rather a set of images that have archetypal power and value for you. The oracle I was initiated into is called *The Druid Animal Oracle*, and there are many other animal oracles out there. In *The Druid Animal Oracle*, each animal image is connected to a Northern European indigenous animal. Each animal has different stories associated with it and represents different kinds of traits and archetypal truths. From a shamanic perspective, what we are dealing with is essentially the group soul of the animal and the wisdom that each animal holds and has to offer to humanity. There are now a number of excellent oracles available on the market. Each has its own character and provides a way to develop a link to the inner world.

Oracles can convey messages from your soul. Your soul speaks in symbolic images, and the oracle is your metaphorical, image-based, common vocabulary. By creating a language in which you can talk back and forth to your soul-self, you allow yourself to gain access to wisdom and information. Developing your oracular skills is an art like any other art. Once you have an oracle that you're drawn to, it becomes a living means of continual dialogue between self and soul.

If you do not have an oracle, you are essentially losing one of the main ways that most of humanity has had to help guide them through the process of living a human life. It seems silly *not* to work with what you can and what most of humanity has used for thousands of years to help guide them.

. . . .

EXERCISE

Begin Using an Oracle

The next assignment in this course is to find yourself an oracle, draw cards from it, and engage with it as a communication system between self and soul.

To find an oracle, the first thing to do is ask your soul to please bring you to an oracle system. The simplest way to find possible oracle systems is to walk into a spiritual bookstore and go to the oracle section. Look at the different oracle decks and see what catches your attention. Or, using your mobile phone, search the apps for oracle cards. Find something with art that attracts you and that has a pantheon of deities, angels, or animals that call to you. Use your intuition to find the right kind of oracle.

Once you acquire a system, simply follow the directions provided for engaging with the oracle and the energies and beings it is a connection to. Almost all oracle authors have an explanatory section to help you know how to ask a question and how to use the cards they created. After you are comfortable with one oracle system, feel free to explore a few others. Find your own way to work with them.

Write about your experience in your spiritual journal.

. . . .

FORMING A SACRED MAGICAL IDENTITY

One of the premises of our path is that we are the partial weavers of our own personality. With our soul as our guide, we develop our capacity to co-create a more authentic identity and destiny.

To sustain our path, an identity-shaping process needs to take place. When you are forming a new identity, whether joining a club or starting a new profession, various steps go along with it. For instance, if you take up a sport, then acquiring the equipment you need to play the sport is vital at some point. From a theatrical perspective, you gather props to make others believe that you are seriously engaged and committed to the activity but also to demonstrate such to yourself. Likewise when you decide to take up a spiritual practice, you can orient your outer life to correspond with your intention.

How do you create a sacred magical identity, one that is mystical and shamanic? As we described earlier, the first step is to find a space to reflect upon your intention to build a spiritual practice and connect with your soul. One of the easiest ways to define that space (and humanity has been doing it forever) is to build an altar of some kind. An altar can be any number of materials, including a stack of your favorite books.

Place important spiritual items on your altar, including the oracle you found. Maybe place something from each of the four directions. You might find a stone, a feather, some kind of wand, and a cup for water—any sacred objects that can represent the journey into the transformative process of the four elements over the four seasons of the year.

Also place something to represent pure Awareness itself. It could be a sphere of stone or perhaps a mirror. One of the classic methods of recognizing reality, or pure Awareness, is looking in a mirror, into your own eyes, and sensing that there is an Awareness watching from behind your eyes and mind. This is one of the reasons that throughout history, statues of various deities were created with realistic eyes—so that worshippers could go and see Awareness reflected back in them. The priests would start a ritual, create lots of magical tension, and then suddenly reveal the deity's eyes and—bam!—awakening.

It might seem that most people have not built altars. In fact, the whole time you were going to school, if you had a desk at home, it was an altar to the deities of learning, such as Ganesha. You created a space where the sacred activity of studying occurred. So your goal now is to gather items that take on sacred energy as you work with them and put them in the space of the altar so you can begin to build an identity. Like any other identity-building process, building an altar is slow, so take it one step at a time. There can be a synchronistic process that unfolds in which you find the exact items that you need. Some of them are probably already in your room. They might be items you have gathered that seemed to have some kind of resonance or value that you intuitively sensed was important. Gather those together and build a small altar to the transformation process that nondual shamanism and the Way of the Mystic-Wizard are all about. By doing so, you will validate your new path and give it concrete form. Making it tangible is vital. It is the same reason that (traditionally) a man presents a woman with a ring when he asks her to marry him. Without the ring, it is not "real." It takes energy and earthly resources to buy a ring, and to get the money for one takes commitment, and commitment takes discipline, follow-through, and grit. These are all things one traditionally wants in an earthly spouse and also in a spiritual practitioner. They indicate the capacity of a person to stay on task when the going gets tough.

Also start gathering together some sacred clothing that reflects your practice. Like an actor creating a character in a play, you need a wardrobe to make the character believable to the "audience," which, for now, is yourself.

Ask yourself: What clothes do I wear? What items, what jewelry, would give value to this new aspect of my own character and life? The common religions built up their traditions over hundreds of years in just this way, one person at a time. You are essentially starting your own private religion, and creating the sacred garb is essential. It might be that you wear a particular shirt, or a scarf given to you by your grandmother.

For both objects and clothing, anything that represents your connection to the spiritual world, to the ancestors, to all the aspects of your sacred life will work. You do not need to know what the items mean with your left brain. Use your intuition and feeling sense to discover if they fit, and the soul will guide you. The idea here is not to intellectually understand all the symbols in your sacred life, but rather to let them have symbolic and transformative energy of their own. We let them reveal to us their meaning over time, and we let them deepen. To allow the items you find to develop symbolic meaning, you must practice negative capability.[14] Think of symbolism as a garden: the importance of symbols takes time to grow and then flower. The soul speaks in symbols, and the language of the soul realm must be taught to the egoic self and the mind. The left brain always wants to figure it all out on its own terms, but in this case, the mystery of a symbol's many possible meanings is what makes it valuable.

Next, begin to interact with your altar intuitively. There's no one right way. We are engaging in the instinctual process of building spirituality and religion for ourselves, the way it happened before the world created religious institutions. We are

---

[14] Remember, negative capability is the ability to be in uncertainties, mysteries, doubts, without any irritable "reaching" after fact and reason.

opening ourselves to the inspiration of the soul and an inner and outer world that can speak to us. There might be pieces of different religious traditions that speak out to you. Go ahead and integrate those. Whatever comes to you is between you and your soul, which is how shamans have always managed and created their sacred symbolic items. You are making a new identity to engage in a particular way of life that, by definition, must be unique to you.

For instance, find an image that captures the perfect sort of energetic expression of the Inner Beloved for you. Maybe that image has been in the background for years. Maybe there was some image that you idealized or idolized from your childhood that embodies your beloved. It could be a famous person; it could be an image you came across, or a character from a book who seems to capture so much of what you would love the Inner Beloved to be. Seek an image that expresses the essence of someone supporting you. This is called a spirit spouse in many shamanic traditions, the Holy Guardian Angel in the Western esoteric system, the *dakini* in the Tibetan tradition, and the *fylgja* in the Norse and Anglo-Saxon shamanic traditions.

Once you have an oracle and a soul image, and some items to represent the four elements and directions, then you can begin to engage in a spontaneous ceremony. Again, there is no "right" way. Try to stay away from books that tell you exactly how to do this. All you need to do is listen and be open to being creative. The best instruction I ever got was from a friend named John who said he rolls out of bed every morning, lights some incense, says hello to everyone on his spiritual team, and then sees what happens. I took that most simple of instructions, and it became how my day begins. Then I just listen for what might be next. More often than not, it goes like this . . .

I get some coffee, wash my face, then pick up my journal and write a bit. Then I plan my day on paper to give it some concrete form and commitment; writing out my plans helps

THINK OF SYMBOLISM AS A GARDEN: THE IMPORTANCE OF SYMBOLS TAKES TIME TO GROW AND THEN FLOWER.

me prioritize what areas of my life need attention. I am listening while I plan, and my spirits are with me in that process. Sometimes I sense I need to draw a card from one of the five oracle decks I use regularly. Then I begin what I call my sitting practice. I switch into my sacred robes, light some incense and sometimes a candle, and then sit in meditation.

I always start with the specialized breathing I do and the inner imagery that awakens my light body, the energetic body used to travel the inner world. Then I awaken to or notice the divine presence of pure Awareness followed by the soul's presence. From that state of aligned self, soul, and spirit, I can see and hear much more than when I am in my ordinary consciousness. Insights come to me about energies inside me and in the larger world that need to be managed, processed, or shaped. At times, this is an easy process; other times, when material comes up from the unconscious that my conscious egoic self would rather not face, it becomes emotionally challenging. In those times, I experience typical moments of regression and fear or frustration; they must be processed, and the unconscious elements recognized, held in compassion, and seen through as elements of Awareness itself. For me, doing the inner work is often a visual process. Over time, I learned to look forward to the next time I would be "dismembered" or in some way dissolved or broken up.

After all that, it is time to put my street clothes on, close up the sanctum by folding up the sacred garments and blowing out the candle, give a little thanks, and head off to work, school, or whatever is going on that day. On the NDS section of my website there is a journey that addresses how to do these morning exercises. They must be done by listening in this case because of the transmission that occurs through the recording.

As you can see, this connection activity is not that complicated, but it is a foundation that becomes unshakable. Even when I have no time and skip the robes, I still make it to the sacred seat, sit, light the candle, and become aware of the soul and spirit. The shortest amount of time it can take me is about three minutes. Ironically, the capacity to do your connection exercises quickly can create an ability to connect anywhere. I used to feel like I was cheating when that happened, but then my inner guides helped me see that some time is better than none, and short can be powerful if your intention is focused. With a great deal of time, people often lose focus and float around a lot. With less time, you get down to business. My wife and I raised two boys, and my practice was going on the entire time they were toddlers waking up early, coming to the door of my sanctum, and pressing their little faces to the glass at 6:30 a.m. Some days I would have just sat down and my older son would suddenly be there. He knew exactly when I was awake. I learned to hold my finger up and make him wait for fifteen seconds—and that was all I got on those days. Then I would adjust my wake-up time, and that would last another month before he somehow changed as well, and the process would begin again.

So create your own spontaneous, flexible, nimble, open, and reliable practice structure, and make it as much a habit as brushing your teeth. I call this process "having a fixed structure and a flexible form." The intention you make is fixed, which is the skeleton of your practice, but the form flows with the specific demands of the outer and the inner world as they arise on that day. In this way, your practice thrives, because you re-main adaptable and resist the urge to form deep habitual ruts that can eventually prevent you from accessing the states of consciousness you are seeking. A tennis player trains on a wide variety of challenges so they are ready to adjust when it is a real match. In our practice, every day is a "real match," and every day could be different. Embrace the variation, because it em-powers and strengthens both your endurance and your capacity to listen to how the river is flowing.

PRACTICE METHODS: MEDITATION, ART-MAKING, AND MORE

Ultimately this book is about developing a daily practice that is sustainable throughout your life and that connects you to your soul. The practice is also intended to deepen an awakening to the non-dual presence of pure Awareness. The question is, what methods are you going to put at the center of your practice? The answer is "lots of methods," and each person will have to find their own. But I will give you some ideas of some of the categories that are possibilities.

From the outset, you have the obvious practice methods that people associate with spirituality, such as meditation and prayer. But we can add creative endeavors such as art-making and journaling. The goal is to learn to listen to, and go back and forth in conversation with, the soul. This conversation can be in actual words that you hear coming through your mind, or it could be through impressions and feelings, storytelling in your journal, or poetry or painting. Or it could be in the physical arena such as yoga, tai chi, chi gong, dance, or any other form of movement, from swimming and baseball to badminton and skiing.

Then there are all the ways of strengthening your light body (your energetic body) and upgrading your nervous system just as you can your muscles and mind. The various ways of doing this, such as chakra work and kundalini practice, allow you to utilize more energy. With that, you can channel more spiritual power, manage more complicated tasks, and create more. One excellent program is Awakening Your Light Body by Duane Packer. I have been using it for twenty years, and it changes how you exist in the world.

Each system of working with the light body has experts you can learn from, many of whom now have recorded courses online that allow you to access them. The COVID-19 pandemic, for all its destructive power, was also an epidemic that forced many teachers out of comfortable old ways of doing things (such as weekend workshops and retreats) and into, in many ways, a more accessible and democratic distribution method. I, for instance, now teach through Zoom 99 percent of the time and work with people worldwide rather than only in my neighborhood. Before these newly common technological forms of connecting, one had to uproot one's life and move to a more spiritually inclined town or city to find teachers. This had the negative effect of pulling all those kinds of people together in one place, taking them out of environments where they would be forced to work with and engage with circumstances that challenge them in ways that are vital to genuine engaged spiritual development.

Part of our growth comes from finding like-minded people, but part of it also comes from *not* finding those people, or from falling out with them. In isolation, we find solitude, and in that silence comes the voice of the soul and an emotional reason to look and listen inward. If you have not felt lonely for an extended period in your life, then what motivation do you have to seek in your heart for the divine love that will never leave you?

This book and the entire Way of the Mystic-Wizard is a direct result of my having to walk large portions of my path feeling alone and with only the spirit world to support me. I used to complain vigorously to them about this. Then they gave me various opportunities to be a part of different spiritual communities, and I discovered both the benefits and the disappointments of spiritual community. Spiritual groups are fraught with the dynamics of psychological projection, unrealistic expectations, and all sorts of archetypal shadow material. In addition, when you develop a serious practice on your own,

the spiritual world notices, and it begins to bring you the books and people you need. In my case, it took a year of serious engagement on my own before it seemed the spirit world would take me seriously, and this was after some fifteen years of intermittent spiritual development. This process of commitment and response seems to be much like a serious coach not being willing to take on a new athlete until they demonstrate some commitment and passion for the sport they say they want to be trained in. Many people seek to discover their authentic path, and at first they often overcommit to something that is not in fact their path. The spirit world knows this and waits patiently for the aspirant to bumble along and eventually find the true path, or at least the start of the true path. And each misstep is actually part of finding a way that works for you.

I will never forget when I learned about HE Garchen Rinpoche, who became my primary Tibetan spiritual teacher. A few years earlier, I had dreamed about three dancing women—a white, a green, and a red dancing goddess came to me in the inner world. I did not know that they were all aspects of the Buddhist goddess Tara, but in time, I learned this, and they called me onto their path. White Tara, which means "the loving doorway to evolution and opening of the heart and mind," became my primary yidam deity.[15]

However, despite the books I read and the few Tibetan centers and organizations I visited in my home city, I could find no place where I felt any karmic traction. For three long years, I cultivated and studied on my own and did the best I could. Then one day, I was in our local independent bookstore, and in came an old friend I had met some seven years before in the Episcopal church I had been attending. He had moved on years earlier, and I asked what he was up to. He said he was

---

[15] The yidam is a special deity one works with in meditation as a means toward recognizing one's own awakened nature.

spending lots of time up in Chino Valley at the Garchen Institute. I had no idea what that was. He explained that it was part of the Drikung Kagyu Lineage and that Garchen lived there and was the most realized spiritual master he had ever met. I had been looking hard for a community and had no idea the place existed. My friend offered to take me to the upcoming empowerment ceremony that weekend. I said yes on the spot.

Through that friend I went to my first Tibetan empowerment, took refuge vows and bodhisattva vows, and literally bumped into Garchen, who was then seventy-five, as I came around a corner of the temple building. In the first five minutes he spoke, I knew I had met a great awakened teacher. He did not pull his punches. He spoke directly to Awareness in the room, not to us. He spoke right past our personalities and validated pure Awareness, and I could feel it. I had never met someone who did that. And, as it turned out, his yidam deity was White Tara. I was being called home to my lineage. And to this day, the lineage still challenges me and pushes me to engage and do what I came here to do, including creating this path and the Way of the Mystic-Wizard. For me, Garchen and the entire Kagyu Lineage of Tibetan Buddhism are essentially mystical wizards.

You might ask, why did I not stick with only them and devote myself to that practice and community? The answer is simple, and it is the same reason that my other primary nondual teacher, Peter Fenner, disrobed from being a Tibetan monk after being a professor of Eastern religions for twenty years and then a monk for nine years. He was called to bring all he had learned to a broad Western audience. The wisdom in the Tibetan and other Eastern religious traditions needs to be brought over into the West so that the Western audience can connect and metabolize, just like when Buddhism went from India to Tibet. I had no idea at the time I would be called to create the Institute for Nondual Shamanism (NDS), or that literally only one other person on the planet would be putting together shamanism and nonduality programming. In Tibetan Buddhism, the two streams of wisdom had never been split, but here in the West they had. So it became my calling to find a way to combine them. At that point, the teachers appeared and the path unfolded before me. I then saw that this was what I had been working on combining, in a semi-unconscious fashion, for the prior twenty years.

The intention of our work in NDS is for our transformation to be in service to our souls and Awareness and the world. A group of us are dedicated to this. We do not bring our other needs for communal expression and project them onto the group. Clarity of intent, in this case, is critical. We are not a family, not a tribe, not a church, not a religion. We are a working group with a purpose, a group within which we have a great deal of respect, compassion, and intimacy. We are, in a sense, more like a sports team, with a clear purpose to engage in our own evolution, the difference being that we are Mystic-Wizards rather than athletes. The outcome of the work we do together needs to positively impact the life each member is leading outside the group. If the work does not help people grow and transform their lives and the world around them, then that member fades away.

DEVELOPING YOUR PRACTICES IS AN ORGANIC, AUTHENTIC, UNFOLDING PROCESS.

To give you an example of the evolution of practice, you might start out in one area of meditation and, over time, find a particular kind of meditation that seems to really work for you. You might also develop the capacity to go on inner-world journeys, which is a part of the shamanic path, as well as to do internal world downloads of higher energies to awaken yourself to your light body. These practices help cultivate the transformational process, the bringing about of the integration of self and soul, and the recognition of Awareness. This awakening process can develop suddenly, or over time.

I started out with various kinds of meditation, from Zen to

Christian prayer, and finally found and settled on what seemed to be really effective for me, the Ascension Attitudes by Maharishi Sadashiva Isham (MSI). Ascension is quite similar to what you find in transcendental meditation or in the true meditation taught by Adyashanti, one of the great meditation teachers of our age. I particularly like Ascension because it allows you to work an attitude, which is a mental and emotional stance, into your consciousness so it can transform your consciousness. The attitudes move you ever closer to states of praise and gratitude and love, and they are powerful and transformative. The Ishaya monks teach these techniques (they can be found online).

Learning to make art is also an unfolding discovery process. If you're called to it, it is an opportunity to explore and express yourself and express your soul's authenticity. You become authentic by discovering who and what you are through the mirroring process of art-making. Having built and run an art school and been involved with artists for over thirty years, I can tell you that the authentication process requires years of exploring and trying to understand what is rising up from the shadows, and learning to integrate what was once repressed.

Much like practices such as building your altar and the accoutrements that go along with your sacred life, the process of developing all your other practices is also an organic, authentic, unfolding process. It is not something that is ever really finished. Think instead like a gardener: you are always cultivating the garden. The process is a wondrous seasonal unfolding of the extraordinary power and beauty of life. Some seasons there is a lot of new growth, and other times things are quiet and have switched into wintering mode. Listen and use your oracle to sense what you are being called to do.

Even when the Awareness is mostly habituated, the self is still weeding and planting, because life itself is a season for the soul—and it is the only season in which the soul gets to be mortal and muck around in the material world. There is never an endpoint in this process. Instead, there is a station the train has stopped at, allowing you to rest and look about. Then the train leaves again, on to the next life, the following season, the next place, the next set of people, books, paths, walks, or creative projects. To be done with something is a great feeling, and accomplishment counts just as much as any other stage, so enjoy it when it arises, and then begin again and enjoy the first few steps yet again.

The title of Philip Carr-Gomm's book *Seek Teachings Everywhere* has hidden, unspoken magic in the title. It sounds like it's directing you to be busy with thousands of teachings, but in actuality, by seeking teachings everywhere, you are listening all the time for your soul's guidance for the next place to go. At certain stages of your spiritual unfolding, some practices will be essential. Then some might become less important over time, and yet others might become so second nature as to be like breathing, such as Ascension Attitudes are for me. Every time I use one, I become instantly aware of Awareness and the bliss-field all around. Not a bad outcome of a spiritual practice. And it keeps unfolding. The bliss-field that these attitudes help orient me toward also follows the breath, inhabits the nervous system, and opens up inner space in which new subtle energies can play and work my light body and my physical form. From the bliss-field, you can create reality in a way that does not even occur to you from less subtle states of being that are based on ignorance of Awareness.

There are reasons for certain kinds of practices. Eventually, once you are seasoned, you may come to a series of techniques that give you access to the state of consciousness that is serene and allows you easy access to becoming aware of Awareness and the soul. That is the promise of the path of the Mystic-Wizard and the purpose of my teaching. The goal is to bring these paths to fruition and find your access point to the bliss-field and the promise of the great spiritual teachings of our world. It is not just about awakening to the presence of Awareness in your mind; it is about embodiment in the emotional and physical body as well. As Peter Fenner once said (I paraphrase), "There is a reason the Buddha has a smile on his face; it is because he is in an excellent state of consciousness." It is our natural state, and it is in everyone, absolutely every being, because it is, in fact, everywhere. Thus it is in you and it is your birthright. This path leads to subtle bliss and joy, and the opening of the centers in your physical body and light body allow you to feel what is already there. It is a lot of work, and there is a ton of stuff in the way for most people, but you are not on your own; if you are this far into this book, you are already at the doorway to the path.

THE WISDOM KEEPER

IS IN YOUR HEART;

IT IS YOUR OWN SOUL.

You are responsible for your choices and for shaping your practice with your soul's guidance and insight. Inside everybody is an inner Wise Woman, an inner Wise Man, the Old Grandmother or Old Grandfather figure there to guide you. That is where you will ultimately find whether something is a good fit. It will not always be obvious, and it will not always be easy, because the process itself is seemingly a wild goose chase at times. Sometimes for your soul to get you where you need to go, it moves you from A to B. But it can turn out that going to B was only so that the soul could get you into position to see the place you are really going, which is C. For many readers, this book will be a station on the way to some other path—that is, this book is only a stop at B, not destination C. Or it can be both, and often is. This roundabout process is the only way for the soul to guide you. It is also the nature of the creative process. Being put through the process teaches you a way of being that increases your negative capability and helps you to understand the extraordinary intelligence of the soul and Awareness.

Even though some things will become absolutely foundational in your practice, wandering will still happen. The Way of

the Mystic-Wizard is not a path of finding a guru who is going to give you the answers. The wisdom keeper is in your heart; it is your own soul. When you are asking for guidance, you are asking for your own most profound wisdom; you are asking pure Awareness to guide you and give you what you need to move forward.

THE INNER BELOVED: A REMEDY FOR THE ROMANTIC MYTH OF THE MAGICAL OTHER

There is a beautiful book by James Hollis, a Jungian analyst, called *The Eden Project: In Search of the Magical Other*. Essentially, he posits that as people began to move away from formal religions, the religious instinct did not vanish—it simply sought out another expression. That expression became the new "religion" of romance. It may sound absurd, until you begin to look around at the number of films and books about romantic love and at the adoration expressed when people fall in love. Then there is the cultural approval of that adoration.

The myth of romance has a nearly universal cult following in Western culture. It gives a secular direction for the instinctual desire for spiritual union. However, it is a less-than-successful myth, for it cannot deliver a sustainable result. From a psychological and spiritual perspective, it misidentifies the solution. Much like the quest for spirit that results in failure and collapse and thus the opportunity to recognize pure Awareness, the romantic myth also creates an impossible dream. We seek romantic love, fall in love, and then fall out of love, which opens us to the opportunity of discovering the Inner Beloved. This romance myth would not be an issue if there were some clarity about what is going on and a second myth to adopt when romance fails to deliver on its promised bliss.

Why is this important?

If you were raised without religion, the reality is, you really were not. You were presented with the faith of the quest for the magical other, the soul mate who will complete you, a lifelong pilgrimage in search of "the one." Romance as religion dominates our commerce and intentions as a culture. You were likely indoctrinated into the religion of romance by Disney films and the many other TV programs and books that embody it. What did it teach you? And where does it come from?

The religion of romance comes from the twelfth-century Arthurian romance stories. The idea of the quest to find the idealized female trapped by an evil king originated from that myth. The knight, of course, must go and rescue her. Then they fall in love and live happily ever after. We are all familiar with this myth. However, if you look at the story symbolically rather than literally, it begins to make some sense. From an archetypal perspective, the knight represents the ego-self, moving heroically through a world of struggle and challenge. The princess in the tower represents the soul, the divine aspect that lives above it all and radiates peace, serenity, and beauty. The evil king that keeps her trapped represents the shadow elements that prevent us from knowing our own soul's deep love for us. The soul is symbolized by an idealized feminine aspect of our being because the soul is considered an aspect of the wisdom goddess, Sophia. (It is also Frigga, Isis, and many more.) The egoic self is symbolized by a masculine form, the knight moving through the woods on a horse. It does not matter symbolically what the knight's actual earthly gender is, and as Western culture has begun to outgrow old gender stereotypes, we have seen female-presenting actors embody this knighthood aspect of the ego-self, such as Rey in the last iteration of the *Star Wars* saga. How each actual gender manifests and expresses the heroic journey is not the subject of this book, and many other good books have explored these issues. What matters for our work is that we live through the archetypes of human growth as the archetypal knight who can and must overcome obstacles to grow and fulfill destiny's call.

The romantic quest became, first in the Arthurian myths and later in the broader Western culture, the main avenue of hope for spiritual salvation from our alienated state of consciousness. In time, romance became an avenue through which people could feel the intense adoration and union of falling in love with their own soul as projected out onto the magical other. It temporarily overcomes the illusion of separation, the sense of aloneness in the universe.

The problem with this is twofold. First, there is falling out of love, of course, but second is that we give up the responsibility for our growth to another human being. We can mistakenly reverse our growth and head back in the direction of being an infant. I call this "giving up your gold." The gold is the potential riches of our being and soul and the promise of incarnation itself. The way we get our gold is to engage and grow and deal with life. To give away our gold is an act of regressing to the dependency of a child. It is a refusal to embrace the challenge of incarnation. So what is the solution?

The mythological confusion about romance generates failure and disappointment when we fall out of love. The myth breaks the hearts of many people, some of whom never recover. The antidote to this brokenness is not falling in love again with the next person to come along and hoping the same thing will never happen again. The antidote is a new myth in which the self discovers the soul in her form as the divine beloved in the inner world.

THE GOLD IS THE POTENTIAL RICHES OF OUR BEING AND SOUL, AND THE PROMISE OF INCARNATION ITSELF.

The discovery of the Inner Beloved was, in fact, the secret intention of the troubadours when they created the tales of Arthurian romance. They knew what they were doing. They sought a spiritual path outside the narrow context of the medieval church, which monopolized the expression of the spiritual instinct. So they hid their secret pathway for finding the soul and creating a spiritual union in the stories of seeking to rescue the princess from the tower (or quest for the holy grail, a cup and another feminine archetypal image of wholeness and the source of life). Our goal is to bring that secret path out and make it public. We no longer need to hide from the religious authorities who would have condemned us in the twelfth century for worshipping the divine feminine inside us. In Christianity, it was okay then, as it is today, to have a personal relationship with Christ, but not with a female divine being that is your access point to the spirit. Only Christ is allowed to play that role for some reason. Therefore, an innovation such as a female version of divinity within you threatened the church's power; in fact, when this spiritual instinct found expressions in southern France where the troubadours were most prevalent, a significant religious sect developed called the Cathars. They had rediscovered the worship of the divine feminine Inner Beloved on their own and were eventually ruthlessly exterminated for it.

The problem with unconsciously moving through the myth of romance as a quest for the magical other is that it sets you up for profoundly unrealistic expectations about what an actual earthly other can be for you. You do not see a real person as they are. Instead, projection, a psychological process of displacing your feelings onto another, takes place. Projection is a process you do not realize you are doing; in fact, if you know you are projecting, you are not projecting anymore. In the romantic myth, you project your own idealized inner soul-self onto a person and fall in love with that projection. This can lead to a bond and get you going in a relationship, but, of course, in the end what you're really falling in love with is divine, and no mortal spouse can live up to that, so you "fall out of love." Often we blame the other for our unrealistic expectations not being fulfilled. Even if you see through the myth and you have a loving connection with a spouse that matures and becomes more realistic over time, you are still left with an unfulfilled spiritual instinct with nowhere to go. It is common to have that spiritual instinct and project the same thing onto another new person. Often this becomes a new *unattainable* person, which then makes the romance even more powerful, such as in the Arthurian myths where the lady (soul) is married to the evil king (shadow) and thus beyond reach in socially acceptable norms.

Part of the solution, then, to the limits of the romantic myth is the practice of pulling that projection back and inward and discovering the Inner Beloved, the idealized inner spouse. From a shamanic perspective, it would be called the "spirit spouse." Shamans all over the world have known about the internal magical other for eons. It is a fundamental aspect of the inner world to have a divine being one can relate to and depend on. In the major religions, this idea turned into the process wherein a deity can become one's inner spiritual spouse. The process is fundamental to shoring up the insecurity and deep needs that the self has for attention, love, stability, safety, and praise.

When you find and cultivate a relationship with the soul via the archetype of the Inner Beloved, it changes the course of your life. You go from trying to find the perfect soul mate to finding that divine energy inside yourself. It releases everyone around you from having to fulfill your unconscious projection. Finding the magical other within you and gaining her unconditional love is incredibly powerful, and it's what is actually meant in our culture when people say you must "learn to love yourself."

The trouble with the command to love yourself is that we are not given a way to do so. In practice, you need a divine aspect to love you exactly as you are, for you certainly cannot love yourself as you are. We are all far too aware of how flawed we are for that. We can learn to *accept* ourselves as we are, with all our complex issues, shadow aspects, hopes, and flaws. But the soul can truly *love* you entirely as you are. Perfect love from an immortal being allows us to see that our flaws are part of our humanity and part of the path of incarnation itself, and that there was never anything wrong about any of us. Our alienation and disconnection from the spirit are not our fault. It is, instead, all part of how things work here. It is also the primary driver for spiritual growth and toward our destiny.

In the Way of the Mystic-Wizard, the path is clear for how to move beyond the myth of romance and create better mythology, a better religion for ourselves—one that delivers the desired outcome we all want, which is to be loved, feel connected and cared for, and not have our natural insecurities drive us nuts. We want stable psychological ground to stand on. And it is via the inner world and the inner divine aspect of the soul called the Inner Beloved that we can find this support. However, not everybody is ready for this path. Many are not prepared to give up on the religion of romance in its outer form of expression, which is fine, for it feels good to adore and be adored by a physical being, even if it leads to disappointment when that adoration stops. It takes a spiritual maturity often born of loss to want to move toward a divine love that does not waver.

With the special inner connection established, you can move through the world with a higher degree of autonomy and emotional support. It helps with working with an oracle. It helps with finding your profession. It helps with finding your vocation. It helps with finding community. It even helps with finding an earthly spouse. Essentially, the whole process of moving through life with an inner magical other will right the ship of the self. Often by the time I am teaching this to someone, I

FINDING THE MAGICAL OTHER WITHIN YOU IS INCREDIBLY POWERFUL.

have found that they are quite wounded by the loss of love, often too injured at first to even entertain the idea that a divine being could love them exactly as they are. The resolution and healing of this pain then unfold in the inner world on journeys and in the discovery of inner unconditional love.

Many people are deeply addicted to the myth of romance. And not surprisingly so, because it is the only way we have been shown to find a sense of union with the divine. Therefore, to have it taken away from you—to have the myth busted, so to speak—can really hurt, especially if there is nothing to replace it. The idea is not to abandon the myth of the magical other, but to adjust our orientation. It is about stopping the projecting of our magical other onto the outer world and forcing some person to unconsciously fulfill idealized images and instead finding that inside yourself. Once that is accomplished, you end the process by which you tyrannize others with unconscious expectations in hopes they fill the hole in your heart. This helps you see your earthly spouse for who they truly are and love them exactly how they are.

Loving something as flawed as a human being is a tremendous spiritual accomplishment for any of us. In some fundamental spiritual sense, it is what the sacrament of marriage is all about.

You meet your Inner Beloved on an inner journey on this path, but we also access the inner divine Oneness. And in my experience, accessing both of those is incredibly important; it supports you in the process of your growth and development and spiritual independence. It does not matter which one you find first. If, for instance, you see the Oneness first, you still need to discover the soul that embodies that Oneness. The soul becomes the immortal middle station between pure Awareness and you as a mortal. If you do not cultivate all three levels, something is missing, because the self, the personality, wants a personal love like we had with our mothers. There is something so fundamental and grounded and beautiful about the relationship between a mother and her offspring, whether it be puppies or kittens or babies. As mammals, we are designed to have the inner support that we are looking for from these beings that created us. So think of your soul as having created you. Then build a bridge through the Inner Beloved image to the soul. From there, you can relate to the Inner Beloved as your internal partner. This inner secret marriage becomes a foundation for your life. In so doing, it fulfills the instinct to find spiritual union and overcome the existential anxiety of isolated separation. Then, at some point, that Inner Beloved will pirouette and walk right into pure Awareness and show you the way home. She can give you an access point to formless mystical bliss. A useful book in understanding this special relationship is *Spirit Marriage: Intimate Relationships with Otherworldly Beings* by Megan Rose.

Interestingly, over the many years in which I have introduced this concept to students and taken them on journeys to meet the Inner Beloved, the vast majority of times students meet the Inner Beloved as a female, regardless of their own gender. There is something primal about divine feminine love and its capacity to support the self. So build your daily practice around it. Have a personal relationship with the divine. If you are called to the Way of the Mystic-Wizard, you will work with the spiritual world directly and cultivate a relationship with the divine beloved inside, and both the feminine forms and the masculine forms of the divine will eventually play a role as your journey unfolds.

Journey Five
THE BLUE CRYSTAL CAVE

Take a breath. Relax. Imagine you are floating in the mist, and now you are floating down, *five*, *four*, deeper into the mist, *three*, deeper, *two*, deeper, *one*, and you appear in front of the door to your inner world. Go ahead and step up to the platform in front of the door; place both hands on the door and feel the presence of the inner world behind it, the vastness that it invites you into. Set your intention to travel to the blue crystal cave, to meet with the Inner Beloved.

You hear the door click, and it opens. Step through, and you are walking through the castle corridor. Reach out with your right hand and touch the cold stones; drag your fingers along the wall and see the light behind your fingers. You come to an opening in the wall, the stairs that go down. Walk down the stairs. You find yourself in the common room. There is a beautiful fire going, and there is your cat waiting to say hello. There are also comfortable chairs and a table with a map on it. You notice the addition of a chessboard, and the pieces are set in a specific way. Notice what seems to be occurring there.

And now walk across the common room to the other staircase that goes up to the portal room; go up the stairs, turn right, and you are in the portal room. On the other side of the room is the shimmering portal itself, filled with light, and to the left of it, the cabinet that holds your traveling garb. Go to the cabinet, open it, and put on your traveling robes. Then stand in front of the shimmering portal and reach out your hands so they go into the energy of the portal; allow the energy to go into your body, filling you with a sort of raw inner-world energy and aligning your body-mind to the inner forest.

Step through the portal, and you are standing on the side of a snowy hill, looking out over a beautiful winter wonderland. Snow is falling, but you are warm. When you look up to the sky, it is covered with clouds. Out of the sky flies a beautiful horse, who comes down and lands next to you. This horse is here to help you travel across the inner world. Go ahead and mount the horse, get to know this inner-world being. As you do, the horse gently lifts off and moves over the field, climbing higher into the air.

You are looking down over the forest. The horse flies directly over the path that leads into the center of the forest and the sacred grove that is there. You can see the snow falling everywhere, and eventually you come to pass over the central grove, where you see the tiny dot of a fire at the center. There, next to the fire, is the old woman who guards the flame and makes sure it doesn't go out. You sense and see that she raises her right hand and points to the north. She is aware that you are above, and the horse turns to the north. You look out, and there is the vast mountain range in the distance, and you know there is a path to be followed.

You fly through the air, heading north toward the mountains, over the forest, until gentle hills begin to appear. You fly over those hills until you finally come to the base of a great mountain. There you see a staircase that has been carved into the side of the mountain, and you fly up, watching the staircase wind back and forth, until finally you come to a ledge, and there you see a blue light streaming forth from a cave. The ledge is wide, with plenty of room to land. The horse lands there, and you dismount.

The blue light that comes forth from the cave is inviting and soft. It reminds you of an eternal presence, a peace that lives within you and all things. Walk to the edge of the cave and look in; you see that all of the ceiling and walls are covered with blue crystals. They're giving off an incredible light. The crystals appear to be alive with light. They are shimmering with a blue, comfortable, wonderful light. There, on the ground of the cave, is a comfortable space with blankets. And there, waiting for you, is the Inner Beloved, who has been waiting for you for a long time. Go and sit with your beloved now, and together look out of the cave and see the forest below, the sky above. In this cave, there's nothing to do really but be and rest, to be completely present and commune together. Be comfortable, welcomed, accepted. Spend some time now with your beloved in the blue crystal cave and be at peace.

While you are in the cave, let the blue light of the crystals permeate every part of your being. This is the light of pure nondual Awareness in which everything is reconciled and at peace. There is no anxiety. There is no fear. There is nothing to do, nowhere to go. You can just *be* and enjoy the snow falling outside. Notice how your beloved is completely aware of all the things that you are, all the things that have ever happened to you, and all the things that you have ever done. All things are accepted one hundred percent. All weaknesses, all strengths, all wounds—everything is known and accepted. All of your humanity is loved and blessed.

Experience the cave and your beloved as long as you like . . .

Now, it is almost time to return. Before you leave, hold out your hands, and inside your hands is a gift for your beloved. Open your hands in a cup and offer the gift to them. Then they have a gift for you. Take that gift into your heart and know that you have begun a deep exchange and that a deep bond is beginning to form. And now say your goodbyes. Your beloved lets you know that they will always be with you, always right there, watching, supporting, being the source of your inspiration, guidance, and the love and safety you need.

Walk to the edge of the cave and look out over the vast forest from the north, there on the side of the mountain. Due to its strength, the mountain is the foundation of the world. This is the strength of the bond between self and soul, the beloved in you. Now it is time to get back on the horse and head out. You fly out over the mountain, over the hills, over the forest. Down below again, you see the sacred grove with the fire. You turn to the left, you turn east toward the castle. And from here, as you fly toward it, you can see the hill, the castle with flags flying. Now, fly down to the shimmering portal, slide off the horse, and give your thanks to the horse, for the horse will be back to travel with you to many places in the inner world.

Look out over the forest from the east again one more time, and sense the north, the mountains; see them as you begin to get to know them. And now turn, step through the shimmering portal, and you are back in the portal room. Put away your traveling robes, and head down into the common room. There you can hear the crackle of the fire, and your cat awaits. Now go over to the table on which the map of the inner world is laid, and there you can see where you are in the common room in the castle in the east. Now you can also see the north, where the mountains are, and the blue crystal cave is marked.

Then you notice that there is a small glass vase on the table with one rose waiting for you, from your beloved. It is time to return now; leave the common room behind, and go up the stairs into the hallway. Turn left, then move to the back of the door, and the door opens. You step through and turn, and the door closes. You hear it click, and there on the door is the symbol to your inner world. Place your left hand on the symbol and say in your own mind, *It is done.*

You are rising up through the mist, *one, two,* higher, higher, *three,* coming back to this world, integrating all you saw and learned and experienced into your human body and mind and memory. *Four,* wiggle your toes and your fingers and come fully back into your body and, *five,* open your eyes, fully returned to the outer world.

Take out your journal and write down, before you forget, those things that stand out and that are most important about the journey into the crystal cave.

Part Six

TOOLS FOR UNDERSTANDING YOURSELF

You walk the street in the aftermath—
for once, alone is the best way to be.
You are there, like an ocean.

There are many tools that can help you in your spiritual practice. In Part Six, we focus on tools that help you understand
yourself and your own personality. This process is essential, and
if you find yourself resisting understanding who you are, how
you work, and why, it is worth asking yourself why you resist.
Underneath can be a fear that you are not unique, or a fear of
being pigeonholed. Whatever the resistance, I suggest that in
all aspects of the quest you bring curiosity. Be willing to look
and see. The reward is powerful. To see the structures of humanity liberates you from blaming yourself, and from blaming
others for being who they are.

THE QUEST FOR BALANCE IN EXCELLENCE
AND AUTHENTICITY

I wrote earlier about the four directions. In the north is stone; the south holds the fire staff; in the east is the sword of air; in the west, the cup of water; and in the center is the nondual diamond. A diamond is a traditional way of representing pure Awareness and the enlightened or natural state. It means the indestructibility that goes along with pure Awareness. Our deepest identity is utterly indestructible and is not an object, is not a form, but is more like light itself.

From Carl Jung's ideas and archetypal psychology there developed many modern approaches to transformation. Jung himself was a doctor and also, essentially, a shaman without a drum. He made a path for us into the inner worlds where the insights of psychology and shamanism could be utilized. One of the concepts he developed was the four elements of consciousness, which link to the four directions noted above.

In the north, we have the stone, which is essentially the body or form. For Jung, this is *sensing*, in other words, touch and everything that goes along with being embodied. And in the south, we have the elemental fire, which symbolizes intuitive function, or *intuition* and inspiration. The north-south axis has come to be called the *arational*, meaning not using logic or reason, which is not the same as *irrational*, meaning unreasonable and inaccurate. Arational can be a source of highly accurate insight; irrational cannot. Thus the arational axis does make sense and is reasonable; it's just that the information that comes to you through touch and through intuition is not information that has to be figured out with logic. You just know. If you put your hand on a hot stove, you do not have to try to figure out whether it is hot or cold; you know immediately because of the sensation. That is the arational axis, and everybody has both the sensing and intuiting components of it.

From east to west, Jung drew what has come to be called the *rational* axis. The east is where we have the sword, which is the *thinking* function of consciousness. Thinking is not always logical, but it works to help you discover whether things are true or false. In the west, we have the *feeling* function, which is also a rational process. In other words, you feel whether something seems right or wrong. You can feel your way through an experience this way. Each of these processes—thinking whether something is true or false and feeling whether it feels right or wrong—is rational; that is, there are two sides to it. But neither process is assumed to be logical or correct. Only when a person has learned to use their thinking and feeling functions with a degree of mastery do they gain the powers of those functions. Much of the time, these two functions are used not to generate analytical insight but rather to rationalize a biased perspective that serves to defend a limited self-identity. It takes serious training in the art of thinking and in the management of feeling to be logical and to have the will to see the truth that the rational aspects of consciousness can reveal.

We all have these four types of consciousness that Jung categorized. The structure he created was later adapted into the Myers-Briggs Type Indicator (MBTI), which helps identify which of the four functions of consciousness—sensing (S), intuiting (N), thinking (T), feeling (F)—are your strongest and weakest capacities. Each of us has a primary capacity, one that's very strong in our personality, and a secondary capacity. The primary one is either from the rational axis or the arational axis; the second one is from the opposite axis. For instance, I am what's called an intuitive feeler, an "NF," so I have intuition as my primary arational strength and feeling as my rational strength. I feel my way through life by intuiting patterns and what those patterns mean. Someone else might have thinking as their primary approach and sensing as their second one—an "ST" who is grounded in and thinks about an embodied world. There are four combinations of the consciousness functions (sixteen combinations when incorporating two additional MBTI characteristics, extraversion/introversion and judging/perceiving). None of these combinations is better or worse. They are all simply different aspects of consciousness, and they give you strengths. Think of them almost like superpowers—but of course they also give you weaknesses. We all have some classic "kryptonite" issues.

If you take my situation as an NF, one of the things I am weak on is the true/false rational and potentially logical thinking; issues of being connected to the sensation world also show up. The opposite would be true for someone who is sensing- and thinking-oriented (an ST). When you take the Myers-Briggs Type Indicator assessment, your core orientation is represented by the two letters in the middle, such as I**NT**P or E**SF**J. Our personalities are built around these inner core aspects.

Why does this matter?

On the path of the Mystic-Wizard, we work with these four directions and functions of consciousness with their attendant symbolic elements. In the inner world, we quest after these symbolic forms and work with them in our imagination to better integrate the experiences and perspectives that each engenders. The goal is to balance out the four aspects of consciousness and to become more aware and masterful with each of them. For instance, if I am making a decision, I naturally will intuit the patterns around the decision and assess how the decision feels to me, but it might also be useful to go gather some facts and think about them logically, and then perhaps I should go inhabit what the consequences of my decision might look like in the physical world. If I'm applying to college, maybe I should go see the college, not just look at pictures. A lot is learned by smell, color, and texture that our subconscious uses to determine if something is the right fit for us—whether college, food, clothing, or a mate.

The process of self-balancing is the point of the quest for the four hallows. Throughout the year, we go on a quest for the sacred, hallowed objects. The journey is deeply connected to the earth and to the earth's cycles—the four seasons, the equinoxes, and the solstices—just as it has been for all of human existence, and the investigation is meant to effectively integrate, develop, and mediate these four powerful aspects of human consciousness from the inner world into the outer world. The quest for each sacred object is transformative.

In the summer, when we seek fire and the staff, we meet the energies of consciousness and the inner-world beings that embody and mediate inspiration, intuition, and transformation.

In the fall, we go on the quest for the cup and water and feeling, and what is traditionally associated with the ancestors (the "lineage" of one's emotional life). In the cup's highest manifestation, the cup with the diamond in it is the holy grail. The idea is that through the feeling function, you can, in your heart, awaken not only to the soul but also to pure Awareness. That moves you in time from an individualized love of a particular object or person to what is called in Tibetan Buddhism "great love," or spontaneous compassion.

In the winter is the quest for the stone. The stone is the body; it is sensing and touch, and all the energies associated with an embodiment of your life, your life story, your life destiny. This includes the wounds that you've suffered in your life and the potentials that will unfold and *can* only unfold when you are actually a human being. What is so powerful about the quest for the stone is the discovery of the foundation stone. The foundation stone is the diamond woven into each of the other elements. You end up finding pure Awareness inside the earth, the body itself. The proper foundation of existence is the emptiness of formlessness. This means that the body is, in fact, a holy temple, as are all its manifestations, including sexuality, death, food, and the many pains and pleasures of having a physical body. The diamond is not only hidden in the rough; it literally *is* the rough.

In the spring, we move on to the quest for the sword. The sword is about thinking and the nature of the mind and thought, how thought can be utilized healthily, and how it can also be neurotic and pathological. We seek out the best processes through which to get a handle on the mind, which involves various forms of meditation. The meditation practices that you develop on a day-to-day basis allow you to use the mind for insight and develop wisdom.

We live through this quest for the hallows each year on this path in order to increase the speed and depth of the process of individuation. This allows us to deepen the relationship with the soul as Inner Beloved and develop a sustainable practice that will eventually lead to a fuller awakening. As you can imagine, people's approach to the Inner Beloved, to their practice, to pure Awareness, is distinctly connected to their personality structure and to which of the hallows they have mastery over. Someone who is a thinking person would approach these elements in a different way from someone who's primarily a sensing, intuitive, or feeling person.

There is a lovely uniqueness in the process that I am talking about, and it also becomes an invitation to work in community. We move through the annual cycle together, dedicated to engage in transformation, which brings about the synthesis of self and soul. The journey is an expression of authenticity in one's life and therefore of fulfilling one's potential and destiny in the world. This is the quest for balance, authenticity, and excellence that the Way of the Mystic-Wizard offers.

· ·

EXERCISE

MBTI

To get a feel for what the orientation of your personality is with respect to the four aspects of consciousness, go online to search for and take a free Myers-Briggs Type Indicator test.

Journal about the experience and any insights you gain.

· ·

THE ENNEAGRAM PERSONALITY TYPE SYSTEM

It is challenging to do transformative work when you do not understand what you are working with. Figuring out who you are and what you are is fundamental to the path, because without that understanding you are setting yourself up for confusion. As you do transformative work, it doesn't just happen in your inner world; transformation challenges will come to you in the outer world. If you are not careful and aware of how you function and you fall into dysfunctional behaviors, you can easily create unnecessary collateral damage. You already do cause damage and will again, so it is best to be honest about that from the start. You will suffer, and you will cause suffering, accidentally and maybe even deliberately, depending on whether your shadow takes over at some point and who it blames and attacks when you are under tremendous transformative pressure.

The Enneagram is the single most helpful tool I've found for deepening self-knowledge. It is based on various ancient mystical traditions from Taoism, Buddhism, Sufism, Judaism, Christianity, and ancient Esoteric Greek and Egyptian magic and philosophy, and is used worldwide in government, business, and education. The Enneagram is tremendously insightful, and both sobering and encouraging. With the right book and course, the Enneagram can assist you in developing a high degree of awareness and self-mastery.

I recommend the 1999 book *The Wisdom of the Enneagram: The Complete Guide to Psychological and Spiritual Growth for the Nine Personality Types* by Don Richard Riso and world-renowned Enneagram teacher Russ Hudson. They have, I believe, captured the essence of the system and delivered a powerful book with grace and compassion. I have been using this book since 2000 and used it to develop the art school I founded and ran from 1998 to 2022. The book provides all you need to use the Enneagram system and dive into your personality type, and it provides a pathway toward mastery and freedom. In addition, Hudson's 2021 audio course, The Enneagram: Nine Gateways to Presence, offers over thirteen hours of invaluable insight. The course benefits from Hudson's many years teaching and researching the Enneagram and is, I think, the best place to start. The two together, book and course, give learners a solid grounding. There is also an app called EnneaApp (enneaapp. com) that is enormously helpful in understanding the essence of your own type and others' and is a handy distillation of the entire system.

OVERVIEW OF ENNEAGRAM TYPES

The Enneagram has nine essential types, often referred to simply by their number. The name represents the type's basic approach to life, and each type has a strategy they use to meet their needs. In the list below, the first term after each number comes from the standard Enneagram Institute name; in parentheses are names that students of mine have suggested.

1. The Reformer (advocate, perfectionist, idealist)
2. The Helper (caregiver, mentor, giver)
3. The Achiever (performer, competitor, go-getter)
4. The Individualist (artist, romantic, empath)
5. The Investigator (researcher, scholar, thinker)
6. The Loyalist (guardian, watcher, doubter)
7. The Enthusiast (adventurer, engager, stimulator)
8. The Challenger (protector, leader, general)
9. The Peacemaker (moderator, collaborator, diplomat)

The deeper you get into the Enneagram, the more you see humanity has evolved nine basic ways to deal with the loss of pure Awareness. It may seem absurd that we only have nine basic types, because we are all so individualistic and quirky, but we are all born with similar bodies and psychologies. From far enough above, we all look similar, just as all the flowers in a field of poppies would. Get down close though, and we rapidly become unique. Somewhere between ten thousand feet and ten inches sits the Enneagram. We all had to deal with the loss of our awareness of Awareness; it makes sense that humanity evolved basic ways of successfully coping with that loss. That coping process has served our survival needs. The adaption structures that succeeded in helping us to create mental and emotional stability are what survived. The Enneagram is not radical when seen in this perspective; however, it should not be seen as prescriptive either, for the egoic self is malleable, and so is the actual brain with its many synapses.

The Enneagram system is both self-determining and a self-reporting system. The assessment itself does not always provide a clear answer as to what type you are, but it will offer a few possibilities. Then you must determine your type by reading the narrative descriptions of the types.

Often what you like the least will turn out to be the key to identifying what type you are. For example, Type Ones (Reformers) fear being "corrupt" or "flawed" and want to be "good" and "right"; as a result, they can be hypercritical—and who wants to agree they are hypercritical? The description of your type may trigger you, and you may try to avoid it because you do not like what you are reading. This is common. You do not like it, because it makes something unconscious into something conscious. In essence, the Enneagram reveals just how conditioned your behavior is. We often use our type to cover our fear. When we face fear and develop our type's gift, we can, in time, become liberated.

Additionally, each type has two "wings," the numbers on either side of their primary type, one of which will be more dominant than the other. For example, I am a Two, the Helper, and I have as my main wing the Three, the Achiever, and my lesser wing the One, the Reformer.

The other thing to note is that each type has an integration type and a stress type. The integration type is the direction you go when you are comfortable; it is the path to finding your way out of the limits of your type. For example, when in growth, a Type One (Reformer) goes to Type Seven (Enthusiast), becoming more fun and spontaneous. The stress type is the direction you go when life is going wrong; think of it as the nuclear option for dealing with life issues. A Type One goes to Type Four (Individualist) under stress, becoming resentful and sensitive to criticism. We tend to act out the unhealthy patterns

WHEN WE FACE FEAR AND DEVELOP OUR TYPE'S GIFT, WE CAN BECOME LIBERATED.

of our stress type, so we try to avoid them. And yet, oddly and ironically enough, the stress type is also the final path to our liberation from the unhealthy aspects of our type.

Hudson's wonderful audio course has a final section in which he reveals how our stress type in fact provides the final steps to mastery. (The course is worth that section alone.)

So essentially you have structural access to four of the Enneagram types: primary, wing, stress, and integration (or growth).

The way we often learn about a particular type is by observing a panel of people who share a type speaking about how they function and perceive reality. You can find Enneagram panels of all nine types on YouTube. They can be helpful for determining your type and for understanding any other particular type. Until you have the tools of the Enneagram available, it is all too easy to think that when you or another person acts in a certain way there is something wrong with you or them. There are healthy and unhealthy versions of each type, but there is nothing fundamentally broken about any of them. They are all survival patterns that create the self. In that sense, the types are sacred tools of the soul.

My focus in this book is on how the distortion of each type creates the abilities the soul uses later in development. My approach is a mystical and magical perspective on the Enneagram. My goal is to validate why the quest for the fifth hallow is essential and to reveal how the soul's choice to manifest as it did was for a specific purpose. Our goal here is not to determine that you are a specific type and thus doomed to the unhealthy expressions of that type. The goal is to see your type as a living, moving adaptation to the loss of awareness of Awareness and to develop knowledge and the wisdom to know how to use that knowledge. Your Enneagram type is the key to the pathway of your awakening. Eventually, we end up trusting that the soul is incarnated and oriented toward a specific Enneagram type to

THE ENNEAGRAM TYPES ARE SACRED TOOLS OF THE SOUL.

live a particular kind of life and master a specific set of capacities along the way.

We must be careful how we use the Enneagram. We can easily either demonize or overly value our own type, and in the worst case, we can weaponize knowledge of the Enneagram and use it to put others, or their type, down. Ethically, we want to avoid those possibilities and anyone who is using the tool in those ways. I am here to set you on your path to discovery and help you become more aware, not to arm you with weapons to prove why you are right and others are wrong for how they manifest.

· ·

EXERCISE
Enneagram Assessment

Go online to take the Enneagram assessment. For a small fee you can take it through the Enneagram Institute (enneagram-institute.com). There are a variety of free online assessments as well, though quality may vary. You may not get back a clear answer from the assessment, but your results will offer a few possibilities. Then you must determine your type by reading the narrative descriptions of the types.

Journal about the experience and any insights you gain.

· ·

AN EXAMPLE: MY ENNEAGRAM TYPE

Wisdom and knowledge are very different when it comes to this kind of system. One simple rule is to not tell others what type they are; allow others to determine their own type. In the Enneagram tradition, we are each empowered to report on the types and perspectives we live out every day. However, unless you are a highly trained and skilled Enneagram expert teacher, it is best to speak from what is known. I have been teaching the Enneagram for two decades, but I am not an expert like Russ Hudson, so I will write only about the types that I have easy access to: my own. In this section, I have shared my Enneagram types and used them to exemplify the effect the fifth hallow and the Way of the Mystic-Wizard can have on type development.

As I said, I am a Type Two, the Helper, which is why I am a teacher and a mentor. On one side of me is Type One, the Reformer, who has a sense of the ideal, and on the other side is Type Three, the Achiever. Both of those wings play a role in my life, but the Three wing is more dominant than the One wing, so I am "a Two with a Three wing"—that is, a Helper with an Achiever wing. I get a sense of deep satisfaction from helping people and also from achieving and performing. Typically, one of your wings is more powerful when you are younger, but as you grow, the nondominant wing can emerge more fully. For me, the energy of the One began to move into my life later on and has grown over time. For example, the Reformer inspired me to try to create a better art school. I'd say about 70 percent of the time, I am engaged in two psychological patterns and processes (Two and Three), and about 30 percent of the time, three patterns (Two, Three, and One).

Despite these types, the forces that shape us are often unconscious, which is why we are developing a practice. That way we can become a co-creator with the soul in fulfilling our destiny. Let's look at this idea in more detail with my example.

EACH TYPE HAS HEALTHY AND UNHEALTHY VERSIONS, BUT NONE IS FUNDAMENTALLY BROKEN.

My Primary Type: Type Two (the Helper). The Two is the helper, caregiver, and mentor who underneath does not feel worthy of love and so seeks attention. The goal of the Two is to attract love and attention by helping others. Type Twos want people to give them attention, praise, and love, but, ironically, cannot fully accept it when it does come to them. Seeking attention through helping, and not being able to receive the love and praise, keeps the egoic self locked out of the unconditioned state. The Two is convinced that what they need is outside themselves. The more they help and work, the more bitter and resentful they get that the love and attention is not flowing in their direction. The more that dynamic plays out, the more others unconsciously move away from the Two.

The goal is to observe these behaviors when they arise, have compassion for them, and then return to the recognition of Awareness. The unconscious drive that creates the behaviors evaporates in the recognition of Awareness.

Type Twos are deeply attuned to the underlying unconditional love and bliss of pure Awareness and the soul. But because they have forgotten this consciously, they have become conditioned to seek it outwardly. In their quest for recognition and love, they abandon themselves. The journey for the Two is to come home to the heart center, stop leaping out to help others, and realize they have already arrived; what they have been looking for was always already right there inside them. In this way, the Two can encounter the bliss-field of the nondual and the great love of the soul as a personalized being that is the perfect spiritual companion. Only then can a Two begin to spontaneously arise as the love that they once looked for and longed for. This heals the primordial flaw of the Two, which is pride, or the need to be recognized as having something no one else has so they can finally feel worthy and lovable. If only someone would see how special they are . . . In reality, the soul has always been aware of both the flaw of this pride and the path to its resolution, which is the embodiment of the presence of pure Awareness.

My Dominant Wing: Type Three (the Achiever). My dominant wing is Three, the Achiever, so it is much more conscious for me than my One wing is, perhaps partly because it is reinforced by our Type-Three US culture. The word "achievement" is like a mantra or holy word in American society. Student achievement is how we measure success in schooling—not student satisfaction, or student health, or student authenticity, but student achievement. Measurement is done via tests that utterly ignore the feelings of the student, all so that we can improve "achievement" in the larger population. "Achievement" in the US means having a higher degree of accomplishments and tasks completed in a shorter amount of time with better outcomes. This is "success." The myth tells us that this "success" will give American people better access to better jobs, and those better jobs will make them more money, and then Americans will be what? Happy.

All this achievement is supposed to lead to happiness. But what happens if you work so hard to *achieve* that you make yourself into the kind of person who has no time to even *feel* happy or to enjoy the fruits of your labor? This is the great Three conundrum. What if you end up wildly successful at something you hate doing? The remedy is authenticity, and that is a tricky thing to achieve as a Three.

I would guess that I am using my Three about 30 to 60 percent of the time. Much that I have accomplished, including this book, is born from this achievement-oriented perspective. But at some point it is no longer about achievement for its own sake. Eventually, one must achieve something meaningful to the soul, or else it is an empty achievement. A meaningless achievement does not feel like an achievement at all; it feels like a lie, and the person who creates false achievements feels like a fake. All Threes know this deep inside, and eventually, it drives them to start the journey for the soul and become authentic. If we do not value authenticity as much as achievement, the considerable cultural Three bias and pressure will eat up time and energy with yet more achievement.

The goal of a Three is to be successful by performing well and getting attention for that performance. Underneath, the Three does not feel worthy or lovable unless they have accomplished something "worthwhile" or are performing live in some way that garners applause. However, much like the Two, they are mostly unable to accept this applause when it does come to them, because the entire structure of the Three depends on not feeling lovable unless they can perform well. And the performance never ends. This type can spend an entire life producing and suddenly wake up and feel like they missed life. The doing and accomplishing is a compulsive need to achieve and be recognized. The egoic self is so busy and moving so fast that it is disconnected from the soul and pure Awareness most of the time. The soul moves at a slower clip than the egoic self. This is why meditation and mindfulness are a path toward connection with the soul.

Type Threes do a lot of work that is not their work to do. Much as Twos help people who did not ask for it, Threes will make up things that never needed to be done to avoid slowing down and getting connected. Slowing down brings up feelings they are ill-equipped to deal with. But all that comes crashing down eventually, and the soul will have its day one way or another. Underneath it, the Three knows that there is nothing we need to do, or ever can do, to be worthy. We are, in fact, everything and, therefore, worthy beyond what a measurable system can compute. But Threes do not know this consciously, so they must prove it and seek recognition for their accomplishments.

When they encounter pure Awareness, they suddenly have nothing to accomplish. Everything is always already complete, and the game is up; they are worthy and always have been. It

> THERE IS NOTHING WE NEED TO DO TO BE WORTHY. WE ARE ALREADY WORTHY BEYOND MEASURE.

can be disconcerting to realize all you have done does not actually make you more worthy. There is nothing the universe can do to be worthy of itself. It is inherently worthy, and so are we.

The nondual view allows the Three to question their methods, to lean inward to develop an inner life and recognize the inner lives of others as unique, valuable, and worthy. In time, the Three, who can be embroiled in inauthentic work for the entire first half of life, can become the most authentic of all types. The journey to get there is arduous, but this only makes the accomplishment have that much more integrity and depth. As the Two must stop abandoning Awareness by seeking it in others, the Three must stop leaving Awareness by seeking it in business and work. Awareness is always available, and always ready to be present with us.

My Nondominant Wing: Type One (the Reformer). The Type One is the advocate, reformer, and perfectionist. Their goal is to be perfect and to achieve the archetypal ideal. They (and I) have a connection to and desire to embody the highest potential in life in its idealized form. Ironically, even when things are nearly perfect, they still see the flaw. It can make them tense and want to fix the flaws (or at least point them out). I want things to look good and be the right way.

The One in me is unconsciously aware of perfection at a deeper level, but, because of the loss of awareness of pure Awareness, cannot see that everything is already always perfect. The One's journey is to rediscover the truth and release the universe and the egoic self from the limited misperception that something is wrong here.

The fact that archetypal perfection is unfulfilled here on Earth does not mean perfection does not exist. We can eventually recognize that the ideal draws us toward a better version of life. The process of working toward it is what shapes us as beings. Things need to be messy for beauty to be created and truth uncovered. Once this realization is metabolized, the desire for perfection arises not as a burden but instead as a remarkable skill in service to the soul and Awareness.

It is an immense relief to the mind, body, and emotions to sense into the Great Perfection and remember that all is perfect exactly as it is. Form is formlessness, and formless perfection is all form. Living into this truth is the holy grail of all types, but for the One, it is the release of an internal angst. With nondual insight and Awareness in place, internal mirth arises when the mind seeks to fix what never was broken or imperfect. Then the One goes about fixing up reality with a sense of humor and compassion for self and others.

That gives you a basic introduction to how I approach non-duality and the Enneagram. The last aspect of the Enneagram to look at briefly is your instinctual type.

THE THREE INSTINCTS

In my mind, at least half of what determines our behaviors and approach to life is instinctual, and within the Enneagram you have not only a primary type, a wing, and growth and stress directions, but also an "instinctual stack." Most of us do not fully appreciate the power of the instincts because their influence is unconscious, but the Enneagram's three instincts are crucial in understanding how you show up in the world as your type.

The three instincts are what they sound like: instincts that come from our foundation as mammals and that have evolved over millions of years. In order of their evolutionary development on our planet, the three basic instincts are:

- **The Self-Preservation Instinct** (or Survival): This instinct is about survival needs.
- **The Sexual Instinct** (or Creative). This instinct is about the perpetuation of our species, adaptation and growth, and creative expression.

- **The Social Instinct** (or Connection). This instinct is about connection to another individual and to the group. It is about communication and collaboration for survival and is quite rare on our planet; many species do not have this instinct.

(Note: I use the terms Survival, Creative, and Connection rather than the terms created by the originators of the system, because the terms they chose seemed abstract in the case of "self-preservation," off-putting and possibly misunderstood, limited, or alienating in terms of the "sexual" instinct, and a simple misnomer in terms of the "social" instinct. We are all social beings and the word "social" implies parties, but the instinct is much deeper: it is the bond between mother and child and every other bond you ever create in which there is emotional connection and communication. The connection instinct is how we build friendships, marriages, and community. Therefore, for the rest of this discussion I will use the three terms that I feel fit better with the actual energy of the instinct. Survive, Create, and Connect are also an easy set of terms to remember when you are trying to monitor what is motivating you. Feel free to use my terms, or the older ones.)

These three instincts are the underlying energetic orientations that drive us and constantly move up through our body and into our psychological system. They create in us a feeling of longing and an emotional drive to fulfill that longing. As self-conscious creatures, we humans have the opportunity to witness these instincts, to make conscious choices about how to use the energy and satisfy the craving they create, and to develop the instincts we are less masterful with.

Each person is typically oriented toward one of the instincts. Our strongest instinct drives us to bring that instinct into the world. Then we have a second instinct that's less strong and a third one that's more unconscious. Their order of importance for you is what is referred to as your "instinctual stack."

I imagine that throughout our recent history, say the last hundred thousand years, these instincts were fundamental to helping tribes survive. Having people with the connection instinct being most important helps bring people together. They drum, they dance, they organize the hunt and create emotional bonds. Then you have people who are oriented around the survival instinct. They ensure that all the food that has been foraged is safe, that we have enough for winter, that the spears are sharpened, the huts are well made, and the borders are secure. Then you have the people who are oriented toward the creative instinct, the intensely energetic people, charismatic and creative.

In our modern context, instincts expand into many more activities and expressions. Note that just because you focus on one instinct in the stack doesn't mean that you have mastered its expression in every area of life that it can manifest. You also can easily have too much of a good thing. And from the perspective of your Enneagram type and the creation of your egoic self, it is your primary instinct's energy, or the distortion of it, that drives the behaviors of your primary type. Those behaviors all have positive and negative aspects, and utilized from the place of nondual Awareness, they are liberated and non-neurotic. When they come from an unconscious place, they are just that—running the show and driving us in that direction no matter what, without any awareness of the need they are trying to fulfill. It is these energies that are the source of unconscious addictions.

Instincts left to run themselves are like animals that do not know when to stop eating. But when connected to Awareness, we can open our mental and emotional space wider, sense what is happening, make clearer choices, and surf though the compulsive urge with the help of being awake and aware of Awareness.

This is why spiritual development is so valuable.

AS SELF-CONSCIOUS CREATURES, WE CAN CHOOSE HOW TO USE THE ENERGY OF OUR INSTINCTS.

The Survival Instinct. The survival instinct may sound basic, but it involves many kinds of important activities, including (but by no means limited to):

- Home improvement and vehicle maintenance
- Safety
- Money management, saving
- Time management
- Skills development
- Good work habits
- Persistence, discipline, endurance
- Stress management and life balance
- Comfort, pleasure
- Exercise, sleep
- Professional development

Even if you are primarily oriented toward the survival instinct, there will be areas in which you are strong and areas in which you are weak, and there may also be areas that you are obsessed with beyond reason. Be practical about developing or managing your instincts, and you will gain some mastery over them. To accomplish this requires insight into behavior patterns, the power to resist doing something, and a good reason to resist. It is much harder than it sounds.

A final note on the survival instinct: it is hard to master all of these areas, yet many of them are essential for mastery of life and also for developing an enduring daily spiritual practice. No one starts with proficiency in all areas, and room for growth is what makes the challenge of life exciting and worthwhile. It is also totally reasonable to get help from others—professionals, partners, or family members. The idea is to be honest about and take responsibility for mastery, even if you gain that mastery from a second person.

The Creative Instinct. The creative instinctual energy manifests in many ways that encourage us to grow and explore. It includes (but again is not limited to):

- Projecting charismatic energy
- Interest in or passion for something
- Learning and self-development
- Adventure and exploration
- Finding the right person, clothes, place, or identity
- Moving beyond your comfort zone
- Inspiration, creative flow, creative expression
- Deep focus and involvement
- Union with another or the universe
- Surrender and release
- Seeking meaning and purpose

Without the creative instinct, we would not have a species at all, and in that sense, it is essential. However, it is also intense and vibrant and, when misdirected, can cause all sorts of complex suffering. This is why religions have many taboos around mishandled creative sexual energy, such as incest taboos, and why we have age-of-consent and power-imbalance laws.

Over time, humanity has learned that creative energy is so powerful that it must be managed wisely. However, overly strict control, or outright denial or denigration of creative energy, generates a whole other set of problems, such as deep shame, self-hatred, hatred of life itself, or hatred of the feminine as the source of life.

We now live in a time in which we have the right and the responsibility to learn to manage creative energy with care, compassion, and mastery. Without this energy, no one would mate, and we would have no people, no art, no creativity at all. So it is essential that we learn how to use this instinct wisely, just as we would money or time. Doing so can take years of working to change conditioning and deep structures of self-judgment, but the result is worth it, for this energy is the source of our creative power.

It is also the energy of spiritual and bodily transformation and is symbolized by fire. We utilize this spiritual power source to build the bridge between self and soul, and soul and spirit. In India, this energy is called *kundalini* and rises from the base of the spine through the bodily energy centers (*chakras*) to the top of the head, and allows for breakthroughs and the expansion of consciousness, creativity, wisdom, and compassion. This same energy is also used in all the world's alchemical traditions to build the immortal body of light, which I will discuss further in Part Nine.

From a nondual perspective, the energy expression at the base chakra is no better or worse than the energy expression at the top of the head. The goal is to master the expression of the energy at every center in our body. In doing so, we have access to many skills and powers, including states of subtle bliss that bring about healing and growth and are beautiful for their own sake.

The Connection Instinct. The final instinct is the connection instinct, which is associated with what we call "social skills" today and the ability to relate with others one-to-one or in groups. It includes (but of course is not limited to):

- Managing complex social situations
- Understanding social expectations
- Reading cues, facial expressions, body language
- Understanding the motivations of others
- Being a good parent, a good child, team member, or life partner
- Building and maintaining relationships
- Valuing communication
- Being good at communication
- Volunteering and contributing to community
- Enjoying play and learning by play with others
- Making meaningful emotional connections

This instinct is also about a drive to belong and find the other and/or the group or tribe where you feel like you fit. This need can be fulfilled by a sports team, a religious organization, a particular musical genre or band, or a game you play. Many cultural activities in the world can be a vehicle to fulfill this instinct, even if the activity itself is not inherently for that purpose.

You can see from these lists that some people are driven to be involved in the creation of connection and finding a sense of belonging or meaning in that setting. For others, connection is the lowest instinct in their stack, and they are not driven to participate or connect in the same manner. Knowing the order in which your instincts stack helps you understand yourself and others.

What matters as you look at your instincts is why you do a particular activity. Ask yourself what your underlying motivation is. Are you joining a club to feel belonging and connection, or to find out useful information to help you do better in life, or to create something new? If it's all of the above, which one is most important to you?

You will discover that the three instincts blend and are constantly weaving together in your life. The idea is not that we can or need always to separate them. Instead, the goal is to get a sense of our overall orientation, develop greater awareness about our instinctual needs, and develop some conscious mastery over them. When they are not being fulfilled, we learn to witness how they drive us to try to get them fulfilled every single day. They do this by making us feel that something is missing in our lives, and they usually show up as fear or desire. It is easier to manage these kinds of instinctual emotions when you see what your instinctual nature is doing. Once you correctly identify a longing, rather than flailing around, you can consciously work to fulfill the longing in a unique way that works for you. To become authentic requires seeing yourself clearly and then choosing that which is the best fit for your path.

EXERCISE
Assess Your Instincts

Look at each of the three instinct lists: survival, creative, and connection. Journal about the following:

- How would you rank yourself for each item on the list? Good? Not so good? Still learning?
- What on the list is important to you, and what have you mastered?
- Does any area have mastery over you?
- What is your instinctual stack? That is, which is your primary, secondary, and tertiary instinct?

Then craft a list of skills you are working to develop.

EXERCISE
Your Instinctual Lineage

Once you have a sense of your instinctual stack, spend a little time looking at where that stack came from and the behaviors associated with it. Your stack can be genetic, it can be from learned behaviors, and it can also be influenced by the soul. Try to get a sense of how your behavior was shaped and, therefore, why you show up as you do.

In your journal, write down the names of your primary caregivers when you were growing up. Look for who embodied the Mother and Father archetypes for you (it may not have been your actual mother and father). Then see if you can determine what their instinctual stacks were by making notes of behaviors that reflect the three instincts. For example:

Mother (or mother figure)
- Connection: Strong sense of social responsibility, often attended protests and demonstrations
- Creative: Charismatic and engaging, loved to decorate and move furniture around
- Survival: Spent money on charities important to her, but couldn't seem to save

Father (or father figure)
- Survival: Worked hard (sometimes worked two jobs), saved money almost to a fault
- Creative: Enjoyed sharing moneysaving tips
- Connection: Didn't like big groups, tended to lose track of relationships with extended family

Once you have a list for your parental figures, create your own list and see how your stack and the behaviors you have in each instinct are related to what you picked up from your caregivers. Young human beings, and mammals in general, learn from their parents how to manage the three instincts. Some of it is so ingrained as to be genetically coded. When you see how you learned what you learned, you can choose to make changes rather than being run by your "default settings" all your life.

Lastly, once you have your own list of behaviors, you can craft a plan for developing some mastery in each area. If, for instance, you have little use for the connection instinct, then investigate it a bit and try to develop it. Or, if you are oblivious about how to manage money, then start to take an interest, and learn from others the skills they have. It is not about right or wrong or shame; it is about acquiring some balance and forgiving ourselves for being the way we are created. Evolution designed this stacking focus because it helped us survive, but in today's world, some mastery over every area is needed to thrive. Recognize your patterns, forgive them, and then take full responsibility for your own human development.

LOVE LANGUAGES

The love languages framework offers a practical approach to understanding how you express and expect to experience love. The framework originated in Gary Chapman's 1992 book *The Five Love Languages: How to Express Heartfelt Commitment to Your Mate*, and it defines five ways that people express love: words of affirmation, quality time, physical touch, gift-giving, and acts of service.

The framework promotes an understanding that people come from different places with different expectations for expressing love. When we unconsciously have expectations, we usually create suffering. When we discover our primary love language, we can stop expecting other people to automatically speak in our language.

In addition, if you love people who never speak your language, you can learn how to ask them to speak yours by developing courage and investigating the inner conditioning that habitually looks for love outside the self-soul-spirit structure. This deeply engrained habit takes time and practice to alter, just as any childhood conditioning does, but the quest to do so delivers enormous rewards in terms of spiritual connection and spiritual independence. In doing so we recognize the reality that when we were children most of us learned to love in an outward direction, toward others, as a survival mechanism. However, just because we learned to love outward does not mean that we can solve all our emotional needs as adults through human relationships.

Imagine a chart with vertical and horizontal axes. The horizontal axis represents our relationships with humans (and animals and other outer-world entities). The vertical axis represents dimensions of love between self and soul and spirit. A solid vertical spiritual connection liberates you from an over-dependence on the horizontal, egoic attachment-based love, therefore decreasing codependence and increasing empowerment. Our goal is to find the right balance of each axis, and the presence of pure Awareness on the vertical axis becomes essential to creating a sustainable sense of emotional support and stability as we travel on the Mystic-Wizard path.

After thirty years of working on this issue, I have come to believe that I can viably get about 50 percent of my love needs met from vertical spiritual relationships and 50 percent from horizontal human and animal relationships. Each of us has our own percentage on each axis that allows for developing a real sense of equipoise in life. The key is to figure out this balance for yourself and realize that it is not someone else's responsibility to figure it out or to develop the capacity for you. Additionally, since life is constantly changing in the outer world, it helps to recognize that the stability of your axial percentages of connection will have to be maintained like a garden.

When people die or move away, you can suddenly suffer from a massive reduction of horizontal "life support." This is why the vertical connection is vital as a foundation and why this connection is embodied in your daily practice: so you can lean on your training and your inner-world contacts.

For example, the death of a loved one creates grief. What many do not know (until they experience it) is that grieving eats up vital energy in your self-structure. After my mother's death, my grief counselor advised me to expect to have anywhere from a third to a half of my average amount of fuel for living. She said this drop in energy can last anywhere from six months to three years, but the average is two years. For me, it was about sixteen months. In times like that, when deep psychological processes are taking place, your daily practice becomes an island of stability and predictability.

WHEN WE HAVE UNCONSCIOUS EXPECTATIONS, WE USUALLY CREATE SUFFERING.

About two years after my mother died, my father died, which is not unusual for couples who have been married for forty-plus years. But what that meant was two periods of significant energy loss. In situations like this, when major losses happen so close together, we could experience this lower energy state for four (maybe even six) whole years. A long-term, low-energy grieving process can then become normalized and habituated. We can even forget what life was like before the loss. Our daily practice and the spiritual world help keep us engaged and prevent a deep dive into depression and hopelessness by giving us purpose, love, energy, and connection as we adapt to loss and the truth of our mortality.

. . . .

EXERCISE

Find Your Love Language

Go online or find an app to take a love language quiz. If possible, find the love languages of the people around you too. Write in your journal about what you discovered.

. . . .

ATTACHMENT TYPE AND ENERGY MANAGEMENT

Another essential aspect of yourself to consider is what is called your attachment type, or how you connect with others. The research in this area started in the 1960s and 1970s with psychiatrist John Bowlby and then psychologist Mary Ainsworth; it has since been expanded upon by others.

Attachment type is typically defined in four categories (the specific terms may vary) where the experience in childhood typically influences the adult relational behavior:

- **Anxious-Ambivalent.** Children feel their parents cannot be depended upon; adults tend to be insecure and emotionally dependent.
- **Avoidant.** Children feel unloved and insignificant; adults do not expect their needs to be met and so tend to avoid relationships.
- **Disorganized.** A combination of Anxious and Avoidant. Children often display anger; adults tend to have difficulty managing emotions.
- **Secure.** Children experience a warm parental bond; adults typically can form healthy relationships without fear of abandonment.

As with our expectations about love, since attachment patterns are often formed in early childhood, they can take significant work to change.

Here's how I like to describe attachment types and the relational energy that goes with them: The basic premise is that there is an emotional space that two or more people create. Imagine it as a bubble of emotional energy. People are filling and emptying that bubble all the time, like a gas tank. At any given time, different individuals are pouring energy into the bubble to get connected to each other, or taking it out of the bubble to get away from each other—or even trying to get out of the bubble altogether if someone is pouring too much juice in. This process generally occurs in an unconscious manner, but gaining mastery in emotional energy balancing is fundamental to the Way of the Mystic-Wizard. It is an artform connected to the quest, mediation, and mastery of the four hallows.

If you think of emotional energy as the fuel, or mana, of life, then mastery of managing relationship mana is the only way to become an effective wizard or mystic and be engaged in the complex activities of life. If you avoid learning this mastery, you will fall, and fall hard, when the time comes. This problem is well documented with spiritual teachers who have developed a powerful capacity to teach about and transmit mana, but who lack discipline, ethical clarity, and mastery of the art of energy management. As a result, they create now sadly cliché sex or monetary scandals that are evidence of their lack of mastery of the energetic mana and of the unconscious attachment programs running in the emotionally charged bubbles they create. Just because someone has lots of mana to give does not mean they know how to manage it well. This is comparable to someone who suddenly has a lot of money: having money doesn't mean they know how to handle that money, as evidenced by the many lottery winners who do not fare so well after winning. Accurate knowledge of managing energy requires first that you recognize that you are ignorant and there is something to learn; then a search for someone who has genuinely mastered the issue; and then study and practice, every day, just like an athlete.

Learn your capacities, limits, tendencies, and attachments. Work to overcome fears that cause your reactive methods of misusing emotional energy and, consequently, people. (The Enneagram is the premier system for identifying these patterns and clarifying the path to overcoming them.) Identifying your attachment type helps you understand what is taking place, therefore allowing you to take responsibility for your behaviors and expectations and so stop blaming others for the emotional energy survival game that is constantly unfolding around all of us.

Keep in mind that the more energy you pour into the bubble, the more you will be out of balance with the other members in the space. The more you fill the bubble, the more likely the others are to retreat from the bubble; and if you leave the bubble, the more others are encouraged to fill it. So do not take up the whole bubble with your love and need, or you could end up abandoned; and do not abandon the bubble to protect yourself from the overly emotional and needy, or you could end up alone as well.

This energy management process is like being on a tightrope with another person, where you are tethered to each other with a tension rope that keeps you balanced. Each person must do their part. If you run toward the other person, then the tension in the rope will go slack, and you both fall. If you jerk away from them, the rope pulls them off balance, and you both fall. So the balance of emotional energy requires a kind of mastery of walking a tightrope with others. The more robust your vertical connection to soul and spirit, the more capable you are of filling your needs and providing for another person's needs when the inevitable changes in rope tension come about.

Your daily spiritual practice gives you an extra rope that ties you to a secure eye hook in the ceiling of the world. That strong spiritual rope makes you more capable of not falling off the tightrope if you are suddenly left alone, and it helps you dive down and pick someone up if they fall or jump off. This ability becomes significant in stressful circumstances in life. We frequently see good examples of it on sports fields. When players fail at something, the other players quickly fill the bubble with

YOUR DAILY PRACTICE TIES YOU TO A SECURE EYE HOOK IN THE CEILING OF THE WORLD.

emotional support by giving reassuring taps and hugs. Also, when a player does something extraordinary or scores a goal, they let loose a massive burst of emotional mana, as does the crowd. Other players climb on and jump in to share in that mana. The energy is then distributed and can keep the players afloat in a state of confidence and euphoria for some time.

The classic mistake we make is similar to that of our lottery winners. When we get far ahead early in a match or win at the lottery, the tank is overflowing with mana, and because most of us do not know how to manage a full tank, we spend it fast; once the mana/money starts to go down quickly, we get nervous and try to consolidate and defend it. These are the worst strategies for winning and reveal a lack of understanding and mastery of the egoic self and its reaction to abundance and depletion. In a football game, an early goal can mean euphoria and then a slacking off and defensive posture, but the opposite strategy is more effective: conserve mana and focus euphoric energy on another round of play, until the game is won.

All of this self-awareness on love languages and attachment types and mana management turns you inward. Once you understand that other people are not responsible for creating an ideal emotional landscape for you, it helps you understand why you need the Inner Beloved and the connection with the soul and why your daily practice is so essential. Your daily routine is an island of predictability that is emotionally stabilizing because it creates a pool of energy and connection that sustains you and allows you to flourish. Daily practice generates meaning and purpose, love and harmony, and mana for use in the world. I practice every morning for only about fifteen to thirty minutes, but it is like fueling up at a station. It lasts until about 1:00 p.m., and then it must be done again if I plan on having a demanding afternoon or evening. I am not the first to figure this out. All the major world religions require monastics to pray and connect with the divine realms three to five times a day. Islam even has every regular Muslim (not only the monastics) pray five times a day; additionally, a belief in angels is one of the five pillars of the faith. The Prophet was wise in his deep understanding of the need for mortals to keep a vertical connection with the divine world. This is one of the beautiful parts of Islam.

The great irony is that as you begin to engage with your own soul and the Inner Beloved, several archetypes will come up: the inner Divine Mother or the inner Divine Father and the inner Divine Beloved. And you'll discover that in your own relationship with the divine, you will run your attachment-style programs on the divine just as you do on people. And guess what? The soul knows this and, from a shamanic perspective, so do the spirits of the inner world. The spiritual energies and powers are fully aware of your humanity and how you act out your version of emotional drama. Calling upon the compassionate beings of the inner world and then finding the Divine Father and Divine Mother begins to give you some liberation from the old family-of-origin patterns. Getting into a good relationship with inner powers allows you to heal and balance out your personality, and to potentially avoid deep neurosis or pathological manifestations of need and dependence or fear and avoidance. From this balanced place, the emergence of genuine compassion for others can develop, and you can learn to love them not for what they give you but because they are marvelous manifestations of the radiant Oneness of pure Awareness.

EXERCISE

Find Your Attachment Type

Find an attachment type test online (there are both free and paid options) to get a rundown on how you connect with people emotionally, what you are doing, and its effect on others. Reflect in your journal. What did you find? What surprised you?

VALUES IN ACTION INVENTORY OF STRENGTHS

One final tool to help you understand yourself is the Values in Action Inventory of Strengths (VIA or VIA-IS), a system developed by psychologists Christopher Peterson and Martin Seligman. The creators are well-known researchers in positive psychology who wanted to categorize and help people develop positive character traits. This was in contrast to the well-known *Diagnostic and Statistical Manual of Mental Disorders* (DSM), which categorizes human deficits and disorders (or what are thought to be at the time). The VIA tries to rectify this deficit focus in psychology. Peterson and Seligman's research shows that when people focus on positive character traits they already have, it increases well-being and fends off various negative psychological states. This model helps our practice by providing favorable conditions in which to orient ourselves as we do transformative work.

The system is made up of twenty-four character strengths that fit into six categories:

- **Transcendence:** appreciation of beauty and excellence, gratitude, hope, humor, spirituality
- **Wisdom and Knowledge:** creativity, curiosity, judgment, love of learning, perspective
- **Courage:** bravery, perseverance, honesty, zest
- **Humanity:** love, kindness, social intelligence
- **Justice:** teamwork, fairness, leadership
- **Temperance:** forgiveness, humility, prudence, self-regulation

These traits are universally valued in all religions and systems of moral development, not always at the same level, but they are recognized as essential positive aspects of our humanity. The initial working goal with this system is to find your top five strengths, what the VIA calls your Signature Strengths.

Why is VIA important for those following the Way of the Mystic-Wizard? After looking at the Enneagram and the inner work required to become a healthy expression of your type, it is vital to have a solid positive lens to look at the egoic self. We focused on the gifts that the Enneagram type creates once the egoic self learns to develop an awareness of pure Awareness. Signature strengths are another way to see and create a positive perspective and honor your development path.

Additionally, one of the ironies of the egoic self-structure is that we often are unable to recognize and value behaviors we are good at. The mind tends to see our flaws and focus on what we need to develop. Seeing your strengths is an act of empowerment. Recognize your strengths, validate them, and then look for ways to apply them in more areas of your life.

My top five strengths are not a huge surprise given this book, my professional career developing an art school, and my desire to help others as a teacher and mentor. My signature strengths are an outgrowth of my Enneagram type (Two with a Three wing), my Myers-Briggs type (ENFJ), my upbringing, and this Mystic-Wizard path. They are:

1. Spirituality
2. Perspective
3. Appreciation of beauty and excellence
4. Love
5. Hope

When I looked at these more deeply, I realized that there would not have been a way I could have become who and what I am today without these five being my signature strengths, and that even having them in the order they are was important.

Note that when you do use and observe your signature strengths, the VIA report points out that they feel "essential, effortless, and energizing," in other words, authentic and natural. However, like the Enneagram, sometimes we get feedback that does not feel precisely like who we are. Think of this as a window of opportunity to investigate what is true for you and your soul. Maybe there is a trait that you are strong in but do not want to be, or another one that you want to develop but do not rank high in. This discrepancy becomes a part of your path to developing authenticity. All of us have had aspects of our core self that have been ignored, thwarted, or simply not recognized by others, our culture, or even ourselves. It is a part of the archetypal myth of heroic development to be unrecognized.

My top strength is spirituality, which emerged over many years and didn't feel like a legitimate or valid focus in life until my mid-twenties. Yet, that instinct and strength were there from early childhood. I will never forget the day my aunt, who was a yogi, came to our house to celebrate Thanksgiving Day, and, alone in the central hallway, for no reason at all, she gave me a spiritual book to read. I think I was nine. "What is it?" I asked. "When you're ready," she said, "you will see."

Today, spirituality is the foundation of my entire life, and so she was right. It only took much of my life for me to see what

BY UNDERSTANDING YOUR STRENGTHS, YOU DISCOVER THE CHARACTER BLUEPRINT YOUR SOUL CREATED FOR YOU.

she saw in me. The result of that search for authenticity is this book and the path it expounds. It always takes time to embody an authentic expression of the soul, and the journey to authenticity is a challenging one. In the struggle to become your true self, the challenges are what develop stability of character in the self. In modernity we call it grit.

Finally, Peterson and Seligman discovered that the more you focus on your signature strengths as your basic orientation in your life, the more your life takes on a depth of meaning and purpose. In essence, by understanding your strengths, you are discovering the character blueprint that your soul created for you. With that in hand, you can become the architect of your life and build it out in a way that allows you to express and develop these strengths. This is the definition of living an authentic life. It took me a long time to find my way to a path and life that is a true expression of my signature strengths. That life now gives me a deep sense of meaning and purpose. A purpose-driven life is a soul-guided life. So go find out your signature strengths and start crafting a daily practice and life that embodies them.

EXERCISE
Take the VIA Inventory

Go online to viacharacter.org and take the VIA Inventory of Strengths. See what stands out to you, and write about what your signature strengths mean to you in your journal. This is a magical act of self-empowerment. By articulating what your signature strengths mean to you, you deepen your insight as well as your ability to remember them and use them.

journey Six
THE ROUND TABLE

Take a breath. Relax. This journey takes us to the Round Table.

Imagine that you are floating down to the mist, *five*, *four*, deeper into the mist. *Three*, *two*, *one*. You appear before the doorway to your inner world. Go up and place your hands on the doorway. Get attuned to the inner world. Set your intention to go meet the part of yourself that most wants to be projected in the outer world. You hear the door click, it opens, and you step through. You are in the hallway.

You start walking down the hallway and on your right you pass by the stairs to the common room and keep going. Then on your left, about halfway down the hallway, is a wooden door. As you approach it, the door opens. You enter, walk through a corridor, and are in an antechamber. In front of you is another large double door. You sense the presence of your beloved waiting for you on the other side. The double doors swing open, and you walk into a well-lit room with high windows and a large round table. Around the table are chairs, and your beloved leads you to your chair, which is the chair of the sovereign, which you are.

Go ahead and take your seat; notice what other figures come to join you at this particular meeting of the Round Table. Then open the meeting with your intention to bring forth the next part of yourself that needs to become aware, awake, and integrated, and that yearns to find itself in the outer world.

That part of you steps through a doorway on the opposite side of the room, comes to the table, and takes a seat. Ask who it is, what it wants, and what solutions you can provide to help it get its needs met.

Take as long as you need . . .

Now it is time to return. Bring the meeting to a close. If need be, you can return here to continue your dialogue or transformation. Stand up from the chair, give thanks to all those who came to assist, then walk out through the double doors; your beloved shuts them behind you. You make your way back out to the main corridor and then walk to the back of the door that leads to the outer world. The door opens, you step through, and the door closes.

Place your left hand on the door, saying in your mind, *It is complete*.

You are rising up through the mist. *One, two, three,* coming back to this world and time, *four*. Aware of your body, wiggle your toes and your fingers, gently integrating back into the outer world with the knowledge you gained in the inner world. *Five*. Open your eyes.

Now take a few moments to write in your journal about your experience and what you learned.

Part Seven

TOOLS FOR NAVIGATING THE WORLD

*We realize that we can separate things and
so make them bigger, see more clearly
what we could not see before.*

To continue building our spiritual toolkit, in Part Seven, we move from looking at tools that help you understand the self to looking at tools that help you navigate the world. The first two, the Life Compass and the Solar System of the Self, are original tools that I developed through the years of doing my own work and teaching students. They each help organize the complexity of our lives into a format that makes it easier to comprehend so we can orient ourselves.

THE LIFE COMPASS: SEEING THE MAP OF YOUR LIFE

The following tool for the journey is called the Life Compass. The Life Compass is a concept, a map, and a process I've developed over the past twenty-five years. The original idea grew out of my making lists of what was essential and a priority in my life, while listening for what wanted attention on the page. Then I began to organize those lists and started to create categories for where different intentions or goals fell. As I began to collect these intentions and categories, I worked with the Order of Bards, Ovates and Druids and then with shamanic practices. The Life Compass ritual work is associated with the five directions: north, south, east, west, and the center point. As described earlier, these four quadrants and the center have qualities that are associated with them.

In the north are the mountains of stone. The stone represents being grounded and practical, and embodied in your life and body.

The east is associated with the sword, which represents the air and the wind and the intellect. What is beautiful about this sword metaphor is that the blade is two-edged: it is dangerous because the mind can find and make sense of things, but it does so by cutting things up. And when you cut something up, you can, of course, kill it. So as much as discernment and dividing things and cutting them into pieces can help you understand the parts, it is only one way of knowing, and it is not a holistic way of knowing that inherently creates meaning. Seeing how things connect is what makes sense for us.

In the south are fire and transformation—the "spear of inspiration" that wounds and heals, and sometimes heals by opening an old wound. Inspiration allows you to have great ideas, and is imperative, because intuition arises spontaneously. Yet, inspiration can be cultivated in your life and can become a way of knowing the patterns of the world. This is something that creative people are deeply connected to and try to cultivate throughout their lives.

In the north, you have the stone; in the east, you have the sword; and in the south, you have the spear and the fire of inspiration. Then, in the west, you have the cup, which is symbolic of water and feeling. Feeling is also a way of knowing.

What is powerful about this particular compass perspective is the idea that you can organize your life into these quadrants and their respective qualities. So I began to use this compass as a map to find my way. By writing down the elements of life into a pattern, I could learn what pieces of my life existed and needed tending, and where my life was going. And the Life Compass became a tool that began to fill itself out.

(You are welcome to make copies for your own personal use, but please respect the artist's copyright and do not distribute.)

THE NORTH

In the north, I began to create what I would call the foundation of my life. Three levels emerged. The inner ring, or level one, involved my relationship with my soul, my direct connection with what I call the Inner Beloved. The next ring out was my relationship with the divine in various deity forms. In my case, I ended up being drawn to Norse deities, Egyptian deities, and the Tibetan Buddhist deities White Tara and Chenrezig. These beings populated the second level in the north, and they became my celestial foundation for my practice and life. The

third outer layer became my literal family—my children, my spouse, my extended family, and some of my friends who fell into our family structure. Finally, I was able to lay that all out on the page.

By creating a map in which I placed my soul as the thing inside, the closest thing to my center point, I validated that relationship. The deities that I work with are second, validating the spiritual part of my relationship to the divine. And then the outer ring is the external world manifestation of what I love most, and is my foundation in the physical world.

It took years to develop what I just described. I had to intuit what needed to be articulated and validated as an essential expression of my spiritual instincts and the desire to form a tribe and a bond with the divine. Most of us do not have a native relationship with the soul or a group of deities, yet this type of relationship was commonplace for most of human history. Historically, to *not* have this connection would have seemed abnormal, at the least. However, when religion became highly centralized and autocratic, with many layers of authority between an individual and the divine, the average person began to lose their intimate, personal connection to the divine. Gone was the shamanic perspective to connect with the tribal deities and the ancestors that had prevailed for many thousands of years before city-based civilization began to develop. Only now, in the past forty years, has the instinct to move back to direct revelation and connection to the inner world finally started to return.

One reason shamanism is so popular today is that it is so profoundly democratic and anti-autocratic. We live in a time when the tendency to do what the secular or spiritual authorities tell us has begun to wane, and the right and responsibility to develop our own connection to soul, spirit, and deity has reemerged in the context of our modern secular world. It is just in time too. Finding direction from the soul and the inner world may well be key to helping us overcome the isolated ego-self that is undermining the world's life-sustaining systems. We need inspiration and direction from the inner world.

THE EAST

In the east, I found a strong sense of how I use my mind to make sense of traveling through the world, gathering information and facts and working with them. The first thing in the east, the inner part, was the sacred oracle *The Druid Animal Oracle*. It took many years for the oracle to even appear as something that was a valid manifestation to be on a life map, because, of course, it doesn't exist, or at the time it didn't exist as widely in the world as it does today. Putting the oracle on the Life Compass map validates it as an essential function of human life, consciousness, and communication with the soul. The oracle is about speaking with the soul and the divine.

OUR PLAYING IS THE UNIVERSE BEING AT PLAY.

The next step in the east was how I use my mind to create and study. Level two contains my daily reflections journal, my poetry practice, and ongoing studies in psychology, shamanism, and spirituality—all the ways I use my mind to create.

The last aspect on the outer eastern side, the third level out, also was not there at first due to the intense achievement ethic of our culture. What I found there was *play*. I used my mind to play, to tell narrative stories, like playing role-playing games and reading novels and watching movies and essentially engaging my mind in a playful way like you do when you are a child. Suddenly play became important, because I was able to identify it as a valid activity that brought joy to my life and allowed my mind to explore and enjoy itself for its own sake. Play does not need to have a utilitarian purpose; it just is.

Many of these points on the compass were actually buried in my subconscious, and were expressions of my life that were not

valid or validated. It took years for them to surface and make themselves known. I did not think it was legitimate as an adult to play role-playing games. Why not? Later it would become a multi-billion dollar industry called video games—but that is not the justification either. Ultimately, the reason for play is because play is what pure Awareness is doing. And so play, for its own sake, rejuvenates us by connecting us to pure Awareness through activity. Our playing is the universe being at play.

THE SOUTH

In the south we have the fire of life and, in many ways, the gift we give to the world. The first level in the south is health and taking care of the body, essentially making sure the stream of inspiration can continue to flow by keeping the fuel and fire in the body flowing properly. If you do not take care of the goose that lays the golden egg, then no gold will you behold. Having an inspired relationship with the body and with form is a liberating one. It allows you to enjoy the pleasure of being in a form.

The next level in the south became what I would call vocation. If I have a body that is inspired to move and I have a psychology that springs from it, then what is it inspired to do? As inspiration flows through this form and this mind and this heart, then essentially the question is: What is my vocation? What is the deep truth hidden for me in the gold inside mountain number two of life? What would I do even if no one paid me to do it? What would I do because I love to do it and it feels fulfilling? This is not the same as play. Vocation has a purpose, and usually it requires sacrifices of energy, time, and resources. The work you do in your vocation simply feels like the right fit for you. Part of the Way of the Mystic-Wizard entails digging around to find out what your vocation is. It takes courage and endurance to let your vocation slowly emerge from the soul. The process is lifelong, as the soul may have many avenues of vocation that it wants you to explore and express.

In my case, my initial vocation was teaching poetry at my art school and then also leading narrative role-playing game sessions with my friends' children (ultimately, my adult friends joined in as well). These two areas were a starting expression of my vocational energy; eventually my vocation as a spiritual teacher and writer evolved out of this early expression, and it has emerged more fully in the past ten years. I had no idea where I was heading at first, but I kept exploring and following my hunches and what felt like a good fit. This very book is an expression of my vocation coming to fruition.

Vocation is different from a profession or job. Your work in the world is the next and last layer in the south. Your work is the gift of your labor, or in a sense, the gift of your hands. You get remunerated for your labor. Sometimes your vocation and your work overlap; sometimes they do not. Many people dream: "Oh, if I could just be paid to be the singer that I've always wanted to be, then I'd be happy" (or some other example of imagined greener pastures). But, of course, once you take your vocation and sell it on the open market, it can feel like you have sold your soul out the door. So there can be tremendous value in asking, "What is the profession I've been called to do? And what is the vocation that I would do just because I love it, that no one has to pay me for it because I'll do it anyway?"

In my case, I became a professional educator and started an art school, and was sustained by it. That was the gift of my labor. It was extremely difficult, and many of my life lessons came from engaging with these often overwhelming tasks. Building a school was not on my list of things to do in my life. But doing so has been my greatest teacher. Work and profession is the place where the fire of your energy ends up giving back to the world in a practical and grounded manner. It is where the rubber meets the road, for in work we are forced to face the results of our imbalances and misperceptions. Our mistaken projections come to us over and over until either we grow through insight and realization, or we run away.

In the mythic two-mountain story of a life that is part of the Way of the Mystic-Wizard, the work you are called to is not often your own choice. Rather it gets ahold of you, and you must do your best to master and flourish in that element. It is the rocky path up the mountain of achievement. Doing it, and leaning into it, is required not only for some measure of stability but also in order to develop endurance and insight about your own human nature. In other words, the work is hard for a reason. There is no such thing as easy labor; if it were easy, it would not be labor. You must struggle, sweat, and work in order to develop mastery, capacity, grit, and endurance. And all those traits are developed in the fiery crucible of work. Even if you love your work, it is still labor and still a challenge; otherwise you would grow bored. Hitting your talent ceiling in any endeavor is essential for the expansion of your capacity. This is why on this path, we do not look for a "good" gig; we look for the *right* gig, the one that demands much and delivers on many levels that which the soul demands of you. Through work you prepare the vessel of the self to be the container in which the soul can come to live.

In the south, then, we have the fire that creates and sustains the body; it also sustains and helps create the vocation or calling; and then it sustains and creates the profession or work and the gift of your labor. So you can now see that in the southern part of the Life Compass, you are able to track the expression of your outer life and make distinctions that allow you to comprehend the various areas of the self that need to be developed and maintained for fulfillment to become a real possibility.

THERE IS NO SUCH THING AS EASY LABOR; IF IT WERE EASY, IT WOULD NOT BE LABOR.

THE WEST

The west is the emotional content and the feeling of connection in your life. It is represented by the cup that holds the water of life. That water is what heals the heart and connects us to others and to meaning and value in life. It heals the wounds of the sword and the spear, and waters the earth so that growth can happen.

The inner level in the west contains what I call the relationship with a spiritual companion. Spiritual companions are essential. In Buddhism, this community is called your *sangha*. When you engage in spiritual work, you will have a karmic connection to certain people, and if you set your intention and are fortunate enough to find them, they can be a part of your transformation and help sustain your practice. Although you may love and respect them deeply, a spiritual companion is not an egoic romantic partner. The goal with a spiritual companion is not to project your own inner gold onto them; you do not let them become an idealized, romanticized vision of your own divine soul. This relationship is the opposite of that romantic quest; it is, instead, pragmatic and yet deeply authentic and intimate, and can be with any gender. Caring is essential, and so, too, is the shared intention of doing the spiritual work. This kind of relationship is rare in the modern world and yet is important, because practice is difficult to sustain on your own. Being a monk in the world is not an easy thing, because the world is busy pulling at you. The Way of the Mystic-Wizard requires a dedication to cultivating the power of spiritual companions and also a willingness to let them go on in their own journey with an understanding that maybe you will share in another round of inner-world experience when the time comes, if it is meant to.

The idea of finding one's spiritual companion or companions became famous in a book called *Anam Cara*, which means "soul friend," by a great Irish poet named John O'Donohue, who passed away too early. The *anam cara* is someone who is able to help you in the journey. The relationship must be cultivated, and in our larger culture, because that kind of relationship was in the unconscious, people didn't recognize it much until O'Donohue's book came out. The book's title was initially misunderstood by the New Age world, and "soul companion" became "soul mate." Since romanticism is the most common modern religion, it is no wonder people did not understand the meaning correctly.

Anam cara is a deep and important friendship, and there may be a great distance between the ages of the people in the friendship. It could be twenty-five years, or five years; it could be five months. If you are lucky, you might have two or three different soul friends throughout your life. This type of relationship is archetypal, and is sprinkled throughout mythology and even in family lore. It can show up as the wise aunt or uncle or the fairy grandmother. Or it can be the teacher, mentor, or wise person met on the road. The mere act of putting the concept onto the Life Compass validates it and brings it up from the unconscious.

I was fortunate that a friend of mine invited me into this type of intentional relationship. If he had not invited me into it, I do not think that the archetype of *anam cara* would have manifested to the depth it did and so become an essential part of the Life Compass matrix. When an archetype that has been around for millennia is lost, it does not vanish; it goes underground and awaits a time when it is once again needed in the collective human psyche. The archetype of the Spiritual Companion, or *anam cara*, must be clearly discerned and carefully cultivated, or it can devolve into a normal friendship and even a romance, neither of which serves the purpose of the path.

CULTIVATE SPIRITUAL COMPANIONS, BUT ALSO BE WILLING TO LET THEM GO.

On the next level in the west is something that you give to the world. This falls under the category of volunteering. What are you called to do to volunteer, to make a contribution? This is different from a vocation, in the sense that vocation is some-

thing you do for yourself because you love it; and it is different from a profession, where you are doing something as the gift of your labor and are getting paid for it. Volunteering has its own quality, its own innate sense of archetypal purpose and intention. This is the section under which collective barn-building and any other act of service might go. This is your part in helping humanity, the animal world, or natural world progress, survive, or recover from the conditions of life on Earth.

In my own case, I took something that I loved to do on my own in the play department (the third level in the east), narrative play, and brought it over to the middle level of the Life Compass in the west. I created opportunities for young people to engage in the playful fun of role-playing games. I was able to enjoy myself while I volunteered, and I contributed to my community by creating shared collective play.

It took some time for me to see that service and volunteering were there in the subconscious, waiting to emerge, because my service did not fall into the outwardly typical acts of service, such as working at a soup kitchen. What matters is that you volunteer in a way that is authentic to you. No one wants a grumpy volunteer. And every form of volunteering is a kind of work; it is the gift of your labor for free, a true gift with no expectation of remuneration. For me, preparing four different role-playing games, sometimes two per weekend, was a lot of labor, but it was one that was worth it, because I could see how much people in my community enjoyed it. They needed an escape into the mythic dimension of narrative in order to enrich their lives. I didn't understand that mythic narrative play was an important but missing part of life for many people. So it's essential to find out what *your* form of volunteer service is.

One of my favorite writers, the American humorist David Sedaris, spends a considerable amount of his day (when he is not on tour) picking up trash along the roads near his home in Devon, England. It is by instinct that he picks up trash. It fulfills the innate desire to make a difference beyond the creative vocational work he does as a professional writer and performer. Volunteer service comprises the cakes my wife bakes for our friends' birthdays, the garden we grow and the vegetables we give away, the car you repair for a friend.

All of this is an important part of life and needs to be discovered, expressed, and validated on the Life Compass. If it is not on the Life Compass map, it will likely remain uncultivated, because life gets in the way; if you do not bother to write down an archetype, then your commitment to its cultivation is abstract. There is a reason we sign contracts on paper: a signature is a stamp of your commitment, and so too the Life Compass is a signifier of the active archetypal energies in your life. Volunteering brings an emotional connection from doing something together. Even though we draw satisfaction from the thing we volunteer in, everything is not just for us and our own satisfaction. If you get rid of volunteering, if it just vanishes, something will be missing from your life, and you will feel it but not know what it is.

On level three of the western side of the Life Compass, you find community or tribe. These are the people you feel you can live near and who have something in common with you. You may meet some of these people in a synagogue, church, or temple, or through a sport that you all love, or through hiking or playing video games. Whatever it is, this archetype requires that you cultivate a sense of community. The community and social instincts that all humans have are stronger in some than in others, but they are a part of how human beings keep themselves safe and emotionally connected. These connections provide meaning to life and also to the daily practice you develop, for in doing your practice, you are improving yourself for yourself as well as for your community.

THE CENTER

At the center of the four directions is your spiritual practice, all your tools and techniques, including filling out your Life Compass once a month or so. You place your practice in the center because from your practice, like a flower, grow the petals of your life. You can use the compass to maintain your life like a gardener maintains a garden.

If you do not manage the different aspects of life in your Life Compass, what tends to happen is that one area of your life gets dense and heavy and takes a lot of time and energy until it feels like it is your entire life. Maintaining balance is not automatic. You must learn to ride the bike before you can learn to ride it with no hands.

Imagine that the Life Compass is sitting on a plate that is spinning on a dowel. When one area gets heavy, the plate begins to lean in that area, and you must run over there to deal with it. You expend a lot of energy to put out fires there. Then another area suddenly catches on fire because it is being ignored. Or a category falls off the plate and you are oblivious—until you hear it shatter as it hits the floor. So then you end up running around blindly on your life plate, tipping and untipping all the elements. This can be exceedingly frustrating. Putting out fires your whole life is not a good way to live, but it does create a kind of frenetic, distracting energy.

Instead, consider sitting in the middle of the empty space like a wizard, seeing the different sections of life, understanding that each one of them is a valid and important part that needs to be maintained and connected with, and then managing the elements as CEO of your own life. This is what it means to have a magical meditation practice. Your goal is to see and use all the areas; in so doing, you can chart a course across your life of practice and spiritual and magical growth.

USE THE COMPASS TO MAINTAIN YOUR LIFE LIKE A GARDENER MAINTAINS A GARDEN.

The Life Compass

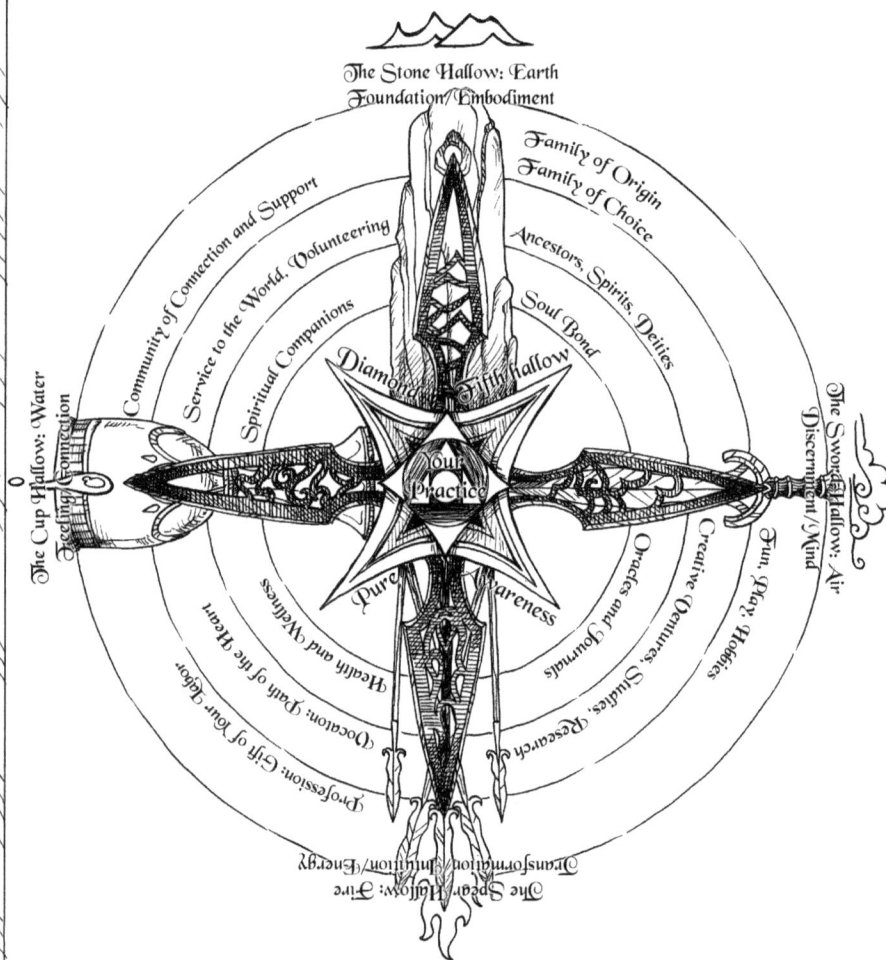

The Stone Hallow: Earth
Foundation/Embodiment

Family of Origin
Family of Choice

Ancestors, Spirits, Deities

Soul Bond

Community of Connection and Support

Service to the World, Volunteering

Spiritual Companions

Diamond Fifth Hallow

The Cup Hallow: Water
Feeling/Emotion

0

The Sword Hallow: Air
Discernment/Mind

Fun, Play, Hobbies

Creative Ventures, Studies, Research

Oracles and Journals

Your Practice

Pure Awareness

Health and Wellness

Vocation: Path of the Heart

Profession: Gift of Your Labor

Transformation, Intuition/Energy

The Spear Hallow: Fire

Fill in and rewrite once a month to track the overall balance and focus of your attention.

Avoiding a section for too long can produce a crisis. Not developing an area will create a blind spot that puts an area in shadow.

EXERCISE

Start Creating Your Life Compass

Take some time to begin developing a Life Compass, using the image on the prior page as a guide. Feel free to draw in your journal or use the blank compass at the beginning of this chapter (also in Appendix C). It will take time to develop your Life Compass, so keep coming back to it regularly.

THE SOLAR SYSTEM OF THE SELF: MAPPING YOUR RELATIONSHIPS

The Solar System of the Self is another tool I created, this one to make sense of relationships and learn to manage them appropriately. Open up your journal to a blank page and put your name in the center. Draw a circle around your name to represent the sun. In the center, with you in the sun, is your soul as the Inner Beloved. Make some kind of symbolic mark that conveys that truth. The planets that will be added around you are the people in your life. (You can also use the template found at the end of this chapter and in Appendix C; you are welcome to make copies for your own personal use, but please respect the artist's copyright and do not distribute.)

The Solar System of the Self charts the different social aspects of your life. Our social reality is essential to our development and to creating meaning, purpose, love, and joy in our lives. By placing yourself and your soul in the center, you symbolize what is true about being an individual ego in the world: you and your soul together are the source at the center of who you are. As a Mystic-Wizard, it is vital to realize that there is no other human in the sun with you. There is no magical "other," other than the soul. You do not die with someone, and you were not born with someone. When you are born, you separate from your mother and become a self, and that is your existential condition throughout the rest of your human life. You can merge with someone for a bit, but to stay combined with anything but soul and pure Awareness is an attempt at regression. Only joining with the soul and spirit gives you a reliable way out of the existential anxiety of being a separate self. The connection between the three levels of your being is what can relieve existential anxiety and empower the self to become what it was meant to be all along, the living incarnation of the soul. Accomplishing this quest for authentic soul expression is the entire point of the path of the Mystic-Wizard. It is a spirituality and practice that is about being *here*, about incarnation and its creative potential.

Your task for creating the Solar System of the Self is to organize the different people in your life into a visual symbolic representation of your social bonds. One of the ways to do this is to make a list of names of all the people in your life. You can separate the list into several categories, such as family of origin, chosen family, friends, acquaintances, mentors, partners, and pets. Then start thinking and feeling about where they are in your solar system. Create a series of concentric rings and ask yourself: "Who is in the first ring around my sun?" The closer someone is to you, the more bonded you are with them, for good, bad, or otherwise, and the closer they are to the sun.

With your primary inner bonds, see if you can determine their possible Enneagram type and instinct, their love language,

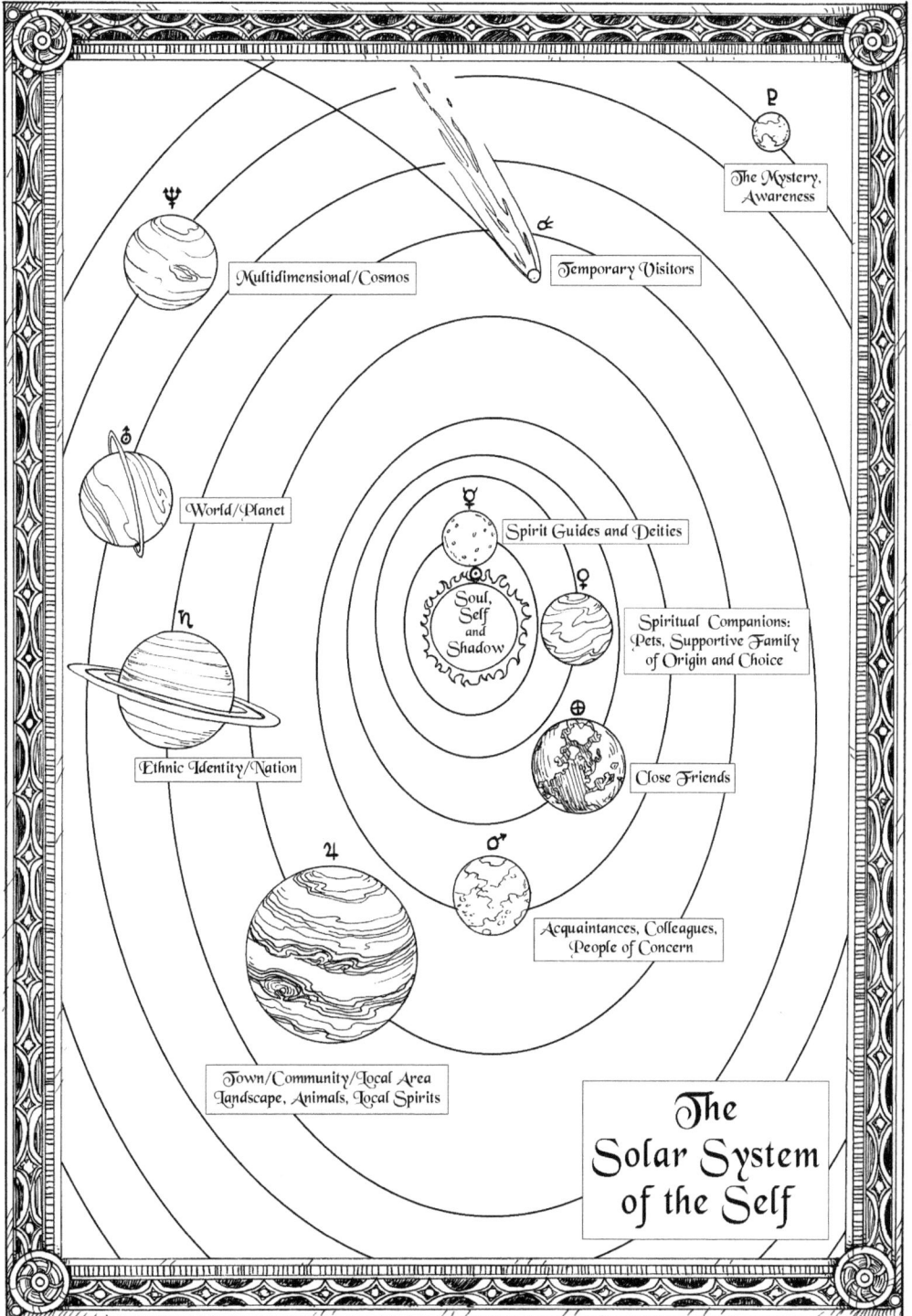

The Mystery, Awareness

Multidimensional/Cosmos

Temporary Visitors

World/Planet

Spirit Guides and Deities

Soul, Self and Shadow

Spiritual Companions: Pets, Supportive Family of Origin and Choice

Ethnic Identity/Nation

Close Friends

Acquaintances, Colleagues, People of Concern

Town/Community/Local Area Landscape, Animals, Local Spirits

The Solar System of the Self

and perhaps even which Spiral Dynamics[16] color they sit in. If you can get a good sense for each person, you can approach some mastery in sustaining your primary bonds.

One of the most mature, compassionate, and caring behaviors in any relationship is to learn enough about another person that you can translate your own reality into the languages they speak. As a Mystic-Wizard, the objective is to gain the capacity to be present with all types of people in your solar system, to sustain and have the compassion, wisdom, and skill to speak their languages. Many people never develop these skills and are perpetually frustrated that others do not speak their own language. The work in this process starts with knowing yourself, and then you can begin to understand those around you. Once you embrace that it is your responsibility to gain this capacity, and not others' jobs to translate your language, you begin to get traction. Learn to look forward to the many ways in which people show up. When you look forward to the differences, you can see the beauty in each person around you. This same ability is what also allows you to make wise decisions about who you let into your solar system and who you move out.

Once you have filled in your first ring, then do the others. The further you get away from the sun, the weaker or less intense the bonds are, until there is almost no bond. The last layer is the space beyond all orbits, which in this case means the public and the world. As you begin to assign positions and understand where people fit in your life, feel what boundaries you need to have or want to have with various people.

Some other questions to ask yourself:
- How many people can I have in my first ring?
- How many can I have in my second ring?
- Is there someone I need to move out of my solar system because they are toxic?

---

[16] Spiral Dynamics is coming up next.

- Is there someone I would like to cultivate a relationship with and bring them in one ring closer? If so, do I know how? Am I afraid to do so in some way?

There are only so many people and just so much time to have intimacy in your life, so the relationships you craft become incredibly important to your life path. By putting yourself through a process of understanding where people orbit in your life, you get an opportunity to craft this "solar system." From that exercise comes meaning for your social life and a foundation for your practice life. The idea is to understand and honor all the orbits of your social solar system and attend to them appropriately.

Some Enneagram types and instinct types are more focused on the outer layers, and some more on the inner layers. Whichever the case for you, attempt to learn to attend to the aspects that are not your natural instinct. The goal is to develop the capacity to master the social instinct at all orbits, from intimacy to the public, in an appropriate and meaningful way without undue anxiety or attachment. The only way that can occur is if you have a strong marriage between self and soul and understand that your practice and your relationship to soul and Awareness always come first.

My elder son, who was only eighteen at the time, came up with a metaphor to describe how this works for him. We were in the kitchen and spoke for about an hour about how being connected to soul and knowing himself as an incarnation affects how he operates and manages his social solar system. He said to imagine yourself on an island of land surrounded by a moat filled with water. You are not hidden behind castle walls out of fear, but you also do not have a bridge to the other side of the moat. Another person can come to the edge of the moat and see who you authentically are. You have nothing to hide, as you know your true source as soul and Awareness and thus have real ontological and emotional stability. Knowing who you are and where you come from, and who the other person on the other side of the moat is, gives you a secure position to base relationships on. That other person can see you, and connect to you via Awareness, soul, and self, but they cannot get over the moat and pitch a tent on your island. In psychological terms, they cannot attach regressive childhood projections and needs onto you that are not your responsibility. You and your soul are complete. You are the incarnation of your soul, an immortal being, and you have a responsibility to own the island you live on and keep it as a sacred space. This is a mature adult orientation to identity that recognizes your existential status in the world. You are alone, in that no other person can fill the spiritual holes in your being. But you are not alone in the spiritual sense. Your soul and Awareness, when discovered and cultivated, can and do fill those holes.

Another way to understand and actualize this idea in your egoic structure is to imagine who you will be after you die. Imagine that all earthly bonds and responsibilities are no longer actionable. And then, after you die, you merge with your immortal soul and feel utterly complete. Who might you be in that case? How would you be with others? Imagine that you need nothing from anyone, as you are sustained by Awareness. When you interact with another being, it is only with the memories of your life that are meaningful as a resource, but with no agenda or attachment to life on Earth. There is nowhere to go; you are just there. Take a moment to imagine it and feel what this sense of completion might be like. Now imagine walking around in life like that. There is the hint of a kind of completeness that is possible. It will not make us immune to suffering, loss, disease, or death, or make us magically powerful like a superhero. It is rather a feeling of acceptance, humility, and also a kind of subtle empowerment and confidence through a union with that which is. It is a paradox that empowerment

IF PEOPLE ARE STOPPING YOUR DEVELOPMENT, ALTER YOUR RELATIONSHIP WITH THEM.

comes by aligning with and surrendering to the deeper realities of our own being. Think of Yoda from *Star Wars*. He had great humility and compassion, all combined into one little package. He was also deeply empowered. That power was always present but rarely visibly used, and it was always a strain on him to use it openly.

The Solar System of the Self lets you chart and consciously craft the expression of your social instinct over time. In your journal you can draw it once and then you can redraw it whenever you feel the need. The arrivals and departures of various people in your life are easier to understand if you can see why things must be that way. People can leave due to conflict or betrayal or death. Stuff happens in the solar system, and by drawing it, you get some measure of control over how you manage your response. Sometimes comets come in, circle the sun, and then leave. This can be powerful and meaningful, or it can be a disaster.

The key principle for the Mystic-Wizard and the Solar System of the Self is this: if people are stopping your development, alter your relationship with them.

If needed, move people out a layer, or move them out entirely, in order to continue on your spiritual path. This does not mean abandoning your responsibilities; it means taking a hard look at any dependencies you may have and the limits of relationships on the horizontal plane (the earthly level). When you reach a threshold in which major change and transformation are in the offing, there is a culling process that removes elements of your life that are no longer needed or that must be taken away to make room for a new level to manifest. This process often involves changes in relationships and where people are located in your solar system. There is nothing wrong with this, but it takes determination, courage, and connection to soul to craft the new constellation of your bonds every time you make a major shift. When these shifts happen, there can be grief and disappointment. It is the nature of attachment that this separation pain occurs. Eventually the soul bond at the center is strong enough that the coming and going of other people on the other layers of the system is less emotionally painful. Slowly you develop an independence from earthly dependency.

The goal at the end of your life is to look back and see that you developed bonds at different levels of your solar system, and that each one had its own value and beauty, and also that the primary marriage of self and soul had the room to grow and deliver you to an embodied relationship with Awareness. The stronger the vertical bond with soul and Awareness, the more liberated you are from childhood attachments and the triggers that make you regress, and therefore the more healthy and respectful your relationships will be.

· ·

EXERCISE
Draw Your Solar System

Draft your own Solar System of the Self in your journal or using the template found on the next page and in Appendix C. Go back through the chapter to consider key questions about who is in orbit around you. Do you need to make any changes?

· ·

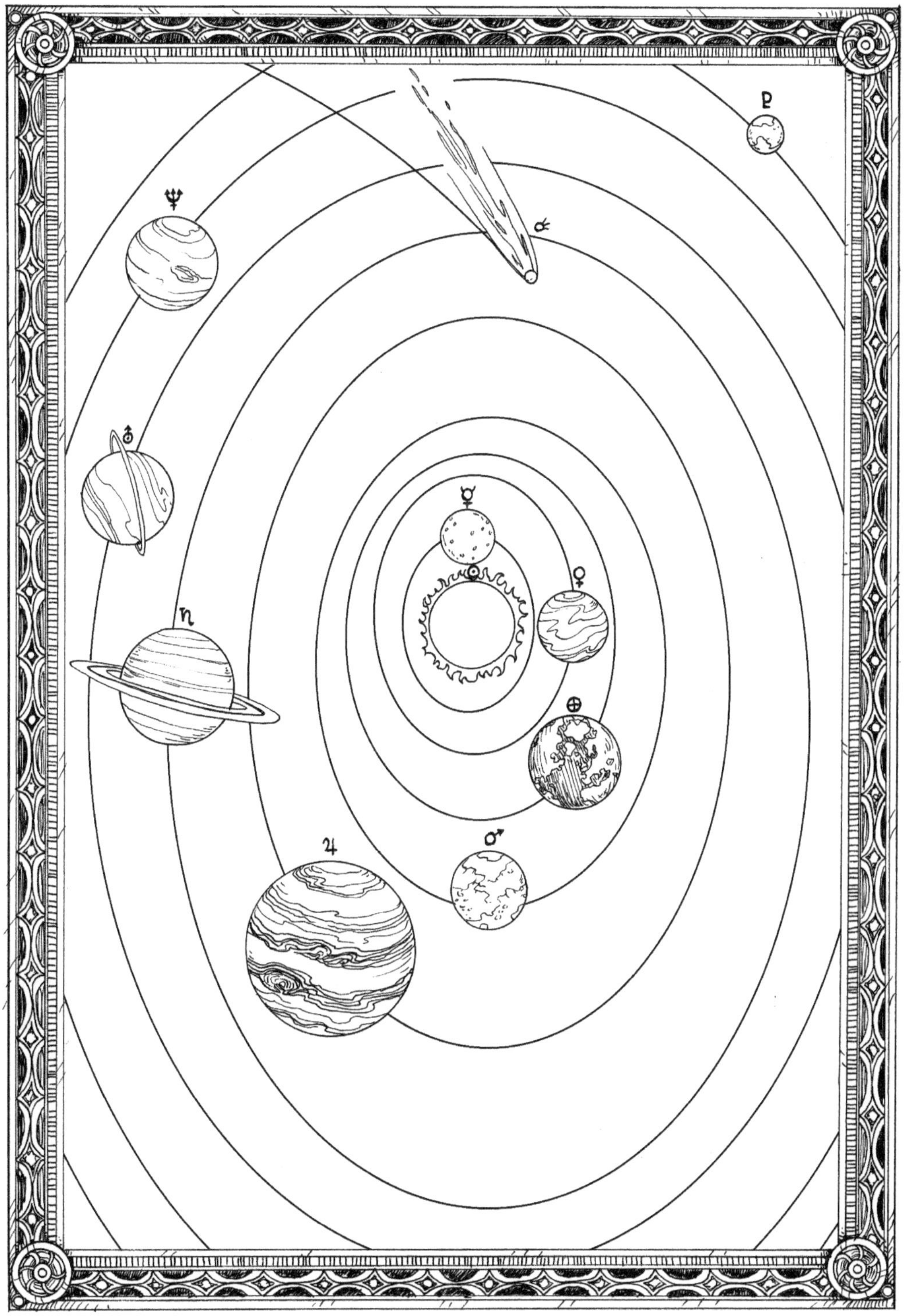

SPIRAL DYNAMICS: KNOWING YOUR WORLDVIEW

Our knowledge of ourselves is always contextualized by the social situation we are in: by our families, our community, the larger country we live in, and the region of the world we live in. Spiral Dynamics is a framework that allows us to understand how those things affect us and to understand our underlying values. Spiral Dynamics is used all around the world by corporations, governments, and individuals, but it may be new to many people, so I will give you a little background about the framework and then you can go read more online.

Spiral Dynamics originated from research undertaken in the 1950s and 1960s by psychologist Clare Graves, a professor at Union College in New York, who was seeking to understand human nature. Why are people different? Why don't we get along? How do people change? How does the human mind respond to the varied conditions around the world?

Graves spent years gathering information from thousands of sources worldwide to help him understand the values in various societies. He did not impose his own bias on the structure of the information; instead he simply identified what people valued and recorded what their living conditions were. He then realized that patterns existed, and a model began to arise. Graves saw that an adaptive process was taking place: one set of solutions to various life issues eventually created new, more complex problems; then another set of more complex solutions were needed with corresponding values; even more complex problems arose, and the cycle repeated. All this formed a spiral of increasingly complex problems and solutions.

Spiral Dynamics, then, describes the development of deep value systems or worldviews, at a personal and collective level, that are used to judge and evaluate the world and thus solve problems.

THE EIGHT SPIRAL LEVELS

The Spiral Dynamics system has eight levels, each assigned a color to help keep them organized and clear. Each value level in the system has its form of expression and society that it tends to generate. Below are the spiral levels:

Spiral One: Beige = Survival. Level one, beige (or sand), is our basic animal herd mentality for survival. We function to stay alive, and those capable of protecting and directing the herd do so. This survival worldview is inside us all, and we see it come out during massive natural catastrophes when people are not thinking: they act from instinct to survive and take care of the group.

Spiral Two: Purple = Security. In level two, purple, we move into the level associated with tribe and family. This is a close social structure in which we feel secure and taken care of, and individuals are willing to sacrifice for the benefit of the tribe, including their lives, if needed. Powerful bonds are generated that protect and allow for tribal or family culture to evolve. This level of the spiral is active everywhere that family or tribe exists, and helps explain the degree to which many are willing to sacrifice for their family. It provides security for each of us to grow up. Purple tribal and family life is led by elders, matriarchs, and patriarchs, and their authority is strong.

Spiral Three: Red = Power. The third level of the spiral expresses itself by rebelling against the constraints of the tribe and embracing the desire to have power for the individual self. It is about becoming King of the Hill or the Queen Bee. Individuals are part of a hierarchical system that is dominated by physical and/or social power. This level can be seen in social structures such as gangs and the mafia and other social networks in which everyone is beholden to the top. At the red level, all relationships are about where you are in the power hierarchy. Orders come from the top down, and the lower-level individuals are always looking for signals from the chiefs above them. In the red level, might does make right.

Spiral Four: Blue = Order. From the power dynamics of the red level, a new order forms in which a more significant law descends to give shape to society and people. It helps overcome the abuses of power of the red level and provides a structured framework for society to manage itself that is not based on "might makes right." Instead, it is *rules* that make right. Following the rules is the new value that defines the moral fiber of an individual. Our societies today are based on this level, as are the major religions of the world. The rules clearly define right and wrong, and no one is supposed to be exempt from them. The reward for following the rules is belonging to society, freedom to act within the culture, and, in most religious cases, a final reward in the afterlife. In the blue level, community goals are more important than individual goals, and a broad sense of purpose and meaning is felt by the individual who is part of this kind of order.

Spiral Five: Orange = Achievement. The orange level is once again an individual level of the spiral. But rather than "might makes right" as at the red level, now achievement in the "game of life" leads to prestige and success. This is the current center of gravity of modern Western society. With the focus on the individual comes rights, as in the Bill of Rights, and opportunities to compete and go on the quest for one's own happiness. Winning the game of life is what is valued, and the blue level's religious focus and delayed gratification to the afterlife moves instead onto games, such as sports. Rational scientific thinking is the shaping force of thought, and the market and capitalistic

ONE SET OF SOLUTIONS EVENTUALLY CREATES NEW, MORE COMPLEX PROBLEMS.

economies thrive at this level. Life is not about performing for a religious, moral order to get into heaven, but rather about individual success in this life as measured by the winnings of the game, which are money, reputation, and influence.

Spiral Six: Green = Connection. The orange level sets up competition between everyone and, therefore, a certain alienation and anxiety about winning. The green level attempts to address the unfortunate results of this winner-takes-all environment. The green level can think from multiple perspectives and empathizes with the emotions and life conditions of others and the earth itself. The green level can see connections between all of humanity and nature, and deeply desires to heal the world and fix what is broken, including the alienation and anxiety. Because of the sensitivity of the green level, there is strong resistance to the levels that came before it. Green can disdain both the competitive, self-serving worldview of the orange level and the overly moralistic and authoritarian hierarchy of the blue level. Green often seeks to understand why the world is so broken and in so much pain. The green worldview blames the previous spiral stages that allowed green to evolve, especially blue's hierarchical paradigm. Green can be antihierarchical and highly relativistic. The idea that no one person or view is better than any other is common, and that idea itself is seen as the actual truth. With all its sensitivity and its cognitive power to see multiple perspectives, the trouble with green is that it can undermine the very ladder that brought it about. Green values tolerance above almost anything else, but can then find itself being highly intolerant of any form of intolerance or any structure that ranks or generates hierarchies of value. This can happen to individuals and in organizations and cultures. It is only at the next level that these complex internal contradictions can be overcome.

Spiral Seven: Yellow = Integral. The yellow spiral is a massive step in which a very high level of complexity in problems can be solved. Yellow develops autonomy from both social pressures and internal conceptual contradictions. Yellow has realized that it actually contains all the other spiral levels, and it finds a way to reconcile them. This is an enormously complex process simply because much of the other levels' values are somewhat contradictory. At the yellow level, the complexity of problems no longer evokes unconscious fear but rather a creative engagement with the problem itself. Yellow sees the world as filled with unique opportunities, and finding one's individual path through it becomes the new highest value. Yellow is the first level that does not feel compelled to convince others of the correctness of their view. Yellow can sense the flow of the larger process through which people, organizations, and society evolve. The yellow individual's goal is only to help contribute to that unfolding and prevent pathological manifestations of the various other levels from taking control. At this level, the universe is seen as one whole living thing, and one begins to wonder how one manifests with the universe through processes such as synchronicity.

Spiral Eight: Turquoise = Holistic. The eighth level, turquoise, experiences a connection with all of life and all of reality, and tends to see all of life as one dynamic, collective organism. This worldview has a balanced vertical/spiritual and horizontal/earthly perspective, thus people can be aware of self, soul, spirit, and shadow inside themselves and in society. There is a perception that many forces are working at many levels, all set in a sea of Awareness. This level is quite rare on the planet now, but it is emerging. All the highly complex problems that our world faces today may well be solved only from this level. This level can sense the entire phenomenon of existence unfolding and, therefore, very complex problems begin to be solved on multiple levels at once. As this new worldview develops, things long kept apart, such as science and spirituality, begin to come together. Abilities long thought to be unique to mystics and wizards will become more common and will be used for both the greater good and for self-development.

· ·

EXERCISE

Take a Spiral Dynamics Assessment

Go online and take a Spiral Dynamics self-assessment (there are a variety of free options) to get a feel for where your values come from. Do the results sound like you? Why, or why not? Write about your experience in your journal.

· ·

INSIGHTS FOR OUR JOURNEY

Spiral Dynamics posits levels of complexity; however, this does not mean people at a later spiral are inherently better or more intelligent. Complexity value is one way of measuring value and an important one for our growth, but so are ground value and essential value.

Complexity value means that that which is more complex is of more value. *Ground value* means that we are all equal and that this all-is-one perspective is the most important. *Essential value* means that that on which all else depends is more important and so it comes first. All three values are important, but if you place one above the other, an entirely different ethical and philosophical position develops. The key in this path is to respect all three types of value equally and try to hold the implications of them in a kind of uneasy balance. This balance forces us to make decisions with less sureness that we are "right," frustrating the rational mind and thus opening us to inspiration. It also forces us to accept life on its own terms even though we are then accepting the existence of pain, suffering, and the seeming injustice of our human condition.

The later levels of the spiral depend on the earlier ones for their existence. In addition, the goal is not to seek out the highest level of complexity and jump into it. Rather, it is to ascertain where you are and seek institutions and people at your level so you can flourish at the level in which your center of gravity floats. From that place, you can develop a practice, such as is described in this book, and work toward greater complexity when the soul draws that forth in your life. And it will.

Note that the spiral levels are not about your ideas; they are about the values that determine how you act on those ideas. Someone can have a sophisticated idea but work on it from a much less complex spiral level. For instance, you could have an idea about solving climate change but act on that idea from the blue level and become a zealot about it. In addition, just as with the Enneagram, at each level of the spiral you can have healthy and unhealthy expressions of it.

From Dr. Graves's perspective, the goal in life is to develop a healthy expression of the level of the spiral you are at, and then grow from there if your living conditions change. In that process, the spiral oscillates from a collective "we" worldview (purple, blue, green, turquoise), centered on communal value systems that value self-sacrifice, to an "I"-centered value system (beige, red, orange, yellow) that demands personal development and authentic expression. Self orientation and collective orientation are the two significant psychological imperatives and poles of human existence, and they are the engine of growth from the time we are children. Humanity desires both an individual expression and a more significant connection to the whole. In this oscillation, we find the energy to go out on our own and make our way, but also to come back and seek connection.

In the Way of the Mystic-Wizard, we are engaged in creating an authentic personal spiritual practice that will help us evolve into unique beings, and yet we are also developing an awareness of Awareness, which connects us to the One Awareness. The mystic seeks union with the ultimate "we," the One, and the wizard seeks the most unique, creative, and potent expression of the "I" that you and your soul can manifest in your life. In this path, the two oscillating impulses are no longer at odds with each other, but rather complement each other and help each other develop. It is a fundamentally creative process that embraces rather than avoids change; however, real change is unsettling and sometimes deeply painful.

The change process creates a dynamic tension in our lives. In the Way of the Mystic-Wizard, we are purposely engaging with this tension. We see it as natural and healthy, despite how hard it is. As we grow our practice and our connection to our inner-world allies, we develop a greater capacity to engage with change and manage the tension and anxiety that change brings up.

Small pressures in life often only require minor adjustments to our practice or our way of thinking and living. But sometimes the internal tensions, or the outer tensions in our work or family life, are intense, and the changes required appear radical. This, too, is natural, and learning to ride these waves of change is part of the point of this path. It is far easier to manage radical change when you have an inner world that acts as an island of predictability. Likewise, if the outer world is stable, then it can be easier to manage a significant inner transformation.

On the quest for the hallows, we are actively engaged in a journey that attempts to transform our limited view so we can fully experience a holistic perception of reality. Expect change, expect tension, and expect your resistance to show up over and

HUMANITY DESIRES BOTH INDIVIDUAL EXPRESSION AND CONNECTION TO THE WHOLE.

over again. Name and embrace that resistance, and ask for help to get you through it. Surrender to the process of being broken and rebuilt, and the entire experience will unfold with much more grace.

It is a widespread understanding in shamanism that the body of light you have in the inner world will go through dismemberment and then rebirth in the process of change. This symbolic inner destruction of the old self is utterly ordinary and necessary for any real change to happen. In this path, we embrace the symbolic inner-world dismemberment process, and in so doing, we are less likely to tear apart our outer world and act out our destruction in ways that harm ourselves and others.

The most significant changes in our life often involve a major value shift and thus a spiral shift. In that process, we always face an identity shift as well. Our sense of self is created at a certain level of the spiral, and when we move, we lose that old self, since we now begin to value different things.

Often this process is shrouded in darkness and loss because we cannot yet see from the new level, but the old level no longer works for us. Lacking a clear vision for how we will end up is not an issue; instead, we need courage, endurance, and trust in the process. The vision will emerge like a flower from a bud when the right conditions appear. The entire process can feel like we have lost our way, and our egoic self resists this anxiety at a deep level, usually holding on even tighter. Ironically, this holding on to the old often generates the energy needed to break up the old ways. This change of level and identity can create feelings of despair, pointlessness, anger, fear, and disillusionment with your old life and the people in it. These are the feelings that come along with death and rebirth, and they are normal. But they are also temporary and transformative.

It is at this point that your practice is priceless, for even your practice will seem pointless, but by that time you'll do it out of a deep habit and you can "keep on," as they say, and with that endurance and commitment you can engage the most profound streams of transformative energy in a container or cocoon you have designed to hold it. That is the ultimate value of your practice.

In those transformative times, we learn to trust the soul and spirit to an entirely new degree. Once accomplished and integrated, we emerge empowered and ready to function at a whole new level. When I was in my late forties, my mother's death from pancreatic cancer and, eighteen months later, my father's death from a brain aneurysm was an utterly transformative experience for me. It felt like the safety net in my life had been removed. It took years to recover, but in all that time, my practice became the place in which the intense feelings of loss and the lessons about death could be learned. In the end, I forged a relationship with my soul and also with the inner Divine Mother and Divine Father that I had never had before and did not know was even possible.

Always with significant changes, we must lose the current world to gain a new one.

Journey Seven
SPRING PLANTING

Close your eyes. Relax. Take a deep breath. You begin now to float down through the mist. *Five*, *four*, deeper, *three*, deeper, *two*, deeper still, *one*.

You appear before the door to your inner world. Notice that around the edges of the door, in the cracks of the stone, small green shoots appear. The natural world is always coming up through the cracks of our created world. Go up and place your hands on the wood of the door and feel the energy of life within it, pulsing, beginning, ready to move up from the earth and into the outer world. Understand that every season, every cycle of the year, the energy withdraws to the center and then returns again—not only to the center of the physical earth and the dirt beneath your feet, but all energy goes into the inner world, breathes in and then breathes out, and life begins again.

You hear the door click and it opens, and you walk through. Walk down the corridor, reach out, touch the stone. Feel that it is alive. The stone has its own consciousness, its own awareness, its own specific type of being. Sense how awareness expresses itself through stone, the solidity, the base, the foundation. Take a right. Go down into the common room. There, the low fire burns. The cat, the chessboard . . . it is quiet.

Take a moment now and summon to you your traveling robes while you are there in the common room. Stand centered, feel the stone beneath your feet there in the place you've come to know, a seeming waystation that is actually the center point, the base, the foundation for all your journeys—your den, the place in the earth, down below, where the animal in you must go. Then sit by the fire and gather your warmth, your power, your place. Feel the subtle joy that permeates this space, feel the comfort.

Then you sense a presence. It's coming here to visit you. You look and there, in a chair opposite you, sits a woman. She is radiant, emanating power. She is the goddess of this season, and in her hands, she holds a potted plant. Go sit next to her. She hands you the small potted plant and says, "Care for this, for it is you." And she has blessed it, given it her energy, allowed you to grow, allowed you to bloom.

Take a few moments and speak with her about the coming season and what might grow, what might bloom in your life, and what mysteries are yet to unfold, for she holds them in her heart.

Now it is time to move onto the next stage of this old, old ceremony. Take the potted plant with you, stand up, give thanks to this goddess. She directs you out of the common room, back the way you came. Go up the stairs, but do not return to the outer world. Turn right and walk down the long corridor. At the end of the long corridor, a light calls to you. As you exit the corridor, you come into an open space, a green square of grass within a cloister walk. There in the center is a great tree.

Go under the arches and to the right you see a space for a garden. The dirt has been turned over. Here you must transplant. Get down on your knees and make a space in the dirt for this young plant. Then, gently with your fingers, remove the plant from the pot and place it in the dirt, covering its roots, gently packing the dirt so that it's stable and solid and yet porous.

Here you plant this little plant, which is your future growing. You notice behind you an old wizard who guards the tree; he appears with a watering can. He will water the plant while you are away, but he hands the can to you now so you can water the plant. You sense the joy in the plant for being alive, growing in the perfect place it's meant to be, protected, the great tree by its side, the old man watching over it, and the goddess witnessing it nearby.

Think now about what this plant represents, what image you hope to bring to fruition, what you hope to grow, cultivate, and tend in your life, for you are the gardener.

The goddess appears by your side, kneels down in the dirt next to you. She places her hand over the top of the plant, and you can tell she is blessing the plant and your vision. Then she steps away, and it is your turn. The three of you stand there witnessing the growth, since the roots of the plant are already reaching out for the water, already seeking nutrients. Hand the watering can back to the old man; he returns to his place beneath the tree, awaiting your return.

Now it is time to return to the outer world. Reach out and take the goddess's hand; feel her power, the power of life itself issuing forth out of the earth that makes life possible. You are a part of this. Sense the joy of creation for coming to life. She tells you to go now and return to the outer world and watch for signs of growth.

Walk back along the long corridor till you come at last to the doorway to the outer world. This time, before it opens, reach out and touch the back of the door; you sense there is moss that has grown on the inside of the door, soft and alive. The door opens, you step through and turn around, and the door shuts and clicks. You can see the green between the planks of the door. Place your hands on the door and sense far, far away, deep in the forest, the stirring of an energy. The Stag Lord becomes aware of your presence. Soon, you will visit him. Soon. Then say in your mind, *It is done.*

Step away from the door, and you are rising up through the mist. *One*, *two*, higher, *three*, returning to this world, the outer world, *four*, higher through the mist. Wiggle your fingers and your toes, fully integrating into the physical world, becoming aware of Awareness around you and the bliss-field of joy until finally you are complete and unified and in the outer world, *five*, and you open your eyes. Now, take some time to write in your journal about your intentions with your potted plant.

PART EIGHT

REGRESSION & INTEGRATION

The twin rivers flow nearer the sea—
anger and love blend into
something there is no word for.

As your spiritual practice develops, you will inevitably face challenges with your shadow self. In Part Eight, we look at what happens when we regress or face challenges and how we can integrate old wounds. This section adds some invaluable techniques to the toolbox of transformation. Without them, it will be hard to manage the changes and demands of the quest for the hallows.

INTEGRATION: BYRON KATIE'S THE WORK

One of the ways that you can do some excellent work on integrating your shadow self is a process called The Work, which was created by a wonderful woman named Byron Katie. Katie is a mystic who had a compelling awakening experience of pure Awareness after being in a desperate place in her life. From that experience, she created The Work, a potent cognitive tool for doing the shadow work on the world and yourself. The Work is available for free at thework.com, and Katie also has several books that can expand your understanding.

In The Work, you ask four fundamental questions, and then generate a series of "turnarounds"—or statements of opposite beliefs—that you use to create a transformative cognitive pathway in your mind.

The questions are:

1. Is it true?
2. Can you absolutely know that it's true?
3. How do you react, what happens, when you believe that thought?
4. Who would you be without that thought?

It's easiest to understand the process, especially the turnarounds, by reading examples on the website. You can also get free support for the process.

The Work helps you learn how to accept what is in existence rather than to constantly fight with it, which causes suffering. In doing so, you transform your mind and what has been locked into the hardwiring of the brain and body for years. The mind is trying to fix problems all the time, but The Work analyzes your beliefs and asks you to question them. Think of it as a process that cracks up the hardened pathways in your brain, breaking the fundamental assumptions you have about the way certain things are. The Work liberates the energy that is trapped in the well-worn paths in your mind. When you think of something over and over and over again, you build a rut in your brain, a literal synaptic pathway, and the opposite synaptic pathway either does not exist or is diminished. The Work gets you to engage with the exact opposite synaptic pathways, and it dismantles the preferences you have built all your life. More often than not, this energy is released through laughter brought on by the sheer absurdity of engaging with the opposite belief. It is a process called "the resolution of opposites," and it is a crucial engine for true transformation.

If you are not willing to crack and dissolve the old pathways and laugh out loud at the absurdity of your own mental and emotional ruts, then you will never be free from the suffering that those ruts cause you and others. As Katie often says, you can be free, or you can suffer—you choose. Many choose to suffer, but the Way of the Mystic-Wizard is a path of liberation through transformation, and it requires courage and a willingness to break the patterns that keep you less than whole and feeling like you are a victim. In the end, there are no victims; there are only the beliefs and stories in your mind that you choose to hold onto and that keep you stuck in painful moments of life. Yes, life has pain, tons of it (that is another issue), but, as Katie says, the suffering is optional. This path requires you to be willing to be much larger than you are right now, to be able to contain more diversity and to hold the many opposites swirling within you. In the end, it turns out that in the light of pure Awareness, thoughts, beliefs, and emotions will self-liberate. They will rise up from the unconscious and extinguish themselves like a brief flame rising in the air; this process, as it happens, becomes the path to continue habituating to the natural state. The beliefs that hold you in bondage through your rejection of reality as it is can become the bridge that leads you out of the prison of suffering.

The Work methodology for releasing cognitive patterns is effective if you are brave enough to use it. I've been using it for twenty years now, and eventually it becomes a way of approaching life. When faced with stuff you would usually avoid, you hear yourself thinking, "I am looking forward to it," and a lightness and power come into you because you know you are burning off yet another layer of resistance to the full extent of reality. Every time you do that, you become freer, more powerful, more loving, and ultimately more able to embody your soul and Awareness. So you do The Work to be free; in becoming free yourself, you free those around you as well as the parts inside you that are held hostage by your deep cognitive patterns and judgments. Most of those patterns were created early in life and are just conditioning, so there is no need to be overly attached to them.

The Work is an important tool in our toolbox. It is not the answer to pain; however, it is a tool for walking the pathway to freedom from suffering.

. . . .

EXERCISE
The Work

Go to The Work website (thework.com) and read about the process. Pick a problematic situation you are facing and use the process to look at it from a new angle. Write about it in your journal.

. . . .

MY EXPERIENCE WITH BYRON KATIE

I had a remarkable experience with Katie one day. I was aware of her by then, and had seen her once, years before at a conference. This day I was at a beautiful hotel with a central atrium and gorgeous, large palm trees. I was at a crisis point in my life. I was struggling to understand how to integrate my own experiences of pure Awareness, because it seemed to be melting my personality and forcing me into transformative situations that were burning up identities and leaving me with nothing left. It was not a comfortable spot to be in at all. I was killing the "I'm in charge here" instinct of the self, and it was not going down easy. Dying to the self can be like that at times.

I had no idea what to do with myself anymore. I gave up. *What am I supposed to do? Where am I supposed to go?* I just prayed for help. Then I got up and walked out of the hotel. I looked up past the sky and passionately thought, *Help me*—and I really meant it. When I looked back down to street level, lo and behold, Byron Katie was walking by. I went utterly into denial that it was actually her. She was with a man and a younger woman. I thought, "Oh, that can't be her. That's not her. That's not possible, not at this exact moment." I proceeded to follow them down the street from a respectful distance. It was Parents' Weekend at the local university, and I thought, "No, that's just some parents with their kid, and the mom looks like Byron Katie." But Katie has distinctive silver hair; she is easy to recognize from a distance if you know what you are looking for.

I followed them all the way down the main shopping street; then the road ran out and I realized they would stop and turn around and see me. They got to the last store, an Abercrombie & Fitch, and the man peeled off into it. The street continued another fifty feet or so, and the two women kept walking. I still was not entirely sure it was Katie.

As it happens, Katie is married to a wonderful writer and

mystic, Stephen Mitchell, who did a translation of the *Tao Te Ching* that I'd read in college almost twenty years earlier. It was the first major spiritual book that I read when I was in college, after reading *Siddhartha* and *Black Elk Speaks* (which are the two books that are basically the origin point for nondual shamanism) in high school.

I went into the Abercrombie & Fitch, and it was completely empty. I kept looking—where did this guy go? I went to the back of the store, and there he was on the floor looking through jeans.

"Are you Stephen Mitchell?" I asked.

He looked up at me and said, "Yes."

"Wow." I told him that I had read his book and said, "And aren't you married to Byron Katie?"

"Yes."

"Was that her walking down the street right outside?"

"Yes."

"I can't believe it," I said.

I then told him about my experience of despair at the hotel and what had just happened.

He laughed. "Things like that happen around Katie all the time."

Because, of course, she's deeply established in pure Awareness. She has deeply habituated her perception of pure Awareness and so, as a consequence, the universe can move miraculous things through and around her all the time.

I told Stephen I was struggling with my experience of pure Awareness and how to engage with reality. It was really messing with me, and I didn't know what to do.

He smiled and said, "You know what? Go out and say hi. Go say hi to Katie."

I said okay, and as I left the store, there she was walking up. Probably one of the more beautiful moments of my life was when she saw me, and I looked into her eyes. Instantly I knew how deeply she had embodied and habituated pure Awareness because it sparkled through her eyes.

She opened her arms and said, "Oh, hi, honey. It's so great to meet you."

I had not even said anything to her yet and she gave me a huge hug! She saw herself in me, of course. We are the same—we are all the same person—and each time a new person finds itself in her, she can do this. It is a marvelous process.

SYNCHRONICITIES INSPIRE WONDER, ALLOWING A NEW WAY OF BEING.

As you do The Work, you connect to the lineage Katie streams out. Meeting her became a turning point in my own life because spiritual growth and spiritual transformation can be a lonely endeavor. In parts of it, you can feel totally abandoned, so to have her show up the way she did was essentially to have reality—to have Awareness itself—direct me to exactly where I needed to be to reinforce that the path I was on—the awakening process—was not some foolhardy quest, but that, in fact, it matters most of all and is for all of us.

I spoke with Katie for ten or fifteen minutes and as I began to explain to her my problem, she just held the space with me, and she reaffirmed that the engagement with reality is exactly as I described: transformative all the time, a great burning up of false identities until something new emerges that uses all the old bricks in a new format and in which wounds become blessings, pathways to teachings, and much more. I went away from that experience with a deep sense of purpose; I knew that even if I didn't know where I was going, there was a meaning and direction behind it. I just needed to keep on moving along the river.

These kinds of miraculous events—synchronicities, as Carl Jung called them—become important in the process of the unfolding of your own transformation and your own journey, for two reasons: one, they can increase your faith in the process; and two, as the miraculous unfolds in your life, a profound sense of joy arises. These events bring back a childlike wonder and with it a kind of innocence, which become the underlying brickwork for a new way of being in the universe.

Innocence and openness to the miraculous eventually allow for a trust in the process of spirit to direct and guide its own incarnation, as well as to provide a method for healing your wounds and empowering you to become a co-creator with pure Awareness. The right books will come to you at the right time. The right book opens to the right page just when you need it. The right person shows up and says the right thing. It is much like how George Lucas imagined the Jedi live—the sense of being connected to the Force, being connected to an intelligent, all-pervasive force. Most of us, in today's world, start from the place Han Solo is in the first installment of *Star Wars*, where he says, "There's no mystical energy field that controls my destiny." Then, in the last film in which he appears (*The Force Awakens*), he says quite the opposite: "Crazy thing is, it's true. . . . All of it. It's all true."

It is a significant breakthrough and a vital worldview shift to understand that the universe is actually alive, awake, and aware, and actively holding space for and encouraging our unfolding expression.

TRIGGERS, REGRESSION, AND RECOVERY: THE DETOUR METHOD

The Detour Method is a simple but powerful tool to help people overcome emotional regression. It serves a similar purpose as The Work, but it is focused on the emotions of the individual rather than their beliefs. The Detour Method was developed by John Lee, an innovative writer, counselor, and teacher in emotional intelligence, understanding anger versus rage, and emotional regression. Lee has written over twenty books in the field of psychological health and trains other therapists on how to handle regression.

To regress means to emotionally return to an earlier moment in history in which you were hurt, angry, abandoned, ignored, or in some way felt powerless. A sliver of you remains stuck at that moment; a psychic pattern that is frozen at that age gets triggered later when certain events unfold in the present. Regressions happen in many situations in our lives. They can be small or large moments, from a conversation about money or politics to folding the laundry to a significant argument. Almost anything can cause regression in a person, and all triggers are highly unique to the individual.

For instance, one of my common triggers is to be forced to pile into one car when a bunch of people are going out to dinner. This takes me back to my discomfort when, in my youth, all five of my family members would climb into the car on Friday evening after a long week to drive three and a half hours into the New Hampshire mountains to go skiing for the weekend. As a child I felt trapped, uncomfortable, forced to go, spoken over, and sort of in prison. So to this day, even if there are only two couples going to dinner, I insist on maximum flexibility and taking both our cars. It may seem a small thing, but the inability to leave at will, to escape from a tight or overwhelming space, either in the car or at a party, generates a regression and a lot of anxiety that is out of proportion to the threat. Having done the New Hampshire drive hundreds of times from age six to eighteen, the pattern in me is fairly strong. That kind of pattern is called *conditioning* and is not easy to overcome. On top of it, my Enneagram pattern (Type Two) for dealing with conflict is compliance, which may sound good from a parent's perspective, but unwilling compliance generates unconscious anger and resentment. And in this case, as an adult, unconscious resistance to compulsion around cramped road trips is a lifelong trigger.

The key is to know yourself and manage yourself with reasonable expectations, true compassion, and a clear explanation to those around you about your limits. You will never get rid of all your triggers, but you can get to know yourself and reduce your triggers' effects and the impact of reactive behavior on others. Being clear on expectations and management of what is tolerable for you is also good practice in managing conflict and expectations with others.

There is a balance between what you must learn to tolerate and what you must learn to *not* tolerate. Not having the capacity to tolerate some measure of your triggers leads to regressive narcissism, egoic inflation, and oversensitivity (the "snowflake" phenomenon), and overtolerating leads to a regressive and often unconscious self-diminishing attitude that generates massive reservoirs of anger and hurt and in some instances can lead to self-harming behaviors (such as cutting, eating disorders, and addictions). It is helpful to notice in yourself behavior that is too insistent or too compliant, for both may be signs that you need time to observe and process what is going on in your life and likely make some adjustments.

THE DETOUR METHOD SUMMARY STEPS

To help you move out of a regression so you can find the real issue at hand, the Detour Method takes you through five steps using the following questions:

1. What are you feeling right now?
2. What does this remind you of? (For example, is there a place or time, or a person who didn't respond to you or pay attention to you when you needed it the most?)
3. What would you have liked to say/do to that person, or have them say/do to you?
4. What do you still need to say/do to that person right now, or have them say/do to you?
5. How are you feeling now?

On YouTube, you can hear Lee take others through the method. Start with "Five Ways to Grow Back Up."

THE DETOUR METHOD ADAPTED FOR THE WAY OF THE MYSTIC-WIZARD

I have expanded the concept of the five steps to fit the Mystic-Wizard perspective. Lee's instructions involve working with a trusted other person; I have added in working with your inner-world allies (I have done both many times). My goal is to help you develop spiritual autonomy by utilizing resources from the inner world when you can, but not to the exclusion of getting outer-world help when you should. Learning to know when to use each is part of the Mystic-Wizard path, and the ability to manage your emotions with inner-world help and to overcome triggered regression events is essential to this path.

Here is the adapted Detour Method process I have used for myself on the Way of the Mystic-Wizard:

1. Bring Awareness to the current situation.

2. Ask yourself if you are stressed, angry, sad, lonely, anxious, annoyed, hungry, tired, or depressed.

3. Breathe deeply and become aware of Awareness and your soul.

4. Ask yourself, "How old do I feel right now?"

5. Ask yourself when in your past you have been in this situation. Sit with this question for a minute, close your eyes, and let your inner guides bring you the information you need. If you are triggered, it will come to you. Give it some time, as there is often resistance to this information becoming conscious. Once you have identified the last time you experienced this situation, then you can work on it.

6. Determine how you wish you could have managed the old situation. What would you like to say that you did not say then? In your inner world, complete that conversation in the way you wish it had gone. This can involve physical responses in the inner world, such as "I wish I had run away," or "I wish I had pushed that person out," or any number of empowering actions. This leads to the possibility of emotional release.

7. What, if anything, do you still need to say to that person in the present? Pull the person up in your inner world and speak to them in the present. This can also lead to emotional release and completion of the event in the present and the past.

8. Ask yourself how you are feeling right now. Determine if you have grown yourself back up out of that regressed moment. You may need more time—maybe hours, maybe days, weeks, or months—to really process an entire complex of regressive patterns. But the goal is to grow up out of the one that has you "entranced" before you act from that wounded place.

MANAGE YOURSELF WITH REASONABLE EXPECTATIONS AND TRUE COMPASSION.

In the Way of the Mystic-Wizard, we are in a long process of growing ourselves up. We are learning to catch our regressions in the moment and grow ourselves back up by becoming aware of Awareness and witnessing patterns as they arise and then letting them go. It is a lifelong process, and you can gain mastery in this process to the point that you look forward to being triggered so that you can liberate yourself from your conditioning. In these higher stages of ability, all the triggers in life become liberators, and slowly they are whittled away to mere shadows of themselves. This can eventually lead to an abiding equanimity. But to accomplish this, you must practice being aware of Awareness and look forward to the next momentary arising of your conditioning. This is not something that most of us are looking forward to at first, but once the egoic self understands the process as a real path toward freedom, and gets a taste of freedom from a regressive reactionary pattern, then it gets on board with the project.

A secret of the Detour Method is that it can become habituated like any behavior, to the point where even as negative thoughts or emotional patterns arise, they self-liberate in the field of Awareness. This capacity usually occurs on the meditation seat and not out in the field of life. In my own experience, taking it out into the field of life is more challenging. However, not only is it possible to walk around liberating all the time, but at some point, once the process has a life of its own, it becomes nearly inevitable.

The Detour Method is about trying to catch your regressions before you damage the world and the people around you. You can also apply The Work by Byron Katie to any regressive issue that keeps showing up in your life. In this way, by looking forward to this pattern showing up again or being retriggered, you can burn it up over time and replace it with another healthy pattern. The goal is to get free. You may need a helper to do so, which can be both in the inner world and the outer world;

I have always had both. The more you work on your triggers and how they are connected to your history, the better you will handle a transformational process.

One final note on regression: not all regression is negative. For example, if you get together with friends from your childhood and suddenly find yourself being playful, using jokes from that time, and enjoying yourself, then you have regressed in a positive fashion. Choosing to regress to a time that puts you into positive behaviors is not a problem, just as having a thought that doesn't harm you is not a problem in The Work. Both the mind and emotions have their negative and positive aspects, and mastery is learning to craft a reality that is beneficial to you and those around you.

A SPECIAL NOTE ON TRAUMA

Many of the methodologies in this book, especially the non-dual practices such as ascension and other forms of nondual meditation, tend to release "stuff" from the unconscious. This is why complementary psychological processes such as The Work and the Detour Method are so important. Our goal is to become more whole and acquire greater mastery, not to become overwhelmed by all our unconscious regressive patterns at once and have a total egoic meltdown. As the egoic self, you are the one who gets to determine the pace of this process. It is not in our interest to overwhelm ourselves and disrupt the steady pace of transformation and growth.

Trauma of various kinds is often the force behind negative thought patterns and behaviors. *If you have experienced severe trauma, you should get the help of a trauma recovery specialist.* Do not try to relive deep traumas on your own, as the triggering of the trauma can make it worse, not better. Trauma specialists help individuals overcome such events and move slowly and carefully into a healed place through methods such as neuro-linguistic programming (NLP), which helps dissolve and release the patterns that the trauma created. It does not erase the experience but rather allows the experience to no longer have repressed emotions attached to it.

In all cases, if you uncover trauma, ask your soul to help you find the professional help you need to heal. The shamanic path has always been a path of the wounded healer. To grow on your magical and mystical path, you are also going on a quest to heal yourself. Creating a daily spiritual practice as a Mystic-Wizard will bring you face-to-face with challenges that are too great for you to handle on your own. Developing spiritual autonomy does not mean doing everything yourself; it means not giving your power and sovereignty away. As you take responsibility for your practice and growth, you will also learn to ask for and find the right healers, shamans, mystics, teachers, counselors, and doctors to help you along your path of healing and em-powerment.

Journey Eight
THE TREE AND THE OLD WIZARD

Close your eyes. *Five, four, three . . . two . . . one.* You appear before your doorway. Put both hands on your door and connect to it, since inside the door there is power, energy that has been hidden.

The door opens. You step through and start walking down the corridor. Drag your hand along the wall . . . Go down the stairs into the common room. Look around and see if you notice anything different. When you look to the left, on the wall is etched an image of antlers.

Now move out of the common room and up the stairs, into the portal room. Go to the shimmering portal, turn toward the closet, and gather your traveling robes. Stand before the shimmering portal and gently push your hands into it. Feel the energy move up your body, transforming you into light and potential. Then step through the shimmering portal.

You find yourself looking out over the forest. Down in the field below stands a stag; it notices you. Start walking down the pathway, then over and down into the field, and cross the field. As you approach the forest, you see two ravens waiting, one perched on the standing stone and one in the tree, and out from the forest steps your animal guardian. Go greet your guardian with love and care and compassion, and then start walking into the woods along the path.

Out ahead of you, two wolves move, in the forest and across the path, showing you the way. Come to the stream; go down and take a drink of water. Purify yourself by splashing your face. Take a drop of water and put it on the top of your head; feel as it moves through and purifies your whole being.

Now go across the stream, stepping on the stone in the middle; on the other side, feel the earth under your feet. As you approach the inner grove, you see a great golden light, shimmering through the trees; something is causing it. As you clear the last tree, you see that it is an absolutely mammoth tree, made of golden light, at the center of the grove. In fact, it has always been there. It reaches all the way up into the sky and all the way down into the earth below.

Go up to the shimmering golden tree of light, gently place one hand on the trunk of the tree, and start to attune yourself to the energy of the tree. Then step into the center of the tree's energy. You begin to rise up through the trunk of the tree, higher and higher and higher. You are traveling along one of the great limbs, and as you move through, you come to some mist and you travel through the mist. As you come out of the mist, you are in a beautiful valley amidst snowcapped mountains, with a river down the middle.

You are standing on a hillside, and nearby appears a flying horse you're familiar with. You get on the horse and she starts flying you across the valley and over treetops, following the river. There is a series of waterfalls that you fly over, and you can see salmon jumping, trying to return to their origin. You come up over the last vast waterfall, and there you see a great lake and a lone peak beyond. You fly over the lake. It is glimmering and utterly clear and beautiful, perhaps the cleanest and clearest water in the multiverse. Up you go, higher still, till at last you come to the top of the lone mountain that looks over the lake. There you see a simple fire burning and an old man sitting by it. The horse lands and gently walks up to the old man, who looks up and welcomes you to come sit by him. You see that he is looking not only at the fire, but also at that which is laid out before him: runes inscribed in bone. He waves you over and says he wants to show you something about how everything works and how the universe flows.

Spend some time with him and with the runes . . .

It is almost time to return. The old man takes a moment, reaches out gently, and scribes a rune on your forehead, the one you need most to help guide you in the next stage of your life.

And then you look out with him over the vast lake, and there you see the entire tree of existence spread out before you—all the worlds, all the beings, high and low. You see that the whole thing is alive. Energy rising from below evolves and grows, attains wisdom and insight, and ripens, and then that wisdom falls back down into the lower realms to inspire yet more growth, more transformation. And you are a part of that. Down in the clear lake, you notice that, coiled at the bottom, is a great serpent, a great silvery serpent, sleeping but aware.

The old man raises his hand and in the air inscribes a rune that you do not recognize—a rune not meant for mortals, but a rune that connects you to him. And the rune creates a doorway, a portal, through which you can return at any time. The portal turns misty, and he directs you to step through . . . and you are in the portal room again, instantaneously returned.

It's time to put away your robes. As you walk back down into the common room, you realize that every gate and doorway is connected. The old man is the Lord of the Gates, who gives access to all the realms and all the worlds so that you, too, might gather wisdom and cultivate the great tree.

Now it is time to return. Leave the common room, and go up the steps. The back of the door, too, has runes shimmering on it, golden runes. The door opens, you step through, and the door shuts. Place your hand on the door, say in your mind, *It is complete . . . and it has begun.*

You are rising up through the mist. *One*, higher. *Two*, returning to this world, the outer world, just one of many worlds in the great Tree of Life. *Three*, aware of your body and infused with the golden light of the tree. *Four*, move your fingers, your toes. Finally, *five*, open your eyes. You are fully returned.

You remember everything. Write about it in your journal.

Part Nine

TRANSFORMATION & MANIFESTATION

What if you found what you wanted most
delivered by a celestial carrier
in an invisible package?

In Part Nine, we look at two practices—transformation and manifestation—that can help you gain a deeper understanding of how the quest unfolds and the requirements and abilities that develop along the way.

THE LIGHT BODY AND THE PRACTICE
OF TRANSFORMATION

The body is a powerhouse of energy. We incarnate to embody and express that energy in many ways. We create civilization, art, children, and much more. In esoteric[17] spiritual paths such as the Way of the Mystic-Wizard, we are also using that energy to build up our immortal light body. The light body then becomes a vehicle for the soul's consciousness to be able to live and move through the many dimensions of light. This is an integral part of the esoteric Tibetan and Hindu systems of Tantra, the Taoist system, and the Egyptian and esoteric Hebrew alchemical paths. All are devoted to constructing the light body out of the life energy of the physical body and to generating a healthy and empowered physical form and energy body. I started with yoga and tai chi in college many years ago and have ended up working with chi gong as a pathway to embody well-being in my body, mind, and emotions, and ultimately in my soul.

So why have you never heard of the light body? Actually, you probably have but don't realize it, because it is esoteric and only sneaks out into the open through stories and religion. The most famous example in the West is, of course, Jesus, who reappeared in his light body after he died. If you look at this

---

17 Esoteric: designed for or understood by the specially initiated alone (Merriam-Webster).

event as an esoteric act of mastery rather than of faith or religion, then it becomes quite an accomplishment. Even the story about his body vanishing is part of the esoteric lore of how the body is used as the raw material and energy to form the light body. This same basic esoteric story can be found in China, India, and Tibet. In all these cases, other esoteric masters have completed the light body as they were dying.

In Tibet, this is part of the exoteric[18] historical record, albeit rare, and is seen as a natural evolution in the development of highly accomplished meditation teachers. It is not supernatural; it is in fact an act of extraordinary transformation, much like a caterpillar becoming a butterfly. In Tibet, an aspect of the light body is called "the rainbow body." (There is an excellent and beautiful book, *Rainbow Body*, by Loel Guinness, which is the first of its kind to really take the subject seriously.) Through meditation and breathing exercises, the instinctual energies of the body are repurposed and drawn inward to transform the nervous system, the brain, and finally the cells into a material that exists at a more subtle vibration. It is a refinement process, much like precious metals are refined from raw ore. This is why alchemy embraces the symbolism of transforming oneself from lead into gold.

As this process of transformation unfolds over many years, you begin to have access to the light body while still in the physical body. The states of consciousness of this body are quite extraordinary, and it is sometimes called "the body of bliss" for this reason. The path to building the light body and being filled with bliss and joy is much like being an athlete. Your whole life becomes a reflection of this increased level of energy, joy, and subtle bliss. You have more power, so you are able to do more in certain ways. You are able to be more engaged, you are able to be more compassionate, more loving, more capable

---

18 Exoteric: belonging to the outer or less initiate circle (Merriam-Webster).

of drawing boundaries, more insightful, and more creative. If you then stop the practices, it will not take long for things to fall apart. There is a famous story about a professional pianist who stated that he had to practice every day to remain a top concert pianist. He reported that if he did not practice for one day, he would notice. If he did not practice for two days, his wife would notice. If he did not practice for three days, then the audience would notice.

Be intentional about what you create, because the world you make will be the world you become accustomed to living in—just like people get used to having a certain amount of money. If there is a sudden dip in cash flow, they often experience a painful adjustment.

It is not only a lack of discipline that may undo your practice. Breaks in routine can happen when you are sick, or when there is a crisis in your life. For instance, the grieving process is a serious spiritual challenge. Yet your practice can, in fact, make the down times in your life better than they otherwise would have been. The antidote to a feeling of pointlessness is your practice. The processing of your pain is your practice; letting go of the past is your practice. Lose your practice, and you will revert back to who you were before you built it, just like when you stop brushing your teeth, you soon get a layer of film over your teeth. Practice remains the most essential thing in your life, so that when life inverts and things fall apart, which they will and they must, you will still have a stable center.

In addition, it is good to have patience with yourself. Sometimes the things that knock you off your practice routine are part of the transformational process. When energies arise from the shadowy unconscious realm, it is not unusual for them to manifest in the outer world first. The classic example from my life is anger rising up. For example, I drop my keys and then kick them under the couch while trying to pick them up. Suddenly I am irrationally mad at my keys, and then it becomes the

THE LIGHT BODY IS NOT SUPERNATURAL— IT IS AN ACT OF TRANSFORMATION.

couch's fault, and then I am angry that couches exist at all. That is what I call an "irrationality slide"—right into the core of the situation, which is that I am furious. But I am not mad at the keys or the couch. Usually I am angry at life itself for delivering me circumstances in which I feel coerced, powerless, fearful, and attacked. We all have to survive moments like that through what I call "survival suppressing," in which emotions go into the underworld, then come back in irrational moments in which we regress to an earlier age and moment. The goal is to process these moments from awareness of Awareness: forgive the couch and thank the keys for opening a doorway to let that response out of the system.

The other goal is to not shed these energies onto other beings and thus create an endless ripple of the very coercion or fear you suffered out in the world. It took a long time for humanity to learn that expressing repressed rage onto another being perpetuated trauma. This seems obvious to us now, but it was not apparent through most of history. If this knowledge of how trauma is perpetuated were the only thing that psychology had delivered to us, it would have been a priceless gift.

The process of transformation is an up-and-down phenomenon. Your practice is the place that centers you and allows you to manage those ups and downs. Developing a body of light gives you access to the bliss-field, and from that place, healing and reconciliation of various aspects of the self can take place.

The most powerful and accessible light body development system I have come across is called Awakening Your Light Body by Duane Packer. I have been pursuing it for over twenty years, and I would not be where I am today without it. Peter Fenner's course, Radiant Mind, is also priceless. Both courses transmit direct access to the bliss-field and unconditioned pure Awareness. These courses were essential for my own development, and they would normally only be accessible in an esoteric setting, but we live in spiritually fortunate times.

Having instant access to the bliss-body of light simply by taking an intentional breath is a gift worth developing. It is also our human birthright and potential. As with any endeavor that involves the mastery of the body, it must be developed and practiced. Very few of us will fully complete the light body in this life, but that doesn't mean it is not worth pursuing, just as any sport you might take up is not worthless simply because you are not going to the Olympics in this life. The benefits of access to the body of bliss are extraordinary; the light body can help heal you and can awaken you to pure Awareness.

Every morning when I sit to practice, I begin by awakening my light body all the way up the central energy channel of the body. Then I turn my attention to pure Awareness, and the recognition of Awareness immediately reduces the sense of separation and alienation that the egoic self creates. Then from above I draw down the purifying power of the Buddhist deity Vajrasattva. Then I take a few heart breaths, which I learned about from Nicki Scully, a wonderful teacher of the ancient Egyptian shamanic path, in which the two energies of peace from above and life-energy from below meet in the heart and mix. From that place, one can enter the inner world for a shamanic journey to visit inner allies and abide with them as one of them.

The path I am speaking about is open to all who are called to it. The energy of the light body will utterly transform you and your life and your view of who you are. May the light of your soul be your guide.

ON THE ART OF MANIFESTING: THE ACT OF CO-CREATION

How does the universe work? Who is in charge here? And how do we get stuff done? These are the questions that the creative art of magic asks of us. The answers are both scientific and magical in that they apply to the traditional outer realm of the sciences and the inner subtle spiritual realms.

The essential magical element of the universe is that things appear out of formlessness. It is fundamentally inexplicable, and we can only ever study what appears on our side of the manifest wall. The universe is making something appear out of nothing every instant of every day. We are interested in that ever-repeating instant of creation as the focal point for our co-creative intentions and manifestations. If you can abide at the edge of the manifest wall and listen for what wants to arise from the soul, you can learn to manifest. The inner journeys in this book and the ones on the NDS section of my website will assist you in learning these skills.

Below I describe the fundamental outlook toward and tactical process of manifestation for the Mystic-Wizard.

THE MAGICAL ORIENTATION

Reality is one thing, and we are in it and of it. We have limited or conditional objectivity based on our perception and the context of any given moment. However, there is no absolute objectivity and never will be on our side of the manifest wall. We are egoic fish in the fishbowl, and we can stick our noses against the side of the glass, but we cannot cross it and remain what we perceive ourselves to be now.

Therefore, we build an approach that engages with our conditional objectivity and the subtle energetic and physical resources available to us, including the soul and pure Awareness. If we hope to be effective, that engagement must have a broad, integral, multidimensional perspective on reality. The more we understand how the levels of reality work together, the better our ability to create. Therefore, we seek to understand rules of manifestation, creativity, and inspiration just as a physicist seeks to understand the universal laws of the physical cosmos.

Here is one of the rules: How you experience yourself—or who you are being—when you create, affects what you make and how it comes into being. You are what you create, and what you create is you. Emptiness is form, and form is emptiness. Know yourself, and you will naturally manifest the miracles within the self-soul waiting to be born.

This seems obvious once you hear it. How could it be any other way? But it has massive implications. If, for instance, you experience yourself as your soul, or your sacred yidam deity or beloved, or pure Awareness, then your capacity for creation and manifestation increases. The best ideas and creations appear when the egoic self is less dominant and the muse, the soul, channels in the material.

An integral approach that includes the multidimensional nature of reality and our being also includes our relative place in this larger universe. Knowing the role of the egoic self as a collaborator with soul and spirit answers the questions, How does the universe work? Who is in charge here? and How do we get stuff done? The answer is, together. Many a would-be wizard or mage has spent a lot of time on egoic rituals and spells, but if you do not have the backup in the spiritual realm and in your own subconscious, it is tough to create and sustain creativity and manifestation. You can easily ask for something your ego wants but your soul does not, and the soul then teaches you a lesson about who knows best. If you doubt this, see *Aladdin* and *Fantasia* by Disney, two movies that make it quite clear what can go wrong.

The egoic self and the soul work together with inner-world guides to manifest the soul's genuine desire and vision and to unfold a fulfilling life plan. This does not mean a total sacrifice of egoic needs and submitting to the Martyr archetype that is so common at the blue level of Spiral Dynamics. But it also does not mean the opposite, that you take on the egocentric archetype of the Warrior-Conqueror at the spiral's red level, becoming a magical tyrant. There is a higher way that involves the sacred manifestation of the marriage of self and soul.

What is in the way of your receiving the things that will support you on your path? Typically it is your own belief that you do not deserve them. These are the programs of unworthiness and unlovability that underlie Enneagram types and egoic structures. To overcome them, you can practice things that serve others first and so gain confidence in manifesting.

HOW TO MANIFEST

I have been working out how manifestation works since 1991, when I first came across the idea. Manifestation is the same thing as creativity. It is a deceptively simple process. Keep in mind that magic does not involve magical thinking, a child-like form of thought in which you misconnect things you do as the only actual cause of events. The total number of reasons for any event is nearly infinite, and that is why you need the soul to help you.

Here are the simple steps for manifestation:

1. Connect with your soul and Awareness, and ask for what you sense wants to arise and come forth.

2. Listen for feedback.
3. Then, in the silence of your practice and the spaciousness of pure Awareness, have a sense that it—whatever "it" is—is done in the subtle dimensions, and simply say, *It is done*, and then *Thank you*.
4. Then forget about it.

That's it. Later, when the time is right for your egoic self to act on something, you will be reminded what you asked for. Usually this reminder comes through some synchronistic event or by your own sudden obsession to move in a new direction or even from a more subtle nudge to check an email, or buy a book, or anything that will move you forward.

Once you have received and given thanks in the subtle inner world, your only job as an egoic self is to respond to the prompts and do your part in the outer world. By doing so, you are changing your own life and personhood to adapt to the arrival of the change. Your response can involve a few large changes or hundreds of small changes (or more), depending on how big the difference in your life may be.

Wanting a thing to appear in your life is not enough; you must also want to become the person for whom that thing is inevitable, and you and your soul must be in alignment with it. A change is unlikely to manifest if you want something but do not want to become the new person required to have it. The more you make yourself into a new you, the more the spirit will bring the synchronistic events that help bring that about. You are writing yourself into the novel of your life and getting the props you need to play your part.

Your daily spiritual practice is an act of magical manifestation, and manifestation is, in fact, your practice. You are transforming yourself all the time. As you connect to your soul and are open to the source of your inspiration, you gain confidence in your new creative capacities and your status as co-creator

YOU ARE WHAT YOU CREATE, AND WHAT YOU CREATE IS YOU.

with the soul. This is how any artist grows as they gain abilities and confidence working in any medium. This is why magic is called the Great Art, and your transformation into an awakened multidimensional being is called the Great Work.

COMMON STUMBLING BLOCKS

The process of manifestation is not particularly complicated, but there are some common stumbling blocks people face, especially when starting out.

Not knowing how to ask. For many modern people whose worldview centers in the orange or green level of the spiral, the idea of asking the transcendent for help can feel strange or embarrassing. If you do not know how to ask to receive from the spiritual realms, admit to your soul that you are clueless, and then just ask how to ask. From that humble request for help, the spiritual bridge between self, soul, and spirit is forged.

Not knowing what to manifest. If you don't know what to manifest, start by asking for things that help others and the world. This way, you gain trust and faith in your capacity and also understand the nature of service. It took me ten years of manifesting a long list of miracles, including millions of dollars and a school building, before I was capable of manifesting things for myself and my family directly. It took me another ten years to master that process.

I was ultimately successful, but it took many years of practice to overcome the underlying beliefs that I was not worthy of personal love, bliss, peace, joy, security, success, and purpose. I went through a psychological and shamanic healing process and a spiritual merging process with soul and Awareness. Learning to embody all those principles more often than not is an accomplishment that serves others as much as it does yourself. Your own empowerment helps to empower others and places you into yet another level of service. Imagine what humanity would be capable of if all of us were able to embody most of those traits most of the time. That is the dream, and the actual great work of our species.

However, if you, like most of us much of the time, are unclear on what to manifest, then stick to this basic but powerful spell sequence inspired by the words of Simon Court. Its intention lies beneath the entire path of the Mystic-Wizard:

What must I be
to manifest
what needs to occur?

Asking from ego and/or intentionally causing harm. You learn to create good luck by asking for it. You ask for it by literally asking the spirit world to handle things. But if you ask for lower-level egoic crap that hurts others instead of helping the situation, you will generate pain and suffering in your life, and the compassionate spirits there to support you will withdraw.

You attract the energies and spiritual beings of the same energy you embody. Embody the truth, and recognize your own nefarious shadow intentions. Face the shadow with compassion, and then choose the higher path. We take the higher approach by seeing through the veil of illusion about the identity of the "other" being anything besides Awareness itself. Even as you do this, you will be humbled by both what you can accomplish and how you distort your primary instinct's power to serve and support your egoic structures.

Always return to Awareness before you ask for something. If you are asking for something and you are not awake to Awareness, then stop yourself. Get your view of Awareness into position first. Then your egoic self will already feel fulfilled, and the desires of the soul will arise, and from there you ask. Oftentimes egoic desires vanish in that moment and never come back. Other desires are soul desires, and others still are deep in the unconscious and must be rooted out by a process I will explain below.

If you ignore my counsel and use what you have learned here to create harmful magic based on the illusion of the egoic self, you will suffer. If you purposely hurt another egoic self, what do you think Awareness is going to do? From the perspective of Awareness, you would be trying to hurt yourself. The only compassionate thing to do would be to show you that that is not a good idea. The only way Awareness can do so is to teach you through returning that negativity to you. Those are the rules. It is hard enough to handle your own shadow desires and your unconscious projection of them without adding to them by consciously using your egoic self to ask for harm to come to other people.

Being stuck in old desires or attachments. Some egoic de-sires vanish in the face of Awareness, and others just seem to stick around . . . There are two ways to get past any old desire or deep unconscious attachment that you can't seem to let go of. The first is to ask to have the thing given to you. The second is to ask for whatever needs to happen to get you over wanting the thing.

I have often said to Awareness and my own soul, "Please give me what I want, or get me over wanting it." This is a spell you are casting on yourself, and it is potent, so be very careful what you ask to get over wanting. By doing so you are asking to be thrown into the deep fiery end of the pool of transformation. Do not ask to get over something you really don't want to get over.

The process that unfolds after using this intention is always humbling, usually involves the type of suffering involved with profound detachment, and, if it goes well, provides deep in-sight into the patterns of your structure that created the desire.

Even after you get over the desire, the underlying imprint of the desire is always there for you to reinitialize and be sucked into. I have found that to burn something off, it can take three complete rounds of invitation to get free. This happens by making it seem like you will get the thing, only to have it taken away, or getting it and realizing it is not what you wanted after all. The soul is in charge of this process, so be prepared to completely forget you asked for this process to happen and then to have it play out in your outer world over the following year.

Only use this kind of asking for things you cannot accomplish in the inner world, and do not ask for absurd things like getting you over wanting to eat, or experiencing love, or the need for joy or money. Your egoic self needs all kinds of things to make life meaningful, and many of them are basic, practical needs. Instead, ask to get over things that come from the distortions of your Enneagram and instincts or from past traumas—things like wanting to be famous, beautiful, or rich, or things like giving away your power, talking too much, or being afraid, sad, or argumentative all the time.

You can start by asking the inner world what would be the best thing to ask for right now.

FINAL THOUGHTS AND RECOMMENDATIONS

There is a famous ancient Mystic-Wizard who said, "Ask and you shall receive." It is a deceptively simple statement. But it is actually a foolproof formula, because if you ask and do not receive, it sets you on the quest to discover how to ask the right way, and lo and behold, you are on the spiritual path. And when you ask and receive, you begin to gain confidence in how manifesting works.

For a much more in-depth discussion on how to manifest, I highly recommend a book by David Spangler, one of the great Mystic-Wizards of our time, titled *The Laws of Manifestation: A Consciousness Classic*. Another book I highly recommend is *Weaving Fate* by Aidan Wachter. What is essential in this book is the simple process of writing thank-you letters in your magical journal from a viewpoint in the future in which what you wanted to manifest has already taken place. You write full of gratitude for the way something unfolded—without giving precise details, so the spiritual world can work it out independently. Wachter provides excellent instructions and in the second half of the book gives ample writing samples. It is a priceless resource from a highly trained and transformed mage who knows his stuff.

In the end, the process of learning to create and manifest is the underlying essence of your Mystic-Wizard practice, because the ultimate artwork is you and your life, and the soul is your pilot in the process. Your long-term goal as a Mystic-Wizard is to become precisely the person you were meant to be and be amazed you pulled it off. Who you become will not be who you thought you were supposed to be or who you idealized yourself to be; instead, those images will later be seen as essential steps on the path of awakening and finding the true way to your authentic self.

Journey Nine

TEMPLE OF MEDITATION

Close your eyes. Take a breath. You are floating down through the mist . . . *Five, four,* deeper . . . *three,* deeper . . . *two,* deeper . . . *one.*

You are at your door. Notice that the door has an energy in it. Put your hands on the door and feel it. Let the energy gently move through your body as you attune yourself to the inner world. And then the door clicks and opens.

You step through and start walking down the corridor. Reach out and drag your hand along the stone wall. Once again, see the light, the trails from your fingers, and then go down the steps to the right, curving down into the common room. There in the common room you see the fireplace, the light coming in . . . Go across the common room and then up the stairs into the portal room. Turn right and face the shimmering portal.

Walk up to the portal, turn to the left, grab your traveling gear, and then stand before the portal with staff in hand. Place both hands, including the staff, into the portal. Once again feel the energy move through your body, and then step through the shimmering portal.

You appear on the mountainside, looking out over the forest. Start walking down the trail on the hill, down to the field, and walk across the field. You come to the edge of the forest and your animal comes out to greet you. Look down the trail into the forest. You notice that the trail itself and the forest and this entire day are filled with a kind of mist, making it hard to see, but there in the distance, the wolves wait. With your animal, start walking down the trail.

Deeper into the forest you go. You come to the stream and pass over the stream. And then the trail to the left along the stream appears. You have walked this trail before, and you start walking alone, following the stream farther and farther to the south, until at last you come to a sanctuary, a hut there by the side of the river. There before the hot fire sits your beloved waiting for you.

Greet your beloved, who turns and points you farther south along the trail. You start walking down the trail again. And this time the trail diverts from the side of the stream and moves to the right, up a low hill, still in the forest. The trail circles around this low hill once. And there's a beautiful pathway through the forest that rises higher bit by bit. You circle around once and come nearly to the top. Then you see some stairs that lead directly into the top of a low wall, and there in the mist you make out a stone building.

Start climbing the stairs, moving up until you finally come to the stone patio in front of the building. The mist clears a little bit, and you move inside. It's a beautiful, domed stone building, comfortable, and in the center is a place to sit and meditate. Go and take your place.

You face outward, and in that place where you're sitting and meditating, you can see that there is an exit straight ahead, and you realize there is one in each of the four directions. You are at the center, and above you a dome opens to the sky. As you sit, look out to the south; the mist clears a little bit, and you can see far in the distance a lonely mountain where the spear of intuition and dragon of fire live.

Now, notice that the mist changes color and begins to turn gold. You are surrounded by golden mist as you sit in this meditation space. Gently become aware of your body of light. Feel the golden light expand out from your heart, mixing and radiating out into the mist. Become aware of Awareness all around you. And then gently, begin to awaken the light body.

Begin at the bottom, and then move up. Allow the energy to gently flow up like a river through the center of your body. As the energy reaches the top of your head, it then cascades around you like a fountain. Take a calming breath; pull the breath in. And then send the energy moving gently upstream through the top of your head so it cascades all around you in unlimited riches of energy.

Now above your head, notice that a divine being has come to gather white pure energy above the top of your head, and then gently bring it down over you, cascading down through your whole energy body, bringing peace and stillness all the way down through your body. Gently take another breath and contract at your base.

Then a powerful red energy moves up gently through the center of your body, all the way up to the crown of your head, again cascading like a fountain all around you. And then again, the divine being's ball of white energy starts cascading down through your body, delivering peace and stillness. What comes down from the top is peace with stillness, and what comes up from the bottom is power and life energy.

Now imagine as you take the next breath that you bring the two—the white energy from the top and the red energy from the bottom—together at your heart, where they mix, and you breathe them in. This is called the heart breath.

Feel the mix in the center of your being. A golden light emerges. Let the golden light fill your whole body . . .

Now it's time to return. Stand up and look around and notice the temple of light's radiance. Notice again the four directions. Give thanks to those beings that came to help you today and then move from the temple to the stairway that leads down the side of the hill to the path.

Begin walking down the hill. You enter the mist again and eventually come to the bottom of the hill, and you're in the forest. You follow the path there, and again meet up with your animal guide along the stream. You come to the sanctuary. Now, as you pass by the fire, you notice there is a peculiar stone in the center that seems to be the source of the golden fire. Retrieve that stone. The flame is heatless and seemingly full of life.

Now walk along the path, back along the stream, until you come to the main path. Cross over the stream; as you do, the mist begins to clear. Slowly come to the edge of the forest. There is the tall standing stone; turn and look at it. Place a hand on top of it. If you look carefully at the stone, you'll see the fire inside of it. It's always been there.

Say goodbye to your animal guide and walk back across the field and up the hill to the shimmering portal. Now turn and step through the shimmering portal. Return your travel implements. Head down into the common room.

Go across the common room, up the stairs and into the hall, until finally you come to the back of the door. The door opens. Step out, and the door shuts. Turn, place your left hand on the door, and say in your mind, *It is done*.

You are rising up now through the mist. *One, two* . . . returning to this world and this time . . . *three, four* . . . bringing back your awareness of all that you saw and witnessed. Wiggle your fingers and your toes. *Five*, open your eyes and you have returned to this world.

Now, write about your experience in your journal.

Part Ten

HEALING, HABITUATION & HAPPINESS

always you seek after
the granite mountain
in the distance

As you progress in your spiritual practice, additional healing may need to take place. Part Ten contains several methods that can help. These short techniques can be used throughout the day and are simple, powerful inner-world tools for managing the journey.

INNER-WORLD TECHNIQUES FOR TRANSFORMATION AND HEALING

Here I provide a few techniques for inner transformation that I have found helpful and valuable over the years, and that can be used and reused throughout your practice. In each case, I mention the teacher I learned it from and, if available, the corresponding book.

THE INNER CAMPFIRE: A SACRED CONVERSATION WITH THE INNER WISDOM KEEPER

This practice is the simple process of using your active imagination to find a place in your inner world that best suits you to meet with your inner Wisdom Teacher, and to converse with them in a form that best suits you.

Find a site where you are comfortable conversing. It could be at the fireplace in the common room, where I often meet with the Weaver, the Goddess of Fate. Or it could be under the World Tree, where a small campfire burns and the ancient noble deities sit. Or you might prefer the magical island where the first shaman shows up to teach at the sacred fire, or possibly the grove where the crone watches over the fire. All of these places are islands of predictable wisdom where you can find solace and guidance.

Then find the form of the Wisdom Keeper that you are comfortable conversing with. In many mythic traditions, it is a female goddess, the Wise Old Woman, who embodies the divine wisdom component of consciousness. Therefore it is not unusual to find various goddess beings at these sites. I am often in contact with Frigga, the Norse goddess of wisdom, and Freya, the first wise shaman. If you wish to meet with the Wise Old Man, there are many wizards, such as Yoda, Gandalf, Merlin, and Dumbledore, and Wizard-King deities, such as Odin, that you may discover.

Remember, the form that these spiritual beings take is for your comfort and in no way reveals the complete nature of their actual identity. For instance, at the start of my path, I was intimidated by powerful Wizard-Kings, so Odin took on the shape of the diminutive yet powerful Jedi master, Yoda. Later, I met Odin on a bench by the sea in a form more closely associated with Odin's mythic traditions, that of the Blue Wanderer.

This practice of using active imagination to speak to the Wisdom Teacher comes from Carl Jung's own deep inner-world experience with his Wisdom Teacher that he discovered and then offered as an example for the larger world. Jung's inner guide was named Philemon. In the biography *Memories, Dreams, Reflections*, Jung recounts his dream when Philemon first appeared to him in 1913. He saw an old man with kingfisher wings and the horns of a bull flying across the sky, carrying a set of keys. Philemon eventually played an essential role in Jung's inner journey and his outer work. Jung wrote in his journals that he would often talk with Philemon as he walked in his garden in Switzerland. He also said that Philemon taught him about the objective reality of the soul and that the spirit teacher helped him formulate and express everything meaningful that he'd ever thought.

The name of Jung's inner being comes from Goethe's *Faust*, and this example shows how a spiritual being can clothe itself in the needed form to help the earthly student access wisdom. In Jung's case, he was deeply affected by *Faust* and its characters, in much the same way I was influenced by Yoda later in the century.

THE INNER ANIMAL CLEARING AND PURIFICATION

This practice was taught to me by Philip Carr-Gomm, the former Chosen Chief of the Order of Bards, Ovates and Druids and a major contributor to the development of the Druid revival of the late twentieth century. I have taught this practice for almost twenty years. It has a tremendous capacity to reveal our inner emotional state and offer opportunities to heal that condition if needed.

Enter the inner forest, and then find a path that leads to a clearing. In that clearing, you suddenly see an animal. Notice its condition. Is it healthy or unhealthy, angry, tired, happy, tortured, or ecstatic? It is not unusual to find that whatever animal is there is in duress. I often find the animal trapped by ropes or weeds, or hanging from a tree, or in some way metaphorically representing how a part of me feels at the time. It is almost always a part of the self that I am unaware needs some attention. For instance, as I am writing this right now, I see a goat, and he is happily eating grass in the middle of the clearing, but his hooves are sucked into the ground about four inches, and he is stuck and unable to move or walk. He is happy but stuck, which is how I feel right now. I am happily writing this, but I also feel stuck in my chair.

What I do next is as follows: I recognize the part of me that is annoyed and feels stuck. I go and pick up the goat, pulling it out of the earth. He shakes off his little legs, and then I place him on top of a small hillock where there is firmer ground for him to stand on. He looks about and enjoys the breeze. Then a beam of golden light from above shines down over him. He absorbs the light.

And I feel much better about the entire situation now.

In this example, you can see how to creatively use the inner world to recognize and transform your mood and state of being. There are limitless ways you can utilize this magical capacity. For instance, you can go to an inner temple and see yourself outside on the steps and see your hidden internal condition. Right now, I see myself on my knees with my forehead on the earth, a bit tired but not broken. Then, a small group of goblin-monks comes forth from the temple doors with a stretcher, places me on it, takes me inside, and puts me in front of the goddess White Tara. She reaches down and touches my forehead with one finger. I suddenly feel blessed. Tara then channels white purifying power into me, and as she does this, my outer body and state of consciousness shift toward a more energized and awakened state.

You can use your imagination to access various beings and objects that are always ready to help you charge up. For instance, you can imagine a ball of white light above your head and have it drop over your body as you walk. Over time you can master energetic magic like this and take more control over your environment. Instead of being pushed around by the energy in any given setting, you can develop your wizardly capacity to manage the environment yourself and even improve it.

My only warning is to be careful once you have developed this capacity. The better you become at this kind of magic, the more responsibility you have. In Buddhism, there is the concept of "right speech," which means not gossiping and tearing people down. I extend this rule to the correct use of imaginal magic. If you use this imaginative power to hurt others, you will pay for it. Eventually, forces in the inner world will align, and you will be shown the error of your ways. When you misuse magic, you

INNER-WORLD BEINGS AND OBJECTS ARE ALWAYS READY TO HELP YOU CHARGE UP.

are functioning from a dualistic perspective and acting like the "other" is not Awareness. On the path of the Mystic-Wizard, in which the nondual insight is fundamental, the farther you go along the path, the more severely unethical behavior will be corrected. If you are not prepared to give up harming others with speech or magic, it is best not to head down this path at all. When you know what you are doing is wrong, making the error elicits a much more significant corrective consequence than a mistake coming from simple ignorance.

Yet despite this, know that we all make unconscious mistakes all the time. Unconscious dualistic thinking and actions always follow us and are why there are inner purification exercises in all mystical and magical traditions. Self-purification with divine help is an integral part of the practice. To be willing to continually purify our unconscious intentions is to recognize, accept, and take responsibility for managing our dualistic nature. We will always have dualistic subpersonalities that get bitter and want to lash out. Our job is to recognize them, process the emotional content, and then see through them into truth. This work is always present in human form; beware of anyone who tells you they are done or complete. Stating that you're finished with purification work is like saying you're done washing your car or taking showers. It means you do not understand where you are and the nature of existence.

THE INNER ROUND TABLE, PART 1: TALKING TO YOUR REPRESSED SELF

In this technique, you go to the inner Round Table and take your seat in the chair of sovereignty. Then you summon up a part of yourself that needs attention and love. In this way, you begin a dialogue with your repressed selves. With kindness, you can love those parts of yourself and beam golden light into them.

In the inner world, raise your left hand over your head; put your right hand over the part of you that is hurt and needs love. Feel a beam of golden light from a divine being come in through your left hand and out through your right. Do this with love and compassion.

This process is an act of feeding yourself the love you need. The concept was created by Lama Tsultrim Allione, an American teacher of Tibetan Buddhism. You can find it and the journey she took to discover it laid out in her book *Feeding Your Demons: Ancient Wisdom for Resolving Inner Conflict*.

Feeding the hungry parts of yourself helps you manage the various regressed aspects of yourself and grow them up into more adult versions. Feeding your hungry selves is also a life-long process that can be brought into your practice as needed. Essentially, any time you find yourself stuck in a regressive state, you can be sure a young part of yourself needs love and acceptance. It is your responsibility to help that part of yourself, which takes the same kind of time, patience, and compassion that you would give to any other person. In truth, if you spend more time growing yourself up in this way, your outer relationships will go much better. The struggles in external relationships are often caused by parts of yourself that cannot manage adult relationships and act out their issues.

THE INNER ROUND TABLE, PART 2: TALKING TO YOUR ENEMIES

Now instead of talking to a part of yourself, it is time to talk to an "enemy." Go to the inner Round Table, but this time summon up another person, dead or alive, with whom you are in conflict. Then speak what you need to say to that person; get it off your chest until you are fully complete. When done, dissolve that person into pure Awareness and realize who you were talking to the entire time. You have been working out your issues with Awareness itself. By disidentifying with people and seeing them as Awareness, you release yourself and them from the dualistic belief that you are you and they are they.

This exercise is potent and needs to be done as part of an ongoing practice. Our dualistic mind is constantly unconsciously getting annoyed with others. But every time you see through them, you set yourself free. This process has a powerful long-term effect of slowly detaching you from the delusion that others do not share your same Awareness.

This process of seeing through the surface self is hard but liberating work. Garchen Rinpoche spent twenty years in a Chinese prison for fighting against the Chinese when they invaded Tibet. His life was made difficult, and he had endless reasons to be angry at the guards and the Chinese people. He could have become a bitter, mean person. Instead, he used every moment as part of his practice. He is the most loving person I have ever met and has many thousands of Chinese followers.

If you are unwilling to see through people to Awareness, that is about you, not about your enemies. If you choose not to see, you are the one imprisoning yourself. If you do not actively work to see, you can quickly become attached to being the victim. We all have varying degrees of attachment to our stories and can always fall back into them.

SOUL RETRIEVAL: A SHAMANIC TECHNIQUE FOR INTEGRATION

We all have slivers of ourselves hiding in places inside us, and they will not come out. You can journey to find one and bring it back with you or have someone who is trained do it for you. However, you will need to work on why that part was hiding, or it will likely return to hiding. In some ways, it is better to do the work I described above and clear the place inside, make it safe to integrate yourself, and then retrieve the part of you that has been hiding. Think of it this way: would you come out of some happy hiding place inside your consciousness if the reasons you went there are still roaming around?

If you ever become a healer, always seek permission from the person and the soul of the person you are dealing with before retrieval. The process of healing and healing work is timed quite carefully by the soul, and to do it too early or too late can cause problems. I have been doing soul retrievals since the early 1990s. However, I will not do one if a person is not trained in inner-world techniques. In my experience, the person will not likely complete the integration process if they cannot do the surrounding healing work.

The techniques laid out above for transformation and healing are some of those I've found most useful in doing this work and in performing the maintenance required to keep up with unfolding growth. If you want to arise and engage with the archetypes of the Wizard and the Mystic in a balanced way and learn to control the inner fire that will create your light body, then you will have to clear the stage. In that process, you will discover that the wounds received become the pathway not only to your healing but also to the exact shape of how you will arise as a spiritualized being.

I wish you well on this path and in your clearing the way for your ascent.

HABITUATING YOUR AWARENESS OF AWARENESS AND THE SPIRITUAL DIMENSION

What you pay attention to becomes habituated or conditioned into your unconscious. So, suppose you gently pay attention to ever-present unconditioned Awareness. In that case, your true nature and its self-liberating activity become parts of the stream of your mental and emotional life. So, too, with being aware of your spiritual allies. Both your spiritual partners and the field of Awareness are always with you, but your focus cannot be on them at every moment, as you have things to do and to pay attention to that we will simply call "your life." So, what to do?

Let's start with what not to do. Don't try extremely hard to pay attention to Awareness and your inner allies all the time. In some mystic systems, the recommendation is to do just that. In my experience, an overfocus on Awareness is essentially a recipe for abandoning the practice altogether. Overfocus means the egoic self tries hard to never lose sight of the truth. The problem is that the egoic structure that is in the way of sensing the presence of Awareness is the very thing looking really hard for it. Instead, choose to generate a subtle, daily, noncoercive intention to notice what has always been there. Then, throughout the day, you will find little moments that remind you of the presence of Awareness and your allies. It is much like intending to reach out and text a friend that day but not writing it down as a task. Make awareness something you would like to do, with no "should" energy involved. It takes some mental finesse and practice to pull this off, because the mind wants to have things to hunt. Save that instinct for those tasks you must do for work and to sustain your life. This practice is much more energetically subtle.

You can use all kinds of little signposts to help you notice throughout the day. For instance, whenever you see an image that embodies spaciousness, love, or beauty anywhere in real life or in the digital world, intend for it to remind you to take a deep breath and notice. Spaciousness is always there, and Awareness is always nudging you, just like a big dog gently leaning against your leg. Set a gentle intention to be available to Awareness like you might be available to a friend. Decide that it is meaningful for you to be connected and aware, and Awareness and your spiritual allies will find you.

Over time, many years, you will find it easier to notice. Eventually, you may even cross a tipping point when you are, in a subtle unconscious way, aware of Awareness and your spiritual allies most of the time. This is a beautiful reality to live in, for the mind's hunt is mostly over, and you need only go hunting when inspired by the soul to do so. And in those cases, when you do hunt, the search happens playfully as a natural expression of the ornament of Awareness.

From a biochemical perspective, every time you notice Awareness and take a breath, you will get a little dopamine hit. This will encourage you in a gentle fashion to keep noticing. Bear in mind that you will need to slowly address the other ways you get your dopamine hits, which may include getting attention from others, ordering things online, or looking at your phone every time you get a notification. The process of altering your being is partly about noticing and partly about cutting away the things that distract you and compete with Awareness.

We are using the same methods here that social media corporations use to get your attention but for our own spiritual growth and well-being. At some point, you will have to make essential choices about what you cut out and what you allow to enter the field of your attention. The digital world is not an innocent bystander in your life. It is deliberately using sophisticated methods of conditioning to try to keep you addicted to coming back to it for your dopamine hit. Let us use those same subtle methods for our own benefit and kick out the machine that wants to control us and get us to open our wallet. Our goal is to gain control of ourselves and, with the help of the soul, to open our hearts to wisdom, love, and compassion, our throats to joy and sacred speech, our minds to creative inner vision, and our bodies to our golden energetic bliss-body. All these potential aspects of our being are the rewards of the Way of the Mystic-Wizard. For those who are genuinely called to the path, these rewards are the gold of life and the true purpose of life.

SPACIOUSNESS IS ALWAYS THERE, AND AWARENESS IS ALWAYS NUDGING YOU.

THE BALANCE BETWEEN PURPOSE
AND PLAY AND THE WISE FOOL:
THE END POINT

One of the problems often experienced on the quest for spiritual development is overseriousness. The path of the Mystic-Wizard is about attempting to be happy, and psychological research has shown that what makes people happy is not being overly serious. If you have a personality and an approach to life that is all purpose, all meaning, all suffering simply to get noble things done (save the planet, save the forests, save the whales), then you will dry out and disconnect from your soul. If you lose enthusiasm, your life becomes joyless, and so do you.

Overseriousness about fixing the world is a problem from the nondual perspective, because there is absolutely nothing wrong with the world—there never was, and there never will be. There is nothing a human being could ever do anywhere that breaks or fixes anything. It is simply not possible.

Despite this, purpose is still fundamental to our well-being, because the opposite of purpose is pointlessness. Pointlessness is when people feel like there is no value to their life, and particularly when there is no point to their suffering. This leads to nihilism, the sense that life has no meaning, so why bother. We are better off with a system where life matters; otherwise, we check out.

Purpose is work that has meaning to it. You are creating something; you are fixing something. You are helping the environment, you are helping people, you are building a new way of living in the world, you are creating a piece of art that inspires others. I am writing a book about practice, for instance.

Purpose is incredibly important and valuable for our unfolding as a species and for finding your authentic destiny.

Yet, to *over*purpose your life is to set yourself up for an imbalance, which is why when you go back to the Life Compass, in the east you find play. Play is the opposite of purpose. Play is for its own sake. Play is, in essence, what the universe is doing. Everything is just happening: the wind is moving, the planet is spinning, the sun is burning, and children are playing. Access to the instinct for play is vital for staying connected to the truth of the natural state of existence around us.

It is the balance of play and purpose in your life that is key. If you lean to the play side, you can become frivolous, and if you lean to the purposeful work side, you can become too serious. The balance of work and play is an attempt to embody the contradiction that nothing needs to be done, and yet doing things is what we are up to as a species. You are stretched between the horns of being and doing, and if you can hold each horn in one hand and ride on top of the great mother cow's head, then you can move along the path with greater equipoise and grace.

Part of your practice then is learning how to play. The further along the path you go, the more you will encounter unprovoked or unmanufactured joy. If you have not engaged with play and cultivated it, you may experience difficult moral questions about what you have done to "deserve" this joy. This implies that you must "do" something to earn joy. But you do not have to, and you cannot. Bliss is not a game of exchange with the divine. It just is, and your access to joy and bliss is an endowment, not a wage for good behavior.

In time you become a living example to the people around you of what is possible. Imagine wandering through the world, going back and forth at will, between intuitively determining your process of being engaged in the seriousness of the world and then engaging in the practice of playfulness and openness.

In Carol S. Pearson's book, *Awakening the Heroes Within: Twelve Archetypes to Help Us Find Ourselves and Transform Our World*, the last archetype is the Wise Fool. As an example of the Wise Fool, we will again reference Yoda from the *Star Wars* saga.

Luke Skywalker heads off to Dagobah to find the great Jedi master Yoda. Luke is seeking a mighty Jedi master, who he hopes can teach his egoic self to be super powerful. This is an appropriate adolescent and young adult behavioral imperative.

Luke finally gets to the jungle planet, and there are no roads, no civilization, none of the symbols of external egoic power, and he is annoyed. He is setting up camp, and he is struggling. Then a little green creature shows up. Go watch the first scene in which Yoda appears, and observe it, because there, at that moment, Yoda is embodying the Wise Fool. He is poking around with his little stick, looking into Luke's refrigerator, and he is pulling crap out, throwing it around like a toddler amused by it all.

Luke is all seriousness. He is all about finding the Jedi master and becoming one himself. He is all about getting the power he is going to use to defeat the evil Empire. He will save the world(s) and has had this attitude since the beginning of the first movie. Now and then he has a moment of childlike enthusiasm; however, mostly he gets serious pretty quickly, especially after he loses his aunt and uncle and friends in the war. This is a natural development of seriousness based on seeing suffering. It is fine, but if the archetypal path of the heroic self leads only to more and more seriousness, Yoda should be the most serious of us all.

But Yoda is there to poke at that self-importance Luke has developed. Luke has no idea that the little green guy is, in fact, the great Jedi master. Then there is a beautiful moment when Luke gets frustrated with Yoda, and he says to himself, "I don't know what am I doing here. We're wasting our time."

Yoda stops playing and takes a deep breath, and then looks

YOU NEED NOT "DO" ANYTHING TO EARN JOY. IT IS AN ENDOWMENT, NOT A WAGE.

up and starts talking to somebody else, someone and something not embodied. Luke does not understand. Yoda is deeply connected to the Force and the inner world and all the souls of the former Jedi masters. He says, "I cannot teach him. The boy has no patience. . . . He is not ready."

Luke is puzzled but eventually realizes that this annoying creature is Yoda and that Yoda is talking to Obi-Wan. Luke says, "I won't fail you—I'm not afraid."

Only then is Yoda deadly serious. He knows what is at stake. He says, "Oh, you will be. You will be."

Yoda's seriousness is couched in the playful amusement of the Wise Fool. He can flip between these aspects of his being at will; Luke cannot. In that scene, the entire journey from the Warrior archetype to Wise Fool and master is illustrated. Yoda is aware of Awareness (the Force) at all times. Yoda's seriousness is guided, informed, and practical because it emerges spontaneously out of the Great Perfection. Open, spacious Awareness and bliss-joy are the source-field of all that is, and so they make an excellent launchpad for awakened, wise, serious, and compassionate action.

This balance of play and purpose is woven into the way of the Mystic-Wizard from the get-go. It is hard to access the Wise Fool at the end of the archetypal journey of a human life if you have not been entertaining the Fool all along. If you develop a vast ego identity around seriousness and purpose, spirit is going to smack you around hard until that mask shatters. It is a painful process if you are overserious. This is challenging for people, more challenging than my description sounds, because in the face of all the pain and suffering in the world, it appears only a serious response is a reasonable response. But that is not the nondual truth. It is indeed the egoic truth that suffering and pain must be fought against at all times. However, the nondual truth and the path of the Mystic-Wizard are different. Suffering and the transformations of our lives are part of the process.

Moving up the spiral over ten thousand years is part of the process. Riding the Tree of Life, called Yggdrasil, which means "terrible steed," is, in fact, painful and terrible. Yet nothing is broken here; it is as it is. We engage from the bliss-field because it is the most effective way to engage and do our soul's work.

If you have any questions about the validity of this reality, watch the movie *Life Is Beautiful.* Roberto Benigni plays a Jewish Italian bookshop owner who employs his fertile imagination to shield his son from the horrors of internment in a Nazi concentration camp. This movie embodies the sometimes insane and torturous predicament of incarnated life and why the path toward self-evolution is of such importance. The film is a comedy-drama, an apt genre description of the balance of play and purpose in the face of horrible evil and the extraordinarily positive effect that choosing this perspective can have on those around you.

In the end, there is no other game in town than life, and no one gets out alive. The game of life involves all the different values in Spiral Dynamics, all the different stages of life, and all the different archetypes and Enneagram types, along with a journey designed to transform us. It requires a loss of innocence. It requires that we become orphans. It requires that we develop the Warrior, Lover, and passionate Creator to go through this journey and be shaped by it. Loss is threaded into the weaving of reality. One can only assume (at least I do) that if there were any other way to do it, it would have been done that way already. We struggle and toil so that the formless can become "vocal with speech," as Emerson put it, and I see no way around that.

So then, make sure that your practice includes games and play for their own sake. Find practices of play that you enjoy— gardening, playing video games, playing tennis, knitting—just playfulness for your own sake. Everyone plays differently. Some people like to create something. They are crafters, like my wife.

They enjoy making stuff, bread, jewelry, meals, and all kinds of different things. Other people need to play something competitive and challenging so they can win. Allow yourself to win, to enjoy playing and winning. Other people, like me, have to string narratives together and do so in role-playing games (RPGs). Other people need strategy games like chess. Some people need to rebuild cars. Some people need to go hiking through the woods and enjoy looking at the flowers and the trees. Some sing, some dance, all for fun.

Play is an essential part of practice because we are embedded in the world. The Way of the Mystic-Wizard isn't an escape fantasy. There is nowhere to go. We are all going to be gone soon enough and in the inner world, so let us enjoy the process of being out here as much as we can, while still recognizing that purpose and contribution are also part of the game of life.

Lastly, when we have integrated play and embraced life on its own terms, then the meaningful and important work we do arises from a place of acceptance and ease, making us more effective and capable. We are much less effective when we are desperately hell-bent on fixing reality and the brokenness of the world. Most desperation prevents us from connecting to inspiration. Through loving what is, as Byron Katie would say, we model the deepest meditation view that exists: the view that there is nothing wrong here at all. And yet our awakened hearts' spontaneous response to suffering prompts inspired action that works to address that suffering in precisely the way that is needed at that moment, just as Yoda would do.

This is the effect of truth and compassion uniting in the beautiful poetry of awakened action. This is the speech of the grail that heals all wounds and restores the wasteland to abundance. May embodying this capacity be your legacy.

Journey Ten
TREE OF LIFE MERGE

Take a deep breath and relax. Prepare to move into the inner world. Imagine that you are floating in a field of mist. Become aware of the mist around you. Start descending down through the mist. *Five*, *four*, deeper. As you go, become aware of Awareness. Form is emptiness. Out of that emptiness arises the mist and the forms and Awareness itself. *Three*, deeper. *Two*, deeper. *One*, deeper still till you are floating in the radiant black void.

Pure emptiness stretches infinitely in all directions. You become aware of Awareness. It enfolds you. It is aware of you. And you are resting in that space, letting the subtle bliss-field of Awareness heal you and transform you. It purifies you from your toes, all the way up your body, to the top of your head, to the tips of your fingers. Become aware of a golden radiant light that emerges from the void.

That golden light is the healing presence of joy and bliss. From that field, an endless ocean of golden bliss Awareness, a blessed body begins to form—a shape, your shape, your immortal bliss-body. Your consciousness rests. There is emptiness within. Emptiness without. Awareness within. Awareness without. Your whole form is filled with the golden bliss-body of light. Here, you can allow the deepest level of healing to take place.

Set the intention that the healing bliss moves all the way outward into your physical form, into your nerves, your whole nervous system, every cell of your physical form. It knows where to go. It knows which cells and which nerves to touch slowly, perfectly, gently. The bliss-field adjusts. Your energetic and physical bodies more perfectly embody, sense, and experience the bliss-field. Each one of your energy centers is permeated by the bliss-energy of unconditioned pure Awareness until, finally, serene stillness sets in. The work is done for now. And the journey begins.

As always, before you, out of the bliss-field, comes the shape of a door. In the swirling mist, the door to your inner world. Your bliss-body floats up to the door and notices that with a mere thought, a mere intention, you can simply dissolve the door. Step through or float through, and reform the door behind you. In the glowing golden corridor of the inner castle, start walking down the hall. Walk straight past the stairway that leads to the common room, toward the light at the end of the corridor.

You come to the end of the corridor and step out into a cloister walk. There at the center is a great radiant tree, and you see it as its energy body. The roots, the trunk and branches, the leaves, the enormous, enormous Milky Way above. And you notice the fruit of the tree, the energetic apples that fall. Streams of energy fall down to the ground, go into the ground, deep in the ground, nourishing the roots.

There at the base of the central taproot is a great pool of radiant energy. And the tree draws the energy up, all the way up through the roots to the trunk and branches. Become aware of Awareness. Notice that this is the bliss-body of the great Tree of Life, wondrous to behold. It calls to you, calls to you, *Join*. It wishes you to join with it. Walk or float toward the center of the tree, under its branches. And there, beside the tree, you sense the presence of the old man. Maybe you can see him, maybe not, the one who is a master of riding through the tree. He holds the space in the door. Go to the trunk of the energy tree and step in. Take a deep breath.

Allow your own energy body to merge with that of the tree. Feel your feet grow into the roots, your arms up into the branches. Feel the wondrous expanse of creation. Now let the tree speak to you through intuition, image. Listen to the message it has for you, or just share in the bliss of its existence.

At the top of the tree, a great energetic eagle rests, and next to the eagle, a small squirrel made of energy. The eagle and the squirrel communicate, and then the squirrel begins to climb down the tree. It climbs all the way down into the central core, where you are. It comes up to you, and in its mouth it has an acorn. It takes it out with its little paws, this glowing radiant acorn from the celestial realms. Hold out your hand. You are given the acorn, and you know where to put it.

Then the squirrel continues its journey down the tree. You sense its journey all the way down to the base, deeper, down, all the way to the pool. And there it gathers up something from the sisters that tend the pool, and it begins its climb up the tree again. Climbing up your energetic body. At last it stands next to you again with something else in its mouth. Out it spits a stone, a black, radiant stone shining with the clear light of Awareness . . . the source point of all existence. Take this gift and place it where it needs to be in your energy body.

The squirrel heads back up the tree to see the eagle.

Now focus your awareness and sit in a meditation pose inside the tree, at the base that connects the trunk to the ground. Sense the place where roots become trunk. These are your roots. From this place you can create. You can set an intention.

Set an intention for yourself, the world, for your life, for connection to your own soul. Hold out your hand and see what symbol arises there as a manifestation of that intention, the intention that comes from you and your soul combined. Cup that symbol, and then gently reach out and bury it in the ground by the tree so that it may grow.

And now, far above you in the highest realms of the tree, you sense the presence of one of your great teachers. The energy of that teacher, that divine being, descends through the tree, comes all the way down, enters the top of your head. And you begin to take on the shape and form of their body, merging, acquiring the bliss-body of one of the fully enlightened awakened ones. Sense their love for you. You will remember this form and this body, be able to return to it as needed in your meditations.

Now with that form integrated into your bliss-body of light, stand up and step out of the tree. It's time to return.

Walk out from under the great branches, through the gate of the cloister. Walk to the corridor and start walking or floating down the corridor, bringing with you all the knowledge, energy, and subtleness of the many realms. You come at last to the doorway to the inner world. With an intention, the doorway dissolves. Float through, turn, and reform the door.

Take both your hands and then gently rest them, not against the door, but very, very close to it. Feel the energy of the door, the radiant bliss-body of the door itself, and bring your hands together in front of your heart. Say in your mind, *It has begun.*

And now you are floating up through the mist. *One*, higher. *Two, three.* Coming back to this world, integrating all the energies from these bliss-bodies into your physical form and your nervous system. *Four.* Wiggling your toes and your fingers. Sensing the body getting in perfect alignment. Bringing the energy home with you to give out into the physical world and your life journey. *Five.* Finally, open your eyes, and you are fully returned to the outer world.

Take a deep breath, and give thanks to the beings that guided you today. Then take notes in your journal.

PART ELEVEN

JOINING THE QUEST

What is left
is only This—
the answer was always the same.

We've reached the end of this book but not the end of the journey. In Part Eleven, I address how to continue on the quest if you feel called to do so.

NDS, THE QUEST & NEXT STEPS

The Institute for Nondual Shamanism (NDS) is the organization I created to investigate the merging of nonduality and shamanism. From NDS and earlier courses I taught grew the Way of the Mystic-Wizard and this book. NDS is an educational nondual shamanic spiritual organization whose members are dedicated to genuine transfiguration of the egoic self and integration with the soul and Awareness. We seek individual development with collective support.

As a transformational community, NDS is devoted to helping people awaken to pure Awareness, develop a daily spiritual practice, and build a connection to their soul and their compassionate spiritual allies. The ultimate purpose and intention of NDS is to support the transformational process in your life and in our species. To clarify what that means, it might be helpful to look at what NDS is not. It is not a church, temple, religion, club, cult, friend group, or family. It's not a counseling session. It's not a monastery, university, or workshop course, or primarily about outer-world expression. NDS does not proselytize or promise any particular goal or outcome, or charge any fees for participation. The Way of the Mystic-Wizard is a uniquely soul-guided path, and for those genuinely called to it, the rewards of cultivating a connection to soul and pure Awareness are enough.

Every year in NDS we quest for the five hallows and deepen our relationship with the inner world and our capacity to mediate the hallows' power into the outer world. In each season, we go on spirit-led journeys. In those journeys, synchronistic events take place in the inner world that contribute to our individual transformation and the development of insight and wisdom. Each member is responsible for the mastery they have developed and their contribution, if any, to the external world. There is a deep trust that develops in such a working group.

NDS has much in common with the tradition of pilgrimage. Pilgrimage is essentially putting yourself through a physical outer-world journey, typically visiting sacred sites, for the purposes of spiritual transformation. The physical challenges that play out on the trip are part of the transformational process. A good friend named Gil Stafford wrote a great book on the nature of pilgrimage titled *Wisdom Walking: Pilgrimage as a Way of Life*, and he has taken people on numerous journeys in Ireland. He says pilgrimage is a metaphor for human life itself.

Making a transformational journey is what we do in NDS, only the trips are in the inner world rather than the outer world. That doesn't mean they are less potent on a psychological level. Each kind of pilgrimage, inner and outer, has its own merits, challenges, and requirements. One of the advantages of the external world pilgrimage is encountering the natural world's healing energies and the challenge of the elements and the path. An outer journey challenges the body and thus the mind, emotions, and egoic self. Walking fifteen miles a day tends to burn through your resistance to genuine insight, as it takes you out of your comfort zone. When I was eighteen, I spent three weeks with a group of nine people hiking through the Rocky Mountains. It was arduous and at times dangerous, and by the time I rejoined civilization, the stillness of my mind was profound.

One of the advantages of an inner pilgrimage is that you can do it over an extended time and without stopping your life.

The inner quest also allows for easier access. Applications like Zoom enable us to participate in the quest from all over the world with little financial or time commitment. In this era, removing barriers to experiential spiritual learning is essential. It is one of the primary motivations for this book and NDS.

If you have read this far, then the Way of the Mystic-Wizard may well be the path you are called to follow for a time. However, if not, no worries. Take anything you learned from this book and find your way forward. Your soul has its own path for you, and you have permission to use any of the ideas I presented in this book to develop your own practice and approach. Find your way to your practice and your soul. The rest will take care of itself.

If you feel called to work with NDS more directly, a path is open to you as well. First, follow the self-study course outlined in Appendix A. It is based in part on the course I taught for many years. It will take about a year to complete and will walk you through the four seasons. There are books to read, journeys to go on, and side courses to take. This book that you have just read is the textbook for that course. Use it as a reference as needed. After you have worked through the material, if interested, reach out via the Contact page on my website and an NDS member will respond to help you start the application process for joining a working group. As you work through the process, and with your soul as your guide, you can determine if NDS is a good fit for you. Acceptance in a working group is not guaranteed, but we treat every application with care. Please note, NDS is an entirely volunteer organization, so response time may vary. If you are genuinely interested, be patient and yet also persistent.

There is no financial cost for NDS membership. Your own time and effort will be your investment. Once accepted into a working group, you can leave at any time and come back at any time. In addition, every year after Midsummer, before the

"THIS IS NOT A CLUB. THIS IS A CRUCIBLE FOR CHANGE AND GROWTH, AND THAT IS WHAT BINDS US."
—NDS MEMBER

quest begins, everyone has an opportunity to ask themselves if they want to continue, take a break, or leave it all behind. Any of those options is acceptable, and moving on is not seen as a betrayal. In addition, you can stop coming at any point, and no one will bother you. You can stop and then come back later, and no one will ask where you have been. In the Arthurian grail quest stories, seekers often vanished and reappeared to each other as their paths crossed and recrossed. Sometimes you travel together on pilgrimage, and at other times you are alone for a spell. Both are legitimate, necessary, and important for learning and growth. Some years we have many travelers, and other years we have a smaller group. Each time, the group is as the spiritual world deems it to be. This organic approach to learning can take some time to acclimate to, because most of us were trained in schools and religious organizations that require specific egoic commitments and associated monetary costs. NDS is calling upon a much older tradition. The only egoic commitment here is to listen to your soul and inner allies.

SEEKERS OFTEN CROSS PATHS, THEN TRAVEL ALONE, AND THEN CROSS PATHS AGAIN.

The activities of NDS are supported by anonymous donations made once a year. The costs to keep NDS going are minimal, such as website upkeep, so we do not need to gather significant resources. In fact, not working with many resources frees everyone up to listen for what wants to arise next rather than worry about the investment made and the expected return. This is the same way pilgrimage works. You walk, and if you stop, you stop. The choice is yours. There is no finish line for the quest, or awards or certificates or degrees conferred. There is the relationship with the soul and your awareness of Awareness and the new life that blossoms from that connection.

The goal of NDS is not to expand or grow or monetize itself. NDS is not trying to become anything more than it already is, a loosely affiliated group of Mystic-Wizards who support each other in our inner quest for mastery of the five hallows. We do not advertise, and we have no business model or aspirations of any kind other than our individual spiritual aspirations. The entire endeavor is empowered by the inner world, and if and when the inner world withdraws its energy from the group, NDS will vanish. If you have come upon this book many years after its publication, NDS may no longer exist in the outer world. Such is the way.

May you find your own way, with meaningful sacrifices made and authentic rewards gathered.

Journey Eleven
THE STAG LORD

Now we begin the final journey to meet the Stag Lord, from this place where you are aware of Awareness, aware of a golden bliss-field. You are surrounded by this golden mist, this presence, and you are floating down, *five, four*, deeper, *three*, deeper, *two*, deeper still. There is only formlessness. There are no things yet in the universe. And then *one*.

There, floating in the mist, you see a door, a portal. You generate a body made of light, energetic, beautiful. You float up to the doorway, reaching out with your hand. Sense the inner world, forming, creating, emerging out of pure Awareness. The door clicks and slides open, and you float into the castle of the mind, going down the corridor, reaching out with your hand of light, tracing your fingers along the stone, light trailing from them.

You take a right and go down the stairway that curves down into the common room. The room takes shape in front of you. The fire comes to life, and your cat, the map, the chess table. Now move through the room and go up the stairs on the other side until you come to the entrance to the portal room. Move in, turn right, and there at the end of the room, a shimmering portal awaits. Go up to the portal, and, as you do, bring forth your traveling robes, staff, belt, ring, and sword, and boots, and a bag—everything you need to move through existence. All of it is made of light and empty, but it is there, and it is not there. It is both.

Step up to the shimmering portal and place your hands into it. Feel the energy move into your light body, charging you, purifying you. Feel how it moves out from your light body into your physical body in the outer world, also purifying your physical body, and then step through the portal.

You are standing on a hillside overlooking the beautiful forest. The clouds have broken above, and the sun shines through onto the snowy landscape.

Now you walk down the hillside into the field and go across the field until you come to the edge of the forest and the standing stone. There are two ravens in the woods, and two wolves. Go up to the stone and place a hand on the stone. Feel the strength, the power, and the solidity. Let that strength move into your form.

Out of the forest steps your animal guardian, bringing you love and power. Connect with your animal. In the cold, share breath. Breathe each other's breath, and then allow yourself to merge with your animal, bringing the power of your animal into your form and vice versa. Feel it infuse your energy body, feel its strength.

You move into the forest, guarded and protected by the wolves and the ravens, down the path leading you deeper into the woods. You come to the stream that is frozen over. Carefully cross the stream, and deeper and deeper into the forest you go. As you get closer to the inner grove, along the path to the right side you notice two stones for the first time. On the left two large boulders, two large stones, form a kind of gateway. On them appear to be ancient carvings. Notice the carvings.

Step through the stone gateway and you are at the edge of the grove, and there at the center by itself is the lonely fire. Someone has been keeping it going through the night. Go up to the fire and warm your hands. The fire gives a small portion of itself as a flame that lands in your palm. It shall lead the way. It flies off through the air, taking you on a path to the north. Follow along.

The snow gets deeper. The clouds above cover the sky until finally you come to the edge of the forest, and before you is a great hill. Behind the hill, you can see the mountains rising, but here before you, a path winds around the hill and up to the top. At the very top of the hill, the stag stands between two trees. Move up the hill, following the path that winds around until at last you come again to another stone gateway.

The top of the hill is a flat plateau where the stag waits. He reaches out with one of his hooves and pushes the snow away; down below is some grass. Step through the gateway, with the intention of meeting with the Stag Lord. Walk up to this ancient being who has existed since the beginning of the universe. Reach out and place your hand on his forehead and commune.

The Stag Lord indicates the gateway that the two birch trees create. You see that there is a pathway through, and the pathway is for you alone. He guards the way. If you are ready to step onto the path to the next stage of this life, this season, then walk through the gateway of the trees. See what you see . . .

And now it is time to return, but before you go, offer a blessing to the land. Lean over, place both your palms on the ground, and gently give thanks for the earth, the Stag Lord, and the paths.

Now it is time to move back down the hillside, spiraling around, until the path at last comes to the place where it joins the forest. You notice something you did not notice before—that at the bottom of the hill there is a cave entrance and a stone archway. Out of the cave comes water from a small spring, and a small trickle of water has begun to flow down to the stream. Now walk along the stream's edge and back into the forest. There the wolves and the ravens meet you and guide you back to the central grove. And there you see the fire again, and the small fire elemental returns to the flame from which it came.

You leave the central grove and move back through the forest, along the path and through the gateway of the stones, over the frozen stream, back, back, back to the edge of the forest, where the standing stone is. And there on the standing stone, the image of a man with antlers is impressed into the stone: the Stag Lord. Now give thanks to your animal guardians and helpers as they separate from you, and then move across the field and up the hill. Turn and look out over the forest. Sense the presence of the Stag Lord, all throughout the forest. He stands at the edge, sees you, bows his head.

Now turn and step through the shimmering portal. Then go back through the portal room, down into the common room, and over to the map where you see that in the north there is a hill, and upon it the image of the two trees, the gateway to new life, and the symbol of the Stag Lord. Place your hand on it. Here is the place you return when it is time to move on, time to transition from one thing to the next, to start a new life.

And now it is time to return to the outer world. Leave the map and go up the stairway. Turn left, and go to the back of the door, which opens. Step out into the golden mist, and the door shuts. Place both hands on the door, then say in your own mind, *It has begun.*

And now you are rising up through the mist. *One*, *two*, aware of Awareness, *three*, aware of your body, *four*, your fingers and your toes reintegrating all the energy of the inner world into your physical form and all that you need to remember into your physical mind, *five*.

Open your eyes, and you have returned to the outer world, completely intact, integrated. Now take some time with your journal to write about what stood out in this particular journey.

The Land of the Ancient Ones
(The Inner World)

I have come to the end and found that
what I was seeking was with me
from the beginning.

APPENDIX A: SELF-STUDY COURSE

If we were to meet in person and discuss a self-study course for the Way of the Mystic-Wizard, the readings and courses below are the core of what I would suggest you investigate first. Each is a treasure; however, that does not mean that you must read every word.

Let your soul be your pilot: learn to listen for the next bit of wisdom or knowledge you need. Learning is an art form and a creative process. It unfolds like life, with many unexpected turns and wonders. Let go the idea of studying the way you did in school—to accomplish something or to "get it done." The Way of the Mystic-Wizard is a path and a journey—simply put, it's a way through life. For those called to it, the rewards of journey are found on the path itself, for the way never ends.

BOOKS AND READINGS

Awakening the Heroes Within: Twelve Archetypes to Help Us Find Ourselves and Transform Our World by Carol S. Pearson

Feeding Your Demons: Ancient Wisdom for Resolving Inner Conflict by Tsultrim Allione

Growing Yourself Back Up: Understanding Emotional Regression by John Lee

A Little Book on the Human Shadow by Robert Bly

A Mind at Home with Itself: How Asking Four Questions Can Free Your Mind, Open Your Heart, and Turn Your World Around by Byron Katie and Stephen Mitchell

"Spiral Dynamics – A Way of Understanding Human Nature" by Sharon Ede (https://www.magethenovel.com/blog/spiral-dynamics-a-way-of-understanding-human-nature)

Synchronicity: The Inner Path of Leadership by Joseph Jaworski

Weaving Fate: Hypersigils, Changing the Past & Telling True Lies by Aidan Wachter

What We May Be: Techniques for Psychological and Spiritual Growth through Psychosynthesis by Piero Ferrucci

The Wisdom of the Enneagram: The Complete Guide to Psychological and Spiritual Growth for the Nine Personality Types by Don Richard Riso and Russ Hudson

AUDIO COURSES

These courses can all be found on Sounds True (soundstrue.com).

Radiant Mind: Teachings and Practices to Awaken Unconditioned Awareness by Peter Fenner, PhD

Realizing Unconditioned Awareness: Nondual Experience as the Ultimate Medicine by Peter Fenner, PhD

Shamanic Meditations: Guided Journeys for Insight, Vision, and Healing by Sandra Ingerman

APPENDIX B: ADDITIONAL RESOURCES

These are a few of the texts, teachers, organizations, and lineages that are mentioned in this book or have influenced the Way of the Mystic-Wizard.

LINEAGES AND INFLUENCES

Shamanism and Druidry

Norse and Anglo-Saxon Shamanism

Egyptian Shamanism

Foundation for Shamanic Studies: Core Shamanism

Martin Duffy: Irish Shamanism

Sandra Ingerman: Shamanism

Caitlín and John Matthews: Arthurian and Celtic Shamanism and myth

Carla Meeske, Spirit Healer: Shamanic training

The Order of Bards, Ovates and Druids

Philip Carr-Gomm: Druidry

Nonduality

Adyashanti: True Meditation

Ascension Attitudes by Maharishi Sadashiva Isham (MSI)

His Eminence Garchen Rinpoche, The Kagyu Lineage of Tibetan Buddhism,
    Vajrayana Buddhism, Mahamudra, Dzogchen, and Deity Yoga

Peter Fenner and Radiant Mind: Teachings on nonduality and teacher training

Psychology

Roberto Assagioli: Psychosynthesis

James Hillman: Archetypal psychology

Carl Jung: Depth psychology

Tools and Theories

The Enneagram: The Enneagram Institute, Russ Hudson's books and courses

The Myers-Briggs Type Indicator (MBTI)

Values in Action Inventory of Strengths (VIA or VIA-IS) by Christopher
    Peterson and Martin Seligman

The Work by Byron Katie

BOOKS

Anam Cara: A Book of Celtic Wisdom by John O'Donohue

The Bardic Book of Becoming: An Introduction to Modern Druidry by Ivan McBeth with Fearn Lickfield

Black Elk Speaks by John G. Neihardt

The Crystal and the Way of Light: Sutra, Tantra, and Dzogchen by Chögyal Namkhai Norbu

The Eden Project: In Search of the Magical Other by James Hollis

The Eye of Spirit: An Integral Vision for a World Gone Slightly Mad by Ken Wilber

Falling Upward: A Spirituality for the Two Halves of Life by Richard Rohr

The Five Love Languages: How to Express Heartfelt Commitment to Your Mate by Gary Chapman

The Leap: The Psychology of Spiritual Awakening by Steve Taylor

The Magic of Pathworking: A Meditation Guide for Your Inner Vision by Simon Court

Memories, Dreams, Reflections by C. G. Jung

The Power of Myth by Joseph Campbell with Bill Moyers

Psychosynthesis: A Collection of Basic Writings by Roberto Assagiolo

Rainbow Body by Loel Guinness

A Religion of One's Own: A Guide to Creating a Personal Spirituality in a Secular World by Thomas Moore

Seek Teachings Everywhere: Combining Druid Spirituality with Other Traditions by Philip Carr-Gomm

Siddhartha by Hermann Hesse

The Soul's Code: In Search of Character and Calling by James Hillman

The Speech of the Grail: A Journey toward Speaking That Heals and Transforms by Linda Sussman

Spirit Marriage: Intimate Relationships with Otherworldly Beings by Megan Rose

Tao Te Ching by Lao Tzu, translation by Stephen Mitchell

The Tower of Alchemy: An Advanced Guide to the Great Work by David Goddard

The Treasure Within: An Archetypal Unfolding to Your Infinite Potential by Shannon Pernetti and Diane Steinbrecher

The Tree of Enchantment: Ancient Wisdom and Magic Practices of the Faery Tradition by Orion Foxwood

The Tree of Visions: Visionary Traditions of the Western World by David Nez

The Underworld Initiation: A Journey towards Psychic Transformation by R.J. Stewart

The Way of Wyrd by Brian Bates

Wisdom Walking: Pilgrimage as a Way of Life by Gil Stafford

COURSES

Awakening Kundalini: The Path to Radical Freedom by Lawrence Edwards

Awakening Your Light Body by Duane Packer

The Enneagram: Nine Gateways to Presence by Russ Hudson

The Tantric Consort: Awakening through Relationship by Reginald A. Ray

ORACLES AND TAROT DECKS

The Anubis Oracle: A Journey into the Shamanic Mysteries of Egypt by Nicki Scully

The Beowulf Oracle: Wisdom from the Northern Kingdoms by John Matthews and Virginia Chandler

The Complete Arthurian Tarot by Caitlín and John Matthews

The Druid Animal Oracle by Philip and Stephanie Carr-Gomm

The Enchanted Map Oracle Cards: A 54-Card Deck and Guidebook by Colette Baron-Reid

Mystic Wanderer Oracle Cards by Austeen Freeman

The Mystical Dream Tarot: Life Guidance from the Depths of Our Unconscious by Janet Piedilato

The Threads of Fate Oracle by Blaire Porter and Brit June

Sacred Traveler Oracle Cards: A 52-Card Deck and Guidebook by Denise Linn

OTHER RESOURCES

EnneaApp (enneaapp.com)

"Five Ways to Grow Back Up" (The Detour Method) YouTube video by John Lee

APPENDIX C: TOOL TEMPLATES

On the next pages you will find templates of the Life Compass and the Solar System of the Self. They are also available on the Book page of my website, matthewthomasbaker.com. (Several of the other illustrations are available for closer viewing as well.) You are welcome to makes copies of these for your personal use, but please respect the artist's copyright and do not distribute.

ACKNOWLEDGMENTS

I want to express my deepest gratitude to those who assisted in the creation of this book. First and foremost, the One, the Three, and the Inner Beloved, who all guide me.

Thank you to all those members of the Institute for Nondual Shamanism (NDS) who have been working diligently for years in the inner world for their transformation and for the betterment of the world: Aiden Kane, Janine Kane, Arielle Moosman, Francine Hershkowitz, and Sarah Whalen, and especially Shannon Pernetti, who wrote the foreword and whose support, wisdom, companionship, and suggestions have been priceless. Thank you to Shannon also for writing *The Treasure Within*, a book that encouraged me to write *The Way of the Mystic-Wizard*.

A special thanks to Callista Mincks for suggesting this book needed to be written, and for writing many of the footnotes that explain important terms and ideas, and to Chloe Dubisch, an invaluable editor who helped with early revisions of the book. Thank you to Matthew Spencer, who created the fabulous cover art titled *One-Eyed* as well as the interior illustrations and maps, all of which were constant reminders of the meaning of the project and the source of inspiration from which it flows. Special thanks to my editor and publisher, Karin Wiberg, for her dedication, enormous editorial talent, and commitment to the vision of creating a beautiful book. This book would not be what it is without her and her team at Clear Sight Books.

Thank you to both friends and colleagues who encouraged and supported this project and the course it is based on, especially John Silkey, an NDS member who read and edited an entire draft of the book, and Kim French, Sunita Przewlocki, Tamara Wells, John Perovich, Jennifer Quinn, Courtney Page-Bottorff, and Sabrina Husain Bajakian, who all provided moral support by helping me believe I had something worthwhile to say. Thank you also to John Newcomer, who has known me the longest and whose sense of humor and impeccable memory for our shared childhood proved invaluable throughout the pandemic, when this book began to take shape.

In addition, I would like to thank my spiritual mentors: professor of religion and true mystic, the late Ralph Slotten of Dickinson College; writer and spiritual teacher Philip Carr-Gomm for bringing Druidry to the world through the Order of Bards, Ovates and Druids, and acting as a mentor over these last thirty years; Stephanie Carr-Gomm, who with Philip ran the druid order and also created *The Druid Animal Oracle*, which was the magical start of my journey; Carla Meeske, my root shamanic teacher, for training me and for her endless enthusiasm for all my work; the London Open Drumming Group and Shenoah Taylor, who leads it and who created such a supportive community during the pandemic; Geoff Fitch, Terri O'Fallon, Tara DeNuccio, and Thomas McConkie for the Pacific Integral school and the GTC program; Peter Fenner for sharing his nondual teaching methods and for helping me live into the experience of unconditioned Awareness and for directly transmitting the bliss-field of emptiness; Byron Katie for The Work and for being in exactly the right place at the right moment; Ken Wilber for his hugely impactful pointing-out instructions in *The Eye of Spirit*; the late Makari Ishaya, for her support in the awakening process; Caitlín and John Matthews for *Hallowquest*; R.J. Stewart for *The Underworld Initiation* and for explaining and validating the transformative power of pathworking in a group; and Sandra Ingerman, for her book *Soul Retrieval*, which was the first book I read on Shamanism, and for encouraging me to write this book and seek out my own authentic shamanic expression and calling. Without these teachers and their many books and teachings, I would have had no shoulders to stand on and no hope of completing this project.

In addition, to His Eminence Garchen Rinpoche, I offer my deepest gratitude for generously taking me into the Drikung Kagyu Lineage and for the priceless empowerments that continue to unfold and support the awakening process. Thanks also to the late Derk Janssen, the Mystic-Wizard of Prescott, for believing in me, reading my stars, and long ago recognizing I would someday have something unique to offer the world. To Gil Stafford and Chad Sundin for their example of how to live into one's spiritual calling with all the challenges that entails. And to all the members of the five families group who, by hosting and embracing a meaningful community life informed by care and compassion, have made life worth living. You know who you are, and may you all thrive.

A special thanks for supporting and encouraging my path and life goes to my sister, Elizabeth Purcell; my brother, Charles Baker; my dear friend Randi Kent; and my dear deceased parents, whose unconditional support is what has made my life, this book, and this path possible.

Finally, thank you to my family: my wife, Betsy Rosenmiller, my sons, Owen and Nate Baker, and of course Chowder and Addie, who have passed on to the happy hunting grounds. They are the living treasure that keeps me going day to day and are the foundation stone of my life.

Matthew Thomas Baker has been engaged in spiritual study, transformation, and arts education for over thirty years. Matthew earned an MFA in creative writing from Arizona State University and a master's degree in psychology and counseling from Prescott College, focusing on adolescent development, depth psychology, shamanism, and transpersonal psychology. He also completed a seven-year spiritual study course through the international Order of Bards, Ovates and Druids and tutored others in the course for several years.

At the age of thirty, while reading traditional Buddhist "pointing-out instructions" written down by Ken Wilber in *The Eye of Spirit*, Matthew experienced a spontaneous awakening and recognition of the conscious Awareness that all beings share. That awakening radically altered his view of himself, people, and even objects in the world. Everything appeared to be spontaneously arising out of one awake field of Awareness. During the years since, he has been learning to live into that initial insight, and unconditioned Awareness is always accessible to his mind and heart. In addition, the intelligence of Awareness and the soul has burned down and rebuilt his personality, leaving no figurative stone untransformed. Matthew suspects that the transformational process never really ends, for there is always more that can unfold on our human journey as we grow into wiser, more compassionate, and more creative beings.

Matthew is the founder and spiritual director of the Institute for Nondual Shamanism, and currently lives and teaches in London. He can be found online at matthewthomasbaker.com.

Milton Keynes UK
Ingram Content Group UK Ltd.
UKHW051306080224
437498UK00009B/122

9 781945 209277